Lecture Notes in Business Information Processing   542

Series Editors

Wil van der Aalst ⓘ, *RWTH Aachen University, Aachen, Germany*
Sudha Ram ⓘ, *University of Arizona, Tucson, USA*
Michael Rosemann ⓘ, *Queensland University of Technology, Brisbane, Australia*
Clemens Szyperski, *Microsoft Research, Redmond, USA*
Giancarlo Guizzardi ⓘ, *University of Twente, Enschede, The Netherlands*

LNBIP reports state-of-the-art results in areas related to business information systems and industrial application software development – timely, at a high level, and in both printed and electronic form.

The type of material published includes

- Proceedings (published in time for the respective event)
- Postproceedings (consisting of thoroughly revised and/or extended final papers)
- Other edited monographs (such as, for example, project reports or invited volumes)
- Tutorials (coherently integrated collections of lectures given at advanced courses, seminars, schools, etc.)
- Award-winning or exceptional theses

LNBIP is abstracted/indexed in DBLP, EI and Scopus. LNBIP volumes are also submitted for the inclusion in ISI Proceedings.

Geylani Kardas · Ivan Luković ·
Boris Milašinović · Aleksandar Popović ·
Łukasz Radliński · Mirosław Staroń ·
Jakub Swacha · Adam Przybyłek
Editors

Software, System, and Service Engineering

S3E 2024 Topical Area, Held as Part of FedCSIS 2024
Belgrade, Serbia, 8–11 September, 2024 and KKIO 2024
Held as Part of SEAA 2024, Paris, France, August 28-30, 2024
Revised Selected Papers

Editors
Geylani Kardas
Ege University International Computer Institute
Izmir, Türkiye

Boris Milašinović
University of Zagreb
Zagreb, Croatia

Łukasz Radliński
West Pomeranian University of Technology in Szczecin
Szczecin, Poland

Jakub Swacha
University of Szczecin
Szczecin, Poland

Ivan Luković
University of Belgrade
Belgrade, Serbia

Aleksandar Popović
University of Montenegro
Podgorica, Montenegro

Mirosław Staroń
University of Gothenburg
Gothenburg, Sweden

Adam Przybyłek
Gdańsk University of Technology
Gdańsk, Poland

ISSN 1865-1348 ISSN 1865-1356 (electronic)
Lecture Notes in Business Information Processing
ISBN 978-3-031-84912-1 ISBN 978-3-031-84913-8 (eBook)
https://doi.org/10.1007/978-3-031-84913-8

© The Editor(s) (if applicable) and The Author(s), under exclusive license to Springer Nature Switzerland AG 2025

This work is subject to copyright. All rights are solely and exclusively licensed by the Publisher, whether the whole or part of the material is concerned, specifically the rights of translation, reprinting, reuse of illustrations, recitation, broadcasting, reproduction on microfilms or in any other physical way, and transmission or information storage and retrieval, electronic adaptation, computer software, or by similar or dissimilar methodology now known or hereafter developed.
The use of general descriptive names, registered names, trademarks, service marks, etc. in this publication does not imply, even in the absence of a specific statement, that such names are exempt from the relevant protective laws and regulations and therefore free for general use.
The publisher, the authors and the editors are safe to assume that the advice and information in this book are believed to be true and accurate at the date of publication. Neither the publisher nor the authors or the editors give a warranty, expressed or implied, with respect to the material contained herein or for any errors or omissions that may have been made. The publisher remains neutral with regard to jurisdictional claims in published maps and institutional affiliations.

This Springer imprint is published by the registered company Springer Nature Switzerland AG
The registered company address is: Gewerbestrasse 11, 6330 Cham, Switzerland

If disposing of this product, please recycle the paper.

Preface

In an increasingly digital world, software is the foundation of modern society, driving everything from critical infrastructure and industrial systems to everyday applications on our smartphones. Being architects of this digital landscape, software engineers play a pivotal role in shaping the technologies that underpin business, healthcare, education, and entertainment. Their work is fueled by ongoing advancements in research, with new methodologies, tools, and frameworks continually emerging to address the growing complexity of software systems.

The Conference on Practical Aspects of and Solutions for Software Engineering (KKIO) has been dedicated to addressing these challenges since its inception in 1999, focusing on bridging academic research with real-world industrial applications. Traditionally held in Poland and serving mainly Polish academics, KKIO took a significant step in 2024 by becoming a track within the Euromicro Conference Series on Software Engineering and Advanced Applications (SEAA). This strategic shift aims to attract a broader, more international audience and promote global knowledge exchange. SEAA 2024 took place at Sorbonne University in Paris, France, from August 28th to 30th, expanding KKIO's reach and impact in the software engineering community.

Another prominent platform for fostering collaboration and knowledge exchange in the field of software engineering is the Software, System, and Service Engineering Topical Area (S3E), part of the Federated Conference on Computer Science and Information Systems (FedCSIS). With its roots also in Poland, FedCSIS has grown into an international conference that brings together a variety of disciplines under one umbrella. S3E 2024 included two specialized Thematic Sessions: Advances in Programming Languages (APL) and Model Driven Approaches in System Development (MDASD). The S3E Topical Area, held in Belgrade, Serbia on 8–11th September, 2024, addressed the fundamental challenges of developing reliable, efficient, and effective software systems.

In 2024, KKIO and S3E received 18 and 25 submissions respectively. Following a rigorous single-blind peer-review process, with at least three reviews per submission, KKIO 2024 accepted 7 full papers and 3 short papers, while S3E 2024 accepted 9 full papers and 3 short papers. The accepted papers were presented to engaged audiences at both venues, sparking valuable discussions that enriched both presenters and attendees while highlighting promising directions for future research. After the conferences, selected authors were invited to submit revised and extended versions of their work for this post-conference monograph. The final selection includes three papers from KKIO 2024, and five papers from S3E 2024.

We deeply appreciate everyone who contributed to the success of our research events. Our sincere thanks go to the authors for their invaluable work, the attendees whose active engagement fostered enriching discussions, and the dedicated Program Committee members for their time, effort, and insightful feedback. We also extend our gratitude to the chairs of both the FedCSIS and Euromicro DSD/SEAA conference series. Finally, we wish to express our sincere thanks to the team at Springer for their instrumental role in the publication of this volume.

We hope this monograph proves a valuable resource for your professional and academic endeavors and offers an engaging reading experience. We warmly invite you to explore our upcoming events at https://dsd-seaa.com/kkio/ and https://2025.fedcsis.org/main/s3e.

January 2025

Geylani Kardas
Ivan Luković
Boris Milašinović
Aleksandar Popović
Łukasz Radliński
Jakub Swacha
Mirosław Staroń
Adam Przybyłek

Organization

KKIO@SEAA 2024 Organization

Program Committee Chairs

Łukasz Radliński	West Pomeranian University of Technology, Poland
Mirosław Staroń	University of Gothenburg, Sweden
Jakub Swacha	University of Szczecin, Poland

Steering Committee

Marek Bolanowski	Rzeszów University of Technology, Poland
Bogumiła Hnatkowska	Wrocław University of Science and Technology, Poland
Stanisław Jarząbek	Białystok University of Technology, Poland
Aleksander Jarzębowicz	Gdańsk University of Technology, Poland
Sylwia Kopczyńska	Poznań University of Technology, Poland
Piotr Kosiuczenko	Military University of Technology in Warsaw, Poland
Lech Madeyski	Wrocław University of Science and Technology, Poland
Mirosław Ochodek	Poznań University of Technology, Poland
Aneta Poniszewska-Maranda	Łódź University of Technology, Poland
Adam Przybyłek	Gdańsk University of Technology, Poland
Mirosław Staroń	University of Gothenburg, Sweden
Michał Śmialek	Warsaw University of Technology, Poland
Bartosz Walter	Poznań University of Technology, Poland

Program Committee

Mohammad Alshayeb	King Fahd University of Petroleum and Minerals, Saudi Arabia
Ilona Bluemke	Warsaw University of Technology, Poland
Piotr Błaszyński	West Pomeranian University of Technology, Poland

Marek Bolanowski	Rzeszów University of Technology, Poland
Leszek Borzemski	Wrocław University of Science and Technology, Poland
Alena Buchalcevova	Prague University of Economics and Business, Czech Republic
Włodzimierz Dąbrowski	Warsaw University of Technology, Poland
Anna Derezinska	Warsaw University of Technology, Poland
Arpita Dutta	National University of Singapore, Singapore
Mariusz Flasiński	Jagiellonian University, Poland
Denys Gobov	National Technical University of Ukraine Kyiv Polytechnic Institute, Ukraine
Krzysztof Goczyła	Gdańsk University of Technology, Poland
Paweł Góra	University of Warsaw, Poland
Dávid Halász	Masaryk University, Czech Republic
Sebastian Herold	Karlstad University, Sweden
Bogumiła Hnatkowska	Wrocław University of Science and Technology, Poland
Zbigniew Huzar	Wrocław University of Science and Technology, Poland
Irum Inayat	National University of Computer and Emerging Sciences, Pakistan
Aleksander Jarzębowicz	Gdańsk University of Technology, Poland
Frank Johnsen	Norwegian Defence Research Establishment, Norway
Marija Katić	Medicines and Healthcare Products Regulatory Agency, UK
Wiem Khlif	University of Sfax, Tunisia
Sylwia Kopczyńska	Poznań University of Technology, Poland
Piotr Kosiuczenko	Military University of Technology, Poland
Marek Krętowski	Białystok University of Technology, Poland
Martin Kropp	University of Applied Sciences and Arts Northwestern Switzerland, Switzerland
Maria Lencastre	Escola Politécnica de Pernambuco - UPE, Brazil
Lech Madeyski	Wrocław University of Science and Technology, Poland
Bartosz Marcinkowski	University of Gdańsk, Poland
Jakub Miler	Gdańsk University of Technology, Poland
Durga Prasad Mohapatra	NIT Rourkela, India
Jerzy Nawrocki	Poznań University of Technology, Poland
Ērika Nazaruka	Riga Technical University, Latvia
Michael Neumann	Hochschule Hannover, Germany
Yen Ying Ng	Nicolaus Copernicus University, Poland
Arne Noyer	Ostfalia University of Applied Sciences, Germany

Mirosław Ochodek	Poznań University of Technology, Poland
Necmettin Özkan	Gebze Technical University, Turkey
Mel Ó Cinnéide	University College Dublin, Ireland
Subhrakanta Panda	Birla Institute of Technology and Science, Pilani, India
Andrzej Paszkiewicz	Politechnika Rzeszowska im. I. Łukasiewicza, Poland
Rui Humberto R. Pereira	Instituto Politécnico do Porto, Portugal
Manuela Petrescu	Babeş-Bolyai University, Romania
Aneta Poniszewska-Marańda	Łódź University of Technology, Poland
Adam Przybyłek	Gdańsk University of Technology, Poland
Sonja Ristić	University of Novi Sad, Serbia
Adam Roman	Jagiellonian University, Poland
Bruno Rossi	Masaryk University, Czech Republic
Mika Saari	Tampere University, Finland
Małgorzata Sadowska	Wrocław University of Science and Technology, Poland
Sławomir Samolej	Rzeszów University of Technology, Poland
Gheorghe Cosmin Silaghi	Babeş-Bolyai University, Romania
Michel Soares	Federal University of Sergipe, Brazil
Janusz Sosnowski	Warsaw University of Technology, Poland
Zenon Sosnowski	Białystok University of Technology, Poland
Andrzej Stasiak	Military University of Technology, Poland
Krzysztof Stencel	University of Warsaw, Poland
Jacek Stój	Silesian University of Technology, Poland
Tomasz Szmuc	AGH University of Science and Technology, Poland
Marcin Szpyrka	AGH University of Science and Technology, Poland
Michał Śmiałek	Warsaw University of Technology, Poland
Adam Trendowicz	Fraunhofer IESE, Germany
Bartosz Trybus	Rzeszów University of Technology, Poland
Dimitri Van Landuyt	Catholic University of Leuven, Belgium
Anita Walkowiak-Gall	Wrocław University of Science and Technology, Poland
Bartosz Walter	Poznań University of Technology, Poland
Krzysztof Wnuk	Blekinge Institute of Technology, Sweden
Konrad Wrona	NATO Communications and Information Agency, Netherlands
Włodzimierz Wysocki	West Pomeranian University of Technology Szczecin, Poland
Andrzej Zalewski	Warsaw University of Technology, Poland
Janusz Zalewski	Florida Gulf Coast University, USA

x   Organization

Zbigniew Zieliński   Military University of Technology, Poland

S3E@FedCSIS 2024 Organization

Topical Area Curators

Ivan Luković	University of Belgrade, Serbia
Aleksandar Popović	University of Montenegro, Montenegro
Ayça Kolukısa Tarhan	Hacettepe University, Turkey
Marjan Mernik	University of Maribor, Slovenia

Reviewers

Muhammad Ovais Ahmad	Karlstad University, Sweden
Srdja Bjeladinovic	University of Belgrade, Serbia
Vladimir Dimitrieski	University of Novi Sad, Serbia
Arpita Dutta	National University of Singapore, Singapore
Ferhat Erata	Yale University, USA
M.J. Escalona	University of Seville, Spain
Gabriel García-Mireles	Universidad de Sonora, Mexico
Arda Göknil	SINTEF Digital, Norway
Aleksander JarzĘbowicz	Gdańsk University of Technology, Poland
Igor Jovancevic	University of Montenegro, Montenegro
Kalinka Kaloyanova	University of Sofia, Bulgaria
Nenad Krdzavac	Leibniz Information Centre for Science and Technology, Germany
Bartosz Marcinkowski	University of Gdańsk, Poland
Boris Milašinović	University of Zagreb, Croatia
Sanjay Misra	Østfold University, Norway
Necmettin Ozkan	Kuveyt Turk Participation Bank, Turkey
Mert Ozkaya	Yeditepe University, Turkey
Sonja Ristić	University of Novi Sad, Serbia
Bruno Rossi	Masaryk University, Czech Republic
Milan Segedinac	University of Novi Sad, Serbia
Jose Luis Sierra	Universidad Complutense de Madrid, Spain
Maria João Varanda Pereira	Instituto Politécnico de Bragança, Portugal
Vassilios Vescoukis	National Technical University of Athens, Greece

APL@FedCSIS 2024 Organization

Thematic Session Organizers

Geylani Kardas	Ege University International Computer Institute, Turkey
Marjan Mernik	University of Maribor, Slovenia
Pedro Rangel Henriques	Universidade do Minho, Portugal
Boštjan Slivnik	University of Ljubljana, Slovenia
Ivan Luković	University of Belgrade, Serbia
Jan Janousek	Czech Technical University, Czech Republic
Maria Joao Varanda Pereira	Instituto Politecnico de Braganca, Portugal

Reviewers

Ankica Barisic	Université Côte d'Azur, France
Darius Blasband	RainCode, Belgium
Zoltán Horváth	Eötvös Loránd University, Hungary
Paul Keir	University of the West of Scotland, UK
Tomaz Kosar	University of Maribor, Slovenia
Pablo E. Martínez López	Universidad Nacional de Quilmes, Argentina
Boris Milašinović	University of Zagreb, Croatia
Mert Özkaya	Yeditepe University, Turkey
Jaroslav Porubän	Technical University of Košice, Slovakia
João Saraiva	University of Minho, Portugal
Jose Luis Sierra	Universidad Complutense de Madrid, Spain
Hasan Sozer	Ozyegin University, Turkey

MDASD@FedCSIS 2024 Organization

Thematic Session Organizers

Boris Milašinović	University of Zagreb, Croatia
Ivan Luković	University of Belgrade, Serbia
Jeff Gray	University of Alabama, USA
Marjan Mernik	University of Maribor, Slovenia
Sonja Ristić	University of Novi Sad, Serbia
Juha-Pekka Tolvanen	MetaCase, Finland

Reviewers

Ankica Barisic	Université Côte d'Azur, France
Drazen Brdjanin	University of Banja Luka, Bosnia and Herzegovina
Milan Celikovic	University of Novi Sad, Serbia
Haiming Chen	Chinese Academy of Sciences, China
Mohammed Erradi	Mohammed V Souissi University, ENSIAS, Morocco
Krešimir Fertalj	University of Zagreb, Croatia
Ralf Härting	Hochschule Aalen, Germany
Mirjana Ivanovic	University of Novi Sad, Serbia
Geylani Kardas	Ege University International Computer Institute, Turkey
Slavica Kordić	University of Novi Sad, Serbia
Tomaz Kosar	University of Maribor, Slovenia
Nenad Krdzavac	Leibniz Information Centre for Science and Technology (TIB), Germany
Dragan Maćoš	Beuth Hochschule für Technik, Germany
Manuel Mazzara	Innopolis University, Russia
Gordana Milosavljevic	University of Novi Sad, Serbia
Pedro Rangel Henriques	University of Minho, Portugal
Bran Selic	Malina Software Corp., Canada
Jose Luis Sierra	Universidad Complutense de Madrid, Spain
Boštjan Slivnik	University of Ljubljana, Slovenia
Vassilios Vescoukis	National Technical University of Athens, Greece
Manuel Wimmer	Johannes Kepler University Linz, Austria

Contents

Practical Aspects of and Solutions for Software Engineering (KKIO'24)

Optimizing Agile Performance Metrics: Practical Challenges and Strategic Implementation Insights 3
  Kevin Phong Pham and Michael Neumann

Automatic Task Classification of Software Projects for Planning and Simulation 30
  Włodzimierz Wysocki and Mirosław Ochodek

LogGenST: A Framework for Synthetic Log Generation Using LLMs for Smart-Troubleshooting 64
  Sania Partovian, Francesco Flammini, Alessio Bucaioni, and Johan Thornadtsson

Software, System, and Service Engineering (S3E'24)

Blockchain for Public Transportation: Digital Identity and Transaction Verification Architecture 87
  Hidayet Burak Saritas and Geylani Kardas

Enhancing User Experience in Artificial Intelligence Systems: A Practical Approach 113
  Alexander Zender, Bernhard G. Humm, and Anna Holzheuser

S3E'24 – Thematic Session on Advances in Programming Languages (APL)

Programming Cocktail Analysis Based on the Cognitive Load Theory, a First Approach 135
  Alvaro Costa Neto, Maria João Varanda Pereira, and Pedro Rangel Henriques

S3E'24 – Thematic Session on Model Driven Approaches in System Development (MDASD)

Improve the Design Workflow of Hardware Engineers Using a Textual DSL With Immediate Graphical Feedback 167
    Twan Bolwerk, Marco Alonso, and Mathijs Schuts

Embedded Systems Security Co-design: Modeling Support for Managers and Developers 206
    Alexander Fischer, Juha-Pekka Tolvanen, and Ramin Tavakoli Kolagari

Author Index 233

Practical Aspects of and Solutions for Software Engineering (KKIO'24)

Optimizing Agile Performance Metrics: Practical Challenges and Strategic Implementation Insights

Kevin Phong Pham[1] and Michael Neumann[2(✉)]

[1] University of Applied Sciences FHDW Hannover, Freundallee 15, 30173 Hannover, Germany
[2] University of Applied Sciences and Arts Hannover, Department of Business Information Systems, Ricklinger Stadtweg 120, 30459 Hannover, Germany
michael.neumann@hs-hannover.de

Abstract. *Context:* The success of software development projects relies on effective software process improvement (SPI), particularly within the agile paradigm that thrives on adaptability in dynamic markets. *Objective:* This study aims to investigate the barriers to effectively employing performance metrics in agile software development and to propose actionable strategies for enhancing their application. *Method:* Leveraging a mixed-methods approach, this research builds upon previous findings by conducting an updated literature review to identify current trends and challenges in performance metrics usage. Additionally, an in-depth case study employing focus group discussions and qualitative data analysis was performed in a real-world agile environment. *Results:* The findings reveal that while metrics such as story points and burn-down charts are commonly utilized, teams encounter significant obstacles including a lack of standardization, transparency, and accuracy. This paper provides a nuanced analysis of these barriers and introduces additional metrics identified from an exhaustive literature review. *Contributions:* This work broadens the repository of performance metrics for agile practices and offers a structured framework to address the challenges uncovered. By combining updated theoretical insights with practical recommendations, it provides researchers and practitioners with a road-map to optimize metric adoption, enabling more robust and effective agile software process improvement initiatives.

Keywords: Agile methods · agile software development · performance metrics · process improvement

---

This paper is an extended version of our conference paper titled *"How to Measure Performance in Agile Software Development? A Mixed-Method Study"* [46]. In the paper at hand, we provide an updated overview of the related work and give more details of our conducted rapid literature review. Also, we added a comprehensive repository of performance metrics for agile software development with a detailed explanation of the most common metrics used in practice.

1 Introduction

Agile software development has emerged to provide an alternative to plan-driven methods. Agile methods such as Scrum, Kanban and eXtreme Programming are characterized by their high degree of flexibility and adaptability, allowing teams to respond effectively to rapidly changing requirements and customer needs [10, 38]. Today, agile methods used worldwide in various different contexts and are thus often understood as state of the art approaches in software development [35].

We know, that the ability of agile software development teams to react to new or changed circumstances is one of the major objectives for companies to use agile methods in practice [67]. While using agile methods measuring teams' performance becomes particularly essential because it fosters transparency within the team [3,55]. This transparency is of high importance for the iterative process of inspection and adaptation that agile approaches emphasize and on which the process improvement relies on [68]. By continuously monitoring and evaluating key performance metrics, teams are able to identify areas where processes can be improved, inefficiencies can be eliminated, and overall productivity can be increased [3]. This iterative approach of inspect and adapt allows agile software development teams to foster continuous improvement [48] (which we also know as Kaizen [34]) leading to central objectives using agile methods in practice, e.g., stay aligned with customer needs and project objectives effectively. Performance metrics serve as feedback mechanisms that inform the team whether their adaptations are moving the project in the right direction [42]. Effective measurement and analysis of these metrics are fundamental realizing the potential of agile methods in practice, ensuring that the teams adapt quickly and continuously steers the project towards its goals [55]. Thus, agile software development necessitates the use of suitable performance metrics measure and enhance team performance and efficiency [69].

Previous research (e.g., [10,53,60]) emphasize that performance metrics are crucial for understanding, predicting, and evaluating software development projects. Recent studies discussed the reasons using software metrics within agile software development [23,62]. Choosing and using the right metrics can facilitate early problem detection and enhance decision-making within teams [62]. In turn, using inappropriate metrics can introduce bias and lead to undesirable behaviors [55]). Current knowledge and use of performance metrics in agile software development face several challenges. For example, the high variety in estimation techniques [36] or methods provides flexibility for agile software development teams [24,28,66] In turn, this situation also leads to an increased complexity ensuring the selection of the most appropriate metric for a given context, which may lead to inconsistencies in data quality if the chosen method does not align well with the specific project requirements or user capabilities [2].

The comparability of teams is restricted due to the use of different metrics, as the absence of uniform structures allows for varied approaches to measurement [27]. Additionally, the variability in methods can complicate training and standardization efforts across an organization, potentially resulting in misinterpretations and misalignment in strategic objectives.

Thus, the above motivates the objective of our study, which is refined by the following research questions:

- **RQ1:** Which metrics are used in agile software development teams to measure performance?
- **RQ2:** What are real-world challenges agile software development teams face when using performance metrics?
- **RQ3:** What specific performance metrics can be used and optimized in practice to measure project success?

This paper is structured as follows: In Sect. 2, we give a brief introduction on metrics in the area in agile software development and further provide an overview of the identified work related to our studies topic. Section 3 describes our research design. In Sect. 4, we present the results of our study followed by a discussion to present practical implications in Sect. 5. Before the paper closes with a summary in Sect. 7, we outline the limitations of the study in Sect. 6.

2 Background and Related Work

2.1 Metrics in Agile Software Development

Metrics are quantitative measures used to assess, quantify, and monitor various aspects of systems, processes, products, or performances [19,20]. In agile software development, metrics are of high importance role in measuring the performance, quality, and progress of development processes [32].

However, agile methods with their iterative-incremental characteristic differ significantly from phase-oriented approaches (like Waterfall) with the result at the end of the project. Thus, several authors describe agile methods as a reaction to established phase-oriented (or big design upfront [54]) approaches (e.g., [1,71]). For the metrics used in software development, these characteristics led to the situation that established metrics used in traditional settings are not fully transferable to agile environments [22]. Phase-oriented approaches often employ rigid, predefined metrics focused on process adherence and milestone achievement. In contrast, agile methods utilizes more flexible, iterative metrics that evolve with the project, emphasizing both product quality and process efficiency [32]. Metrics in phase-oriented software development are typically quantitative and reviewed at the end of phases (or the beginning of new ones). In turn, agile metrics include both qualitative and quantitative data and are updated more frequently to reflect ongoing feedback and adjustments [32].

This discrepancy highlights the need for developing specific metrics tailored to an agile method in use, a need driven by the increasing popularity of agile approaches [59]. As described in literature, metrics provide objective information that enables precise and comparable assessments [32]. They convert abstract concepts into measurable units, which helps in identifying successes or challenges. Metrics also allow continuous monitoring and control of processes and performance, facilitating the tracking of developments over time [32]. Additionally, metrics serve as a foundation for informed decision-making by highlighting problems, identifying improvement opportunities, and developing optimization strategies [32]. Moreover, different metrics can challenge team members to achieve better results, potentially leading to behavioral changes within the team [32].

Metrics can be grouped into several categories, each with a specific purpose for the tracking and analysis of certain aspects of a project. Some of the main categories are process metrics, product metrics, quality metrics or risk metrics [31]. Each of these main categories can be further distinguished into more specific sub-categories to provide more detailed insights into particular areas or processes. Usman et al. employed a taxonomy design method to systematically and precisely organize various types of metrics [65]. This taxonomy supports structuring the metrics to ensure they are categorized accurately, facilitating better analysis and utilization in software development projects. Performance metrics are quantifiable measures used to evaluate the effectiveness, efficiency, and quality of various aspects of an operation, process, or system. These metrics are crucial for assessing performance, guiding decision-making, and identifying areas for improvement. Previous research and reviews provide a wide variety of performance metrics available, reflecting the diverse needs and goals of different projects and industries [23, 65].

2.2 Related Work

Agile software development has gained significant research interest in recent years as organizations seek to enhance their adaptability and deliver high-quality software solutions in rapidly changing environments [3]. Thus, we searched for primary and secondary studies dealing closely related to the topic of our paper: performance metrics in the area of agile software development.

Though existing primary studies examined the benefits of agile methods and metrics across various industries [32], we identified a lack in literature. We found a notable gap in the literature, especially regarding the application and effects of these methods in regulated sectors such as insurance and pensions. Research in these areas has been limited and focused specifically on certain corporate contexts ([10, 47] to name a few). However, even in the area of secondary studies, we identified a research gap as systematic literature reviews on agile software development have typically concentrated on general best practices, often neglecting the unique challenges of the insurance industry [24, 39]. Research mainly focuses on the adoption of agile methods [12, 37] and the use of metrics to measure their impact [61], with few studies examining how these practices are applied in real-world scenarios, particularly within sectors like insurance that require stringent data integrity and security.

In our previous work, presented in [46], we explored the foundational aspects of performance metrics in agile software development. We identified a gap in the literature regarding the practical application of these metrics and the common challenges teams face, such as issues with transparency, standardization, and accuracy. Our initial findings highlighted the need for a deeper understanding of how these metrics are implemented in real-world settings and how their effectiveness can be enhanced. This current study extends the previous research by delving deeper into the specific metrics identified in our rapid literature review and analyzing their relevance and application in greater detail. The focus has shifted from a broad overview to a more focused examination of the most significant metrics that impact agile software development practices today. Furthermore, this research contributes to the body of knowledge by updating and enlarging the repository of performance metrics for agile development. We address the nuances of each metrics application, offering refined guidelines and best practices that cater to the evolving needs of agile teams. This iterative approach to research reflects the agile principles of continuous improvement and responsiveness to change, ensuring that our contributions remain relevant and practically applicable.

3 Research Design

We selected a mixed-method research design to gain an in-depth understanding of metrics in agile software development. Our research design consists on two different approaches: a) rapid literature review and b) single case study using qualitative data collection and analysis methods. Both research methods were designed, prepared, and conducted using guidelines. In this section, we first explain our research design, followed by a detailed explanation of the applied research methods in the subsections below.

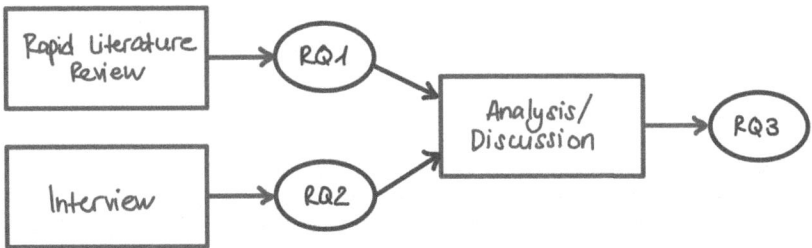

Fig. 1. Mixed-method research approach

Figure 1 depicts our research design and the connection answering our three research questions. Initially, a rapid literature review was conducted to identify, describe, and evaluate documented agile metrics answering RQ1. This phase is essential for the collection of best practices and scientific findings. To investigate the second and third research question, an assessment of the current state in practice was then conducted two different focus groups in a mid-sized company operating in the insurance sector. These interviews are used to determine satisfaction with their currently used methods and processes. Also we wanted to gain industry-specific insights. Recommendations for potential optimizations are finally developed based on these findings, leading to suggestions for improvements that address subsequent research questions.

3.1 Rapid Literature Review

Rapid Literature Reviews are streamlined versions of systematic literature reviews, designed to quickly synthesize available research within a condensed timeframe [8]. By focusing on studies and summarizing evidence more succinctly and efficiently, rapid literature reviews provide timely insights into specific topics of interest often with a dedicated context defined e.g., based on research questions. This approach can efficiently capture and apply current knowledge to improve processes and performance metrics.

We designed, prepared, and conducted the rapid literature review mainly based on the guidelines by Cartaxo et al. [8]. The rapid literature review method followed a three step approach: a) Defining a search strategy including search strings and select scientific search engines, b) defining a study selection strategy applying inclusion and exclusion criteria, and c) data extraction and analysis of the final result set. However, we took some adaptions of the guidelines [8]. We give more information below, when we explain the review process on detail.

Key terms were strategically selected based on the research questions to ensure coverage of relevant aspects. The terms chosen included "agile", "software", "metric", "performance", "mapping", "systematic", and "taxonomy". To optimize the result set by applying a correct search string, we performed test runs using the search engine from ACM Digital Library to refine the search string. In total, we created three final search strings:

- "agile AND metric AND performance AND taxonomy"
- "software AND taxonomy AND mapping"
- "agile AND metric AND systematic"

To capture a broad spectrum of relevant primary and secondary studies, we conducted our search in two scientific databases: ACM Digital Library and ScienceDirect. The final search runs were conducted on 20.11.2023 resulting in a total of 43,088 studies. The result set was narrowed down by using filter settings to apply the inclusion and exclusion criteria related to the systematic characteristics of the studies such as the article type (research articles) and the year range filter (max. 10 years old studies; since 2013) to capture recent trends in the field. After applying the filter settings the final result set consisted of 24,126 studies. A schematic representation of this selection process is illustrated in Fig. 2.

First and foremost, it is worth to mention that we had to handle a massive set of potential relevant studies. As this study is designed as mixed-method study and the rapid literature review was selected because of its characteristic to summarize evident knowledge in an efficient way, we decided to focus on the most relevant results. Thus, we focused the literature review including the study selection process on the first 25 papers per search run (150 studies in total).

However, it is worth to mention that even we screened the other title of the rest of the studies from the result set, we did not find other relevant studies for our rapid literature review. For the result set of the 150 included studies, we performed a three-step selection process-starting with title evaluation, followed by abstract analysis, and culminating in full-text review based on relevance and depth of insight-only 5 scientific papers were ultimately selected for detailed analysis in this study. Further information related to the rapid literature review including the protocol of the study and the selection process are made available at Zenodo [45].

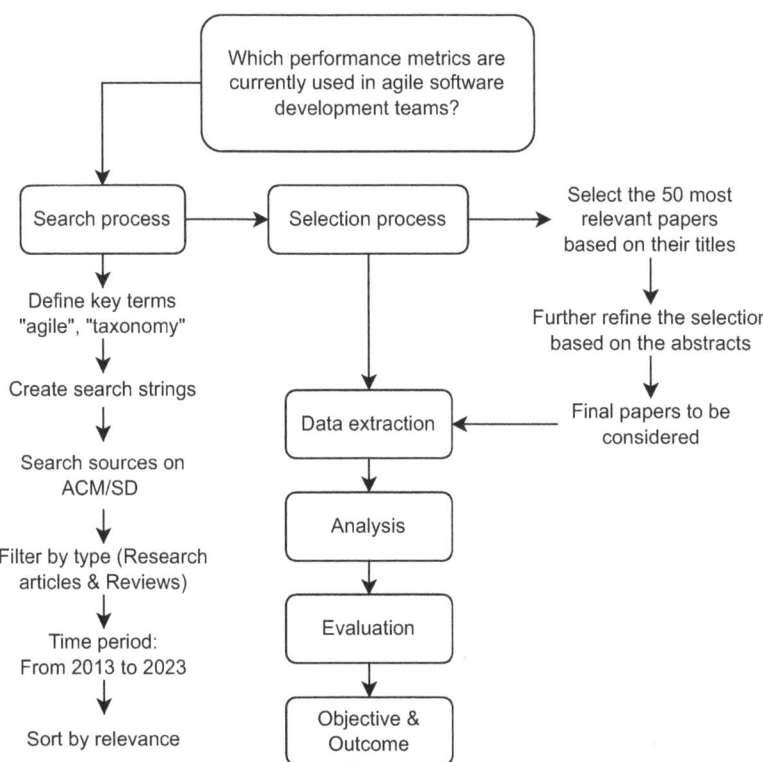

Fig. 2. Schematic representation of the rapid review process for selecting scientifically relevant papers

Study Selection Criteria. The selection of studies for this research was guided by precise criteria to ensure that the included literature adheres to the highest scientific standards and is directly relevant to the focus of our investigation. Considering our research questions, criteria were established to include studies that:

- Report on effort or size estimation using models or metrics.
- Are based on agile software development methodologies.
- Are described in English.

These criteria are designed to capture studies that provide substantial insights into the application of metrics within agile frameworks, thereby contributing valuable data and methodologies to our research.

Furthermore, exclusion criteria were meticulously defined to streamline the review process. Studies were excluded from further analysis if they:

- Do not pertain to effort or size estimation, OR
- Were not conducted using any of the agile software development methodologies, OR
- Are not described in English, OR
- Have not been published in a peer-reviewed conference, journal, or workshop, OR
- Solely focus on a specific performance measurement, such as Velocity, OR
- Do not have available full texts.

These exclusion criteria helped to eliminate studies that might dilute the specificity and applicability of the research findings to the agile context. By filtering out less relevant studies, the review process becomes more efficient, allowing for a focused analysis of how performance metrics are implemented and evaluated in real-world agile software development scenarios. The application of these stringent selection and exclusion criteria ensures that our literature review remains robust and focused, offering a comprehensive foundation for discussing the challenges and strategies associated with using performance metrics in agile environments.

3.2 Single Case Study

We decided to conduct a single case study using a qualitative research approach as we want to create an in-depth understanding of the application of performance metrics in agile software development. For the design and preparation of the study, we used the guidelines from Runeson and Hoest [52] and Yin [72]. As shown in Sect. 2, research results emphasize the importance and benefits of using metrics in agile software development covering different industries (e.g., presented by Misra and Omorodion [32]). However, gaps remain in the literature, particularly concerning their application and impacts in regulated sectors such as insurance and pensions. Consequently, this study focused on examining the use and effects of these metrics within a German mid-sized software development company operating in the insurance sector. Here, we use the anonymized name *Dunder Mifflin Inc.* for the case company. Further information about the case company can be provided upon request and after a proof by the case company. Dunder Mifflin Inc. provides a unique opportunity to understand how agile practices and metrics perform in an environment characterized by stringent regulatory requirements and complex risk management needs.

As mentioned above, the second research method covered qualitative data collection and analysis using two focus groups applying semi-structured interview sessions. Here, we aimed gathering the data with key focus groups within agile software development teams in the case company, selected based on their central roles using performance metrics. The first focus group included Software Developers of various experience levels, providing diverse perspectives on metric application. In the second focus group we interviewed Product Owners, who offer insights into how metrics influence decision-making and product planning. An overview of the participants profiles is given in Table 1.

Table 1. Characteristics of the participants per focus group

	Developer	Product Owner
Sample size (n)	6	2
Average experience in years	11.75	12.5
Average employment period in years at the company	approx. 8.5	12.5
Average agile experience in years	approx. 4.5	5

This approach allows an in-depth understanding of group dynamics and individual experiences related to performance metrics in agile settings. The interview questions were meticulously designed to allow participants from the case company to openly share their experiences, focusing on issues and challenges related to the use of performance metrics. The questions covered various aspects of using performance metrics, including type, frequency and relevance of metrics used as well as existing challenges and success stories. Attention was paid to asking open-ended questions that provided scope for detailed responses and captured the various perspectives of the participants. The interview guideline used is available at Zenodo [43].

We refrained from recording the focus group dates for three reasons: a) Regulatory circumstances in the case company and the resulting consequences for later publication, e.g. through blocking notices, b) Potential effects of the participants with regard to their openness and transparency during the interviews and c) Recordings of group discussions are difficult to transcribe because, for example, it is not always clear who is speaking. Both focus group appointments were conducted in German and onsite in the office of the case company. This data collection approach made informal talks possible and we further were able to consider non-verbal communication. Both focus group were held in January 2024 and took between 30 to 45 min, moderated by the first author.

We performed the data analysis using the field notes and manually created protocols of the focus group sessions. All the data was documented using Microsoft Excel sheets and notes in a text file. In the first analysis step, we merged the data to one Microsoft Excel sheet and categorized the data based on the interview guideline. The data analysis was performed using open coding in accordance with the guidelines by Strauss and Corbin [58] aiming to reduce the complexity of the data. The open coding process led to a comprehensive, but more systematic data basis which we then analyzed in an coding to identify categories.

This two-step data analysis approach enabled a comprehensive analysis of the current state of metrics used in the teams in which the focus group participants operate. Considering ethical reflections related to our qualitative research approach including humans, their behavior and beliefs, we took several actions. First, we guarantee the anonymity of each participant of the study and the case company including all relevant information such as organizational units, software development projects, or even products. Pre-arrangements were made with volunteer participants to ensure structured interviews and we took the consent by all the participants to be allowed taking field notes of the interviews. Thus, participants responses were briefly transcribed by taking notes during the focus group sessions.

4 Results

4.1 Repository of Performance Metrics in Agile Software Development

In this subsection, we present the findings from our rapid literature review and answer our first research question: *Which metrics are used in agile software development teams to measure performance?*

Table 2. Overview of the included studies

Publication-ID: Reference	Research design	Year	Digitial Library
S1: Usman et al. [66]	Systematic literature review	2014	ACM
S2: Chloros et al. [9]	Systematic Mapping Study	2022	ACM
S3: Ram et al. [50]	Multiple Case Study	2019	ACM
S4: Kupiainen et al. [23]	Systematic literature review	2015	ScienceDirect
S5: Lopez et al. [28]	Systematic Mapping Study	2022	ScienceDirect

Following the previously described selection process of the current literature, a total of five studies were retained for detailed analysis. Each of the identified studies (Table 2 provides an overview) provides a comprehensive overview of methods and metrics used in agile software development. However, there are remarkable differences between the identified metrics in several aspects. A thorough analysis of the metrics listed in these studies led to the development of a repository of performance metrics, which documents the metrics in detail and is available at Zenodo [44].

In Study S1, diverse estimation methods were examined, including Expert Judgement, Planning Poker, Use Case Points, Linear Regression, and Neural Networks, revealing a spectrum of techniques that cater to varying project needs and environments. Among these, Expert Judgement and Planning Poker were highlighted as particularly prevalent in agile settings, reflecting their adaptability and team-oriented nature. The study also detailed the use of accuracy metrics such as Mean Magnitude of Relative Error (MMRE) and Magnitude of Relative Error (MRE), alongside Prediction at Level 25 (Pre(25)), to gauge the precision of these estimations. Interestingly, while Balanced Relative Error (BRE) was less frequently utilized, it represents a critical area for further exploration given its potential to provide a more balanced accuracy assessment. Additionally, the analysis underscored a shift from traditional size metrics like Function Points and Lines of Code, towards more agile-centric metrics such as Use Case Points and Story Points, signaling a transformation in metric preferences that aligns with the agile methodology's emphasis on flexibility and iterative development.

In the examination of agile development methodologies, Study S2 provides a valuable overview of the motivations behind the employment of various metrics, although it does not specify which metrics are particularly used for measuring effort. The authors of S2 highlight several key reasons for metric utilization in agile contexts. Metrics are used to:

- Enhance agile processes
- Adhere to protocols in agile methodologies
- Improve software quality during development
- Increase the quality of the source code
- Refine estimates and planning
- Boost productivity

Study S3 delves into the sustainability of metric usage within agile software development, identifying key factors that are crucial for the long-term application of metrics. While specific metrics such as Velocity, effort estimates, and custom metrics are mentioned, the study does not detail these metrics extensively as its primary focus lies on pinpointing success factors for the operationalization of metrics in agile environments. This approach highlights the strategic importance of just choosing appropriate metrics, and furthermore integrating them strategically into the agile workflow to ensure they deliver lasting value. The findings underscore the need for a deeper understanding of how metrics can be tailored and evolved over time to support continuous improvement and adaptation in agile projects.

Study S4 aims to expand the understanding of the reasons for and impacts of using metrics in industrial agile development. Velocity and Effort Estimate are the most frequently cited metrics across the primary studies it reviews. A variety of metrics are employed for performance measurement and information dissemination within teams, illustrating a robust toolkit that supports agile processes. Notable examples include Burn-down Charts, daily check-ins, the number of automatically passed test stages, as well as new and open defects. Additionally, Defect Trend Indicators are utilized to monitor backlog health, and Cycle Time

Metrics track performance over time. The study also notes innovative practices such as the automatic generation of story completion percentages upon test executions, showcasing how agile teams integrate metrics into their daily workflows to enhance transparency and drive productivity.

> **Answering RQ1:** Based on the identified studies we created a comprehensive repository of performance metrics used in agile software development, showcasing a wide range of metrics such as Story Points, Function Points, Velocity, Custom Metrics, Test Coverage, and Lead Time. These metrics demonstrate the adaptability of agile methods to diverse needs and highlight their critical roles in estimating workloads, enhancing estimation accuracy, and addressing errors, thereby underscoring the importance of continuous improvement and flexibility in agile environments.

In Study S5, metrics are tailored to various types of quality requirements (QR), such as response time for specific QR types, demonstrating a nuanced approach to performance evaluation. The study also incorporates Quality Management Indicators (QMI), which serve as general metrics within the quality management context, like delivery speed, measured by average delivery time. Furthermore, S5 enumerates a wide array of specific metrics that span several facets of software development, including builds, issues, requirements, and runtime parameters such as CPU usage, memory consumption, and overall system performance. Notably, for addressing research question RQ1, the metrics concerning requirements, testing, and issues & codes are particularly significant. These metrics provide a comprehensive toolkit for assessing and refining software development processes, thereby enhancing the precision and effectiveness of quality management strategies in agile development environments. In Table 3 all relevant metrics that were found through the conducted Rapid Literature Review are summarized, which will be further examined and evaluated in the following sections.

The variety of metrics presented demonstrates the adaptability of agile methods to various requirements in different contexts. The studies collectively offer an extensive collection of metrics customized specifically for measuring work effort, showcasing the flexibility and depth of metric usage in agile environments.

Based on our analysis, we can highlight Velocity as a key metric for estimating workload in planning future iterations, emphasizing its role in measuring the efficiency and performance of agile software development teams [24,49]. Its widespread use and examination in these studies underline Velocity's important function in planning and managing agile development processes.

Furthermore, metrics specifically designed to assess the accuracy of estimations were prominently featured. Usman et al. [66] emphasize the relevance these metrics serve in evaluating how close initial estimates are to the current outcome or output. This capability is instrumental in refining the estimation processes used in iteration planning meetings. The analysis also highlights that several metrics pertain specifically to the process of error identification and correction [28].

Table 3. Overview of the Various Relevant Metrics in the Reviewed Literature S1-S5.

Publication-ID	Estimation methods and metrics
S1	**Estimation methods:** Expert Judgement, Planning Poker, Use Case Points, Linear Regression, Neural Nets **Accuracy metrics:** MMRE, MRE, Pred(25) **Size metrics:** Story Points, Use Case Points, Function Points, Lines of Code, Number of User Stories, COSMIC FP, Length of User Story
S2	No explicit naming of metrics
S3	Velocity, effort estimate, custom metrics No further differentiation, as the focus is particularly on factors relating to the operationalization of metrics
S4	**Process metrics:** defect count, test success rate, test failure rate, defects deferred, test coverage, test growth ratio, velocity, number of unit tests, completed web pages, cost performance index, schedule performance index, planned velocity, common tempo time, check-ins per day, fix time of failed build, velocity of elaborating features, cycle time, lead time, processing time, queue time, maintenance effort, work in progress, variance in handovers, throughput, queue, implemented vs wasted requirements
S5	**Requirements:** Requirement changeability, Requirements ambiguity, Requirements analysis, Requirements design, Requirements risk, Specification change **Tests:** Failed test ratio, Failed tests fault content function, Path coverage, State coverage, Successful test ratio, Test execution rate, Test performance, Test ratio, Test speed, Tests, Transition coverage **Issues & Codes:** Bugs ratio (number of bugs/LOC), Code changed, Code changed performance, Team productivity

This focus reflects the complexity and multifaceted nature of evaluating the performance of agile software development teams. The variety of metrics related to bug fixing emphasizes the importance of continuous improvement and adaptability to unforeseen challenges in agile methods.

4.2 Overview of Most Relevant Metrics

The methods described in Usman et al. each offer different approaches to measure estimating effort in agile software development. The selection depends on the particular situation, the available data and the preferences of the development team [66]:

– **Expert judgment:** in this method, experts from the development team or other relevant areas are consulted in order to incorporate their assessment and

experience into the effort estimate. The experts use their specialist knowledge to assess the tasks to be completed and estimate the associated effort [13]
- **Planning Poker:** Planning poker is a collaborative estimation method in which the development team jointly evaluates the effort required for specific tasks. Team members hold up cards with estimations, with discussions about differences in the estimations leading to the team reaching a consensus. This method encourages team collaboration and considers different perspectives when forming an estimate [30]
- **Use Case Points:** This metric evaluates the functional scope of a system based on use cases. By analyzing use cases, points are awarded that represent the degree of complexity and effort required for development. UCP enables a structured evaluation of the functional scope and is used to estimate the effort in relation to the use cases covered [11].
- **Linear regression:** This is a statistical method that models the relationship between dependent and independent variables. In terms of effort estimation, historical data can be used to create a regression equation that represents the relationship between various factors and effort [70].
- **Neural Nets:** Neural nets are a subtype of artificial intelligence based on the principle of neurons in the human brain. By training the network with historical data, it can recognize patterns and correlations to derive effort estimates. Neural networks provide an advanced method for effort estimation, especially when there are complex and non-linear relationships between factors [41]

In addition, the paper describes metrics that assess the quality of the estimates and the reliability of the estimation methods used:

- **Mean Magnitude of Relative Error** MMRE is a metric that captures the average amount of relative error across all estimated efforts. The average of the absolute values of all relative errors is determined. The lower the MMRE, the more accurate the estimates are on average [13].
- **Magnitude of Relative Error:** MRE is similar to MMRE, whereby in the absolute relative error for a single estimate is measured in comparison to MMRE. A low MRE indicates that the estimate is close to the actual effort [13].
- **Prediction Interval at 25:** Prediction Interval at 25 (Pred(25)) is a methodology that uses a prediction interval to calculate the probable relative error of an estimate. The interval is chosen so that 25 of the estimates are within this interval. A small pred(25) interval indicates high accuracy, as the estimates are highly likely to lie within this interval [13].

The size metrics described serve to quantify various aspects of software development, be it the scope, complexity or progress of the project:

- **Story points:** Story points are a size metric in agile software development to evaluate the effort required to implement a user story. It is a relative estimate that takes into account the complexity and scope of a task [26].

- **Function Points:** Function points are a metric for estimating the effort required for software that, unlike story points, takes into account aspects such as external inputs and outputs, user queries and database access. They are used to quantify the functional scope of a system [15]
- **Lines of Code:** Lines of code (LOC) indicate the number of lines of code in a software project. It is a traditional but often criticized metric for measuring the scope and complexity of software [15]
- **Number of user stories:** The number of user stories is a metric that measures the scope of an agile project based on the number of user stories defined and to be implemented [14].
- **COSMIC FP:** COSMIC Function Points (CFP) is a variant of Function Points and is an abbreviation for "Common Software Measurement International Consortium - Function Points". It is an international standard metric for estimating the size of software [64]. CFP considers both functional and non-functional aspects, including data movements, interfaces, control functions, and transaction types, providing a more comprehensive view of software size and complexity.
- **Length of User Story:** The length of a user story can be used as a metric to measure the scope and complexity of a single requirement. This can be measured in different units, e.g. number of words or sentences [14]

Ram et al. [50] only mentions higher-level metrics. These play a role in monitoring and evaluating various aspects of the software development process:

- **Velocity:** Velocity is a metric that is used particularly in agile development teams that work according to Scrum method. It measures the amount of work (user stories, story points, etc.) that a team has successfully completed in a sprint. Velocity is often used to estimate future workloads [24, 70]
- **Effort Estimate:** Effort Estimate is a metric that indicates the estimated amount of work required to complete a specific task or project. This can be expressed in hours, days or other units [24]
- **Custom Metrics** Custom Metrics are specific metrics that have been individually developed for the needs of a software project or team. These metrics can relate to aspects such as code quality, test coverage, user satisfaction or other project-specific criteria [24]

Kupiainen et al. [24] name numerous quality metrics, of which the following are particularly relevant:

- **Defect Count:** Defect Count is a metric that counts the total number of bugs (or "defects") identified in the software product during a specified time period. This includes both newly discovered defects and those that have not yet been fixed. The defect count provides information about the quality of the code and the stability of the product [25]
- **Test success rate:** The test success rate is the percentage of test cases that were successfully completed in relation to the total number of tests performed. A high success rate indicates that the software behaves as expected and meets most or all of the defined requirements [25]

- **Test coverage** Test coverage enables to measure how much of the code is covered by automated tests (e.g. unit tests, integration tests, system tests). It is often expressed as a percentage and shows how many lines of code are actually executed and tested during the tests [25]

In addition, the authors [24] lists various metrics for estimating effort:

- **Schedule Performance Index:** The Schedule Performance Index (SPI) is a key figure from the Earned Value Management (EVM), which indicates the ratio of earned value to planned value. The SPI helps to determine how efficiently a team is working compared to the planned schedule [16]
- **Planned Velocity:** Planned Velocity is a metric that represents the amount of work a team plans to complete in an upcoming sprint based on their performance in previous sprints. This metric is used to plan future sprints and set realistic goals [70]
- **Cycle time:** Cycle time describes how much time it takes to move a work unit or task through the production or development process from start to finish. In agile development, this is the time from the start of work on a feature or bug to its completion. Shortening the cycle time can improve a team's efficiency and responsiveness [21]
- **Processing Time** Processing time is the actual time it takes to complete a specific task or operation without interruptions or delays. It refers to pure working time, without waiting times or delays, and is a measure of the efficiency of work execution [21]
- **Queue time:** The queue time describes the time that a work unit waits before processing begins. In production and development processes, this refers to the time that a task or work item spends in a queue before it is processed. The waiting time can indicate bottlenecks in the process and is an important factor for the total cycle time [21]
- **Throughput:** Throughput is the amount of work or the number of units that a system can process within a certain period of time. In software development, throughput often refers to the number of tasks, features or bugs that a team can complete in a given period of time [7].

According to Lopez et al. [28], a large number of quality metrics are mentioned that are geared towards different aspects of quality requirements for software development:

- **Bug issues:** Bug issues are often referred to simply as "bugs". This refers to problems or errors in software that lead to unexpected, erroneous or undesirable events. A software malfunction due to programming errors is often detected through extensive testing even before the application is released. Bugs usually arise due to errors in the coding, such as syntax, logic or data processing errors [6]
- **Bug Types:** Bug types classify errors in the software according to their nature or cause. Common categories include functional bugs, performance issues, user interface bugs, security vulnerabilities and integration bugs. This

categorization helps teams understand the nature of the problems and develop appropriate testing and correction strategies [63]
- **Bugs Fixing Effort:** Bugs Fixing Effort measures the effort required to fix identified bugs in the software. This can be expressed in hours, days or by the number of resources required to fix it. Alternatively, this metric can also be referred to as "Defect Closure Period". A higher effort may indicate more complex or more numerous bugs [17]
- **Critical Issues:** Critical issues are serious problems in a software project that have an immediate impact on the user experience, security or basic functionality. These issues are usually of the highest priority and require immediate action to avoid serious impact on the project or end users [17]
- **Test Execution Rate:** Test Execution Rate measures the speed at which tests are executed, typically expressed as the number of tests per unit of time. A higher rate may indicate efficient test procedures, while a lower rate may indicate bottlenecks or inefficient processes [56]
- **Code Change Performance:** Code Change Performance evaluates how effectively and efficiently changes are made to the code. This can include the time it takes to implement, test and release changes, as well as the impact of these changes on the quality and functionality of the software [51]
- **Requirement changeability:** Requirement changeability measures how easily requirements can be changed or adapted in the course of a project. High changeability can indicate flexibility and adaptability in a rapidly changing environment, but also requires robust processes to manage these changes [29]
- **Requirement Analysis:** Requirement analysis refers to the process of examining the project requirements to get a clear, detailed and understandable picture of what the software should do. This step is crucial for the successful planning and development of a software project [40]
- **Requirement design:** Requirement design deals with the implementation of the analyzed requirements in a structured design that serves as the basis for further development. It includes the creation of diagrams, specifications and models that show how the requirements are to be technically realized [40]
- **Requirement risk:** Requirement risk assesses the potential risk associated with certain requirements. This can include the likelihood of misunderstandings, the difficulty of implementation or possible negative effects on the project if the requirement is not implemented properly [29].

4.3 Challenges While Using Performance Metrics in Practice

Based on the results from our focus group study, we answer the second research question; RQ2: *What are real-world challenges agile software development teams face when using performance metrics?*

The interview involved developers from two different teams at the company, so overlapping responses were observed, especially within the same team where similar metrics are used, and perceptions of problems and challenges are alike.

These interviews provide valuable insights into the practical application of metrics from the developers' perspective, forming a crucial foundation for further discussion and analysis for both RQ2 and RQ3.

The findings reveal that developers at the company utilize a range of metrics and tools in descending order of frequency: Story Points, Four-Eyes Principle, Build Status, Test Coverage, and Person-Days.

Additional metrics such as Runtime Stability, Test Success Rate, Code Quality, Code Smells, and MQ Service Status are also applied. Metrics are typically measured initially in the development process. For instance, Story Points are estimated during the Backlog Refinement every two weeks, where all cards in the backlog are discussed and estimated through oral Planning Poker. Estimates are made as soon as a requirement arises and metrics are adjusted only in exceptional cases throughout the development cycle. The teams primarily use tools like Grafana Dashboard [18], SonarQube [57], Jira [5], and Confluence [4] to measure metrics and monitor progress. This setup underscores the structured yet flexible approach to metric usage in agile environments at the company, highlighting both commonalities and variations in experiences and methodologies among the developers.

> **Answering RQ2:** Qualitative interviews with developers and product owners at the company highlighted the structured yet flexible use of a range of metrics and tools, including Story Points, SonarQube, and Test Coverage, to monitor agile development processes. Key issues identified include the perceived inadequacy of Story Points and challenges with the clarity and accuracy of estimation methods like oral Planning Poker, leading to discrepancies in workload estimates and project management. Product owners emphasized the importance of defining roles clearly and improving communication between teams to enhance project efficiency and transparency.

However, several issues and challenges related to the application of metrics and estimation methods were identified. A recurring issue was the perceived irrelevance or inadequacy of Story Points in some teams, which was attributed by some developers to the lack of commitment to sprints and the absence of Velocity measurement. The oral Planning Poker method was frequently mentioned as insufficiently detailed, and there was confusion about the exact process and estimation method. Developers also reported difficulties using Burn-Down Charts and estimating Story Points for cards. Additionally, the order situation was described as unpredictable, leading to disrupted workflows and changes in prioritization, necessitating adjustments to estimates during the development cycle. This resulted in discrepancies between the initial estimates and the actual time and effort required. It was emphasized that the accuracy of estimates should be reviewed at the end of each sprint to address these discrepancies effectively.

In addition the interviews with Product Owners (POs) at the company provided a broader perspective on the organization's agile methods and practices. POs core competency rely in defining requirements and prioritizing them, offering valuable insights into the product management with regard to the agile software development within the organization. Thus, they enabling a more comprehensive assessment of the software processes in use. Technical requirements are developed through close interactions between various teams and committees (e.g., communities of practice), with a focus on capturing and evaluating professional needs. Nevertheless, we identified highlighted issues with the precise definition and scope of action of POs, particularly regarding their role and clarification of responsibilities. The evaluation of the use of Story Points presented a mixed opinion. Generally, the method is considered understandable and effective for estimating the scope and effort of tasks. However, concerns about the transparency and accuracy of these estimates were raised, particularly regarding the influence of oral estimates during Planning Poker. An overview of the development process is achieved through regular exchange formats like weekly meetings and the use of the Jira board, with Story Points serving as a unit of measure to track progress and capacity. Regarding quality metrics, the focus is on domain tests, system stability, and performance.

The respondents emphasized the importance of regular interactions with developers to ensure the quality of software solutions. User feedback and the continuous improvement of systems also play a crucial role. Challenges in the agile process were particularly identified in requirements management and the clarification of responsibilities. Issues such as lack of standardization and occasional transparency problems during ticket handover were cited as causes for conflicts and misunderstandings. The POs expressed a desire for clearer definition of responsibilities and improved information exchange between teams to enhance efficiency and transparency in the development process.

5 Practical Implications

In this section, we first discuss practical implications based on the findings presented in the previous section aiming to answer our third research question; RQ3: *What specific performance metrics can be used and optimized in practice to measure project success?*

Analyzing the results of the rapid literature review and the interviews allows to understand the utilization and optimization potential of performance metrics in agile software development teams, including those at the investigated company. While not all metrics described in the literature are implemented at the company (e.g., due to the vast variety available) relevant metrics are actively integrated into the software development process. This indicates that the selection and implementation of metrics are based on a careful balancing process, tailored to meet the specific needs and contexts of the individual development teams. From a more critical perspective, one may also assume, that the high variety lead to a higher complexity selecting a new or even another metric. The analysis of the results of the rapid review provides a guideline to highlight areas for improvement and suggest possible adjustments or additions to metric usage. This comparison between the findings from the literature and the actual practices at the company serves as a valuable foundation for identifying best practices and developing recommendations to optimize the use of metrics in agile software development. The use of Story Points is a common practice in agile software development teams for estimating the effort required for tasks and user stories, as frequently mentioned in the literature and interviews. This method allows for a relative assessment of tasks, enabling teams to gauge the effort of a task in comparison to others without relying on absolute time estimates like person-days. Story Points enhance agility, offering adaptability to changes and uncertainties, and allowing teams to respond flexibly to new information or changes in requirements. However, a notable disadvantage is the lack of objectivity in Story Points, which can lead to inconsistencies and uncertainties across different teams. This variability challenges the comparability of Velocity between teams and could potentially hinder the scalability of agile practices at the enterprise level. Furthermore, if Story Points do not correlate well with Velocity or are not considered binding, it can affect the predictability of work progress. Both developers and product owners at the company have criticized the inadequate determination of Velocity, highlighting this as a significant issue.

Although Velocity is often identified as a key metric for measuring team performance in agile software development, it is not actively utilized within the investigated case company. Velocity is typically used to gauge the amount of work completed (or also described as the acceleration of a team), e.g., number of Story Points, within a specific time-frame, like an iteration. Its measurement can provide planning certainty for future sprints, helping teams predict their capacity and set realistic goals by understanding the average amount of work completed per sprint. This may enable efficient resource utilization and continuous improvement as teams can adjust their used software development processes and methods based on identified trends. However, Velocity's effectiveness can vary significantly between teams due to different definitions of "done" and varying levels of efficiency. This variability can make comparing Velocity between teams challenging and may lead to manipulation of Velocity figures by teams wanting to appear more or less productive. Despite these potential drawbacks, Velocity can be a valuable metric if interpreted correctly and integrated into the broader context of the agile development process. It should not be the sole indicator of project success but rather a tool for ongoing improvement.

Planning Poker as described in the literature and also used in agile teams at the company promotes collaboration and unbiased estimates by allowing open discussion and maintaining anonymity. The method enhances team collaboration by facilitating open discussions on estimates, allowing for the integration of diverse perspectives, which helps in achieving more accurate workload assessments [33]. However, its oral implementation at the company could lead to uniform estimates influenced by prior responses, potentially reducing accuracy. The sequential approach could diminish the impact of varying perspectives and levels of experience. It also allows less room for individual contemplation and reflection, as members must immediately respond to their colleagues' estimations. Despite criticisms from developers and product owners regarding its execution, the fundamental practice of Planning Poker is still positively regarded within the team, suggesting that adjustments to its implementation could enhance its effectiveness. Using Planning Poker cards could facilitate discussions and enhance all team members' involvement in estimation. Structured and moderated discussions ensure that all team members express their views and that diverse perspectives are adequately considered, leading to more accurate and agreed-upon estimations [33].

> **Answering RQ3:** In the context of agile software development within the case company, metrics such as Story Points and Velocity are essential, yet their refinement is necessary to improve performance measurement accuracy. Optimizing Planning Poker and Expert Estimation techniques could enhance objectivity and minimize bias, for instance, by introducing anonymized estimation processes and standardizing task completion criteria across teams. Additionally, the consistent application and evaluation of Velocity can facilitate more accurate sprint planning and resource allocation. Ultimately, refining these metrics and their implementation can lead to improved estimation precision and increased efficiency in agile project management.

Expert Estimations is recognized as a common metric in literature and is frequently used at the investigated company, particularly in release planning. This method allows experienced experts to use their knowledge and skills to provide qualitative assessments of work efforts, leading to realistic and high-quality estimates, especially when the experts are familiar with the specific requirements and context. However, challenges such as varying opinions among different experts can lead to disagreements and uncertainties. Additionally, compared to quantitative methods, Expert Judgement might be less objective and transparent, potentially affecting the traceability of estimates. The reliance on individual expertise can also introduce biases, particularly in the absence of clear guidelines or standardized procedures. Furthermore, the rapid review revealed various other metrics for estimation, including advanced techniques such as neural networks.

The findings presented in literature is mainly more positive about metrics as they help measure, optimize, and manage various processes in agile software development. The aspect of the high variety and the challenges applying such metrics in practice is underrepresented. Metrics are utilized for several reasons, including enhancing efficiency, tracking progress, planning future sprints, and measuring customer satisfaction [9]. It is important to note that implementing improvements through metrics can require additional work, including training, process adjustments, and monitoring new metrics. Thus, a careful balance must be struck between the potential benefits and the additional effort to ensure that the changes provide real value to agile software development teams.

6 Threats to Validity

Though we followed a systematic research design using guidelines for the rapid literature review [8] and the focus group [52], some limitations need to be taken into account. We discuss the limitations of our study using the threats to validity concept, focusing on the measures we took to address the threats to validity below.

Construct Validity: A major limitation in literature studies applies related to the completeness of the identified result set. However, we countered this aspect using a systematic approach with the applied guidelines for a rapid literature review Furthermore, the study selection was performed by applying defined inclusion and exclusion criteria and a cross-check of the selection by the second author. Also, construct validity threats apply for the qualitative focus group approach. First, the length of the focus group sessions took between 30 and 45 min. Such an appointment can be tiring in the long run and thus, affect the quality of the results. For this reason, we did not hold the focus group meetings at off-peak times during the working day, but during core working hours. Sufficient breaks were also planned and implemented.

Internal Validity: Although we prepared the focus groups based on a systematic approach using a rapid literature review, there are some limitations that need to be considered to strengthen the chain of evidence. We took three actions to reduce the risk of bias. First, the guiding questions for the focus group were non-leading questions so as not to induce any implicit direction (e.g., positive or negative affect of metrics application) in the participants. Second, the flow of the leading questions was semi-structured, which allowed us to go deeper into the direction the participants were seeking. Third, we considered a mix of roles, expertise, and experience in the composition of the focus group participants (see Sect. 3 and Table 1 for further details). Also, we are aware that the second focus group were only attended by two participants. However, even if the duo limits the perspectives and dynamics that should arise in the group discussion, we tried to counter this aspect by conducting the second focus group session with well-experienced Product Owners in both experience with agile approaches and the company/industry. Furthermore, we did not record the focus group workshops in order to encourage participation and active involvement during implementation. We are aware that this may have a negative impact on the data quality, so we systematically documented the results and took detailed notes also for the informal talks around the workshops. The focus groups were prepared and moderated by the first author. The second author was involved in reviewing the analysis results.

External Validity: The external validity of the study could be improved by including additional focus groups from the case company or additional cases from other industries and regions. It would also be useful to take agile software development teams with different agile maturity levels under study, as we assume that effects on the selection and successful integration of metrics may apply.

7 Conclusion and Future Work

In this paper, we present the results of our mixed-method study dealing with performance metrics in agile software development. Below, we conclude our findings based on the research questions, before we give a brief overview of our planned future work activities.

First, the results from our rapid literature review show that a wide range of metrics in agile software development is used. For example, several metrics to measure performance or software quality exist and are applied in practice. We decided to create a repository of metrics for agile software development to provide a systematic overview of used metrics. The repository consists of 36 metrics clustered in seven categories. The repository of well-known metrics used in agile software development can be used by both practitioners and researchers applying agile methods in practice to enhance the transparency and possible improvement of their processes in use.

Second, based on the findings from our two focus groups (in a single case study), we found that some metrics (e.g., Story Points) may be inadequate for the given context or the underlying objective applying them to a team. Also, metrics for effort/complexity estimation (e.g., oral Planning Poker) are challenged by misconceptions or misunderstandings how the metric may be applied. However, we also identified that the application of metrics is of high importance as they increase transparency of the teams' outcome and progress during an iteration. Third, analyzing the findings and results from the two other RQs, we found that it may be value-able approach to apply a metric like the Velocity measuring the progress of an agile software development team.

As our study is obviously limited by conducting a single case study, we currently plan to expand the study to other highly regulated contexts like finance or public administration.

References

1. Abrahamsson, P., Salo, O., Ronkainen, J., Warsta, J.: Agile software development methods: review and analysis. (478), 7–94 (2002)
2. Ahmad, M.O., Al-Baik, O.: Beyond technical debt unravelling organisational debt concept. In: Proceedings of the 39th ACM/SIGAPP Symposium on Applied Computing, pp. 802–809. ACM (2024). https://doi.org/10.1145/3605098.3635913
3. Almeida, F., Carneiro, P.: Perceived importance of metrics for agile scrum environments. Information **14** (2023). https://doi.org/10.3390/info14060327
4. Atlassian: Confluence (2024). https://www.atlassian.com/de/software/confluence. Accessed 19 Dec 2024
5. Atlassian: Jira (2024). https://www.atlassian.com/de/software/jira. Accessed 18 Dec 2024
6. Bose, S.: Bug vs error: key differences (2023). https://www.browserstack.com/guide/difference-between-bugs-and-errors. Accessed 06 Dec 2024
7. businessmap.io: 6 agile metrics that matter (2023). https://businessmap.io/agile/project-management/agile-metrics#:~:text=2.-,Throughput,weekly%2C%20monthly%2C%20etc. Accessed 10 Dec 2024
8. Cartaxo, B., Pinto, G., Soares, S.: Rapid reviews in software engineering. In: Contemporary Empirical Methods in Software Engineering, pp. 357–384. Springer (2020)

9. Chloros, D., Gerogiannis, V., Kakarontzas, G.: Use of software and project management metrics in agile software development methodologies: a systematic mapping study. In: Proceedings of the European Symposium on Software Engineering, pp. 25–32. ACM (2022). https://doi.org/10.1145/3571697.3571701
10. Choras, M., et al.: Measuring and improving agile processes in a small-size software development company. IEEE Access **8**, 78452–78466 (2020). https://doi.org/10.1109/ACCESS.2020.2990117
11. Cohn, M.: Estimating with use case points (2005). https://www.mountaingoatsoftware.com/articles/estimating-with-use-case-points. Accessed 07 Dec 2024
12. Dikert, K., Paasivaara, M., Lassenius, C.: Challenges and success factors for large-scale agile transformations: a systematic literature review. J. Syst. Softw. **119**, 87–108 (2016)
13. Fernandez-Diego, M., Mendez, E., Gonzalez-Ladron-De-Guevara, F., Abrahao, S., Insfran, E.: An update on effort estimation in agile software development: a systematic literature review. IEEE Access **8**, 166768–166800 (2020). https://doi.org/10.1109/ACCESS.2020.3021664
14. geeksforgeeks.org: Agile planning and estimation (2022). https://www.geeksforgeeks.org/agile-planning-and-estimation/. Accessed 02 Dec 2024
15. geeksforgeeks.org: Differentiate between loc and function point in software engineering (2023). https://www.geeksforgeeks.org/differentiate-between-loc-and-function-point-in-software-engineering/. Accessed 03 Dec 2024
16. geeksforgeeks.org: Schedule performance index (SPI) - software engineering (2023). https://www.geeksforgeeks.org/software-engineering-schedule-performance-index-spi/. Accessed 03 Dec 2024
17. Goyal, A., Sardana, N.: Performance assessment of bug fixing process in open source repositories. Procedia Comput. Sci. **167**, 2070–2079 (2020). https://doi.org/10.1016/j.procs.2020.03.247
18. GrafanaLabs: Grafana dashboards (2024). https://grafana.com/grafana/dashboards/. Accessed 10 Dec 2024
19. Heimann, D.: Metrics and databases for agile software development projects (2010)
20. Kaner, C., Bond, W.: Software engineering metrics: what do they measure and how do we know. In: Proceedings of the International Software Metrics Symposium (2004)
21. Kojic, M.: Takt time, cycle time, and lead time explained (+ calculators) (2022). https://clockify.me/blog/business/takt-time-cycle-time-lead-time/. Accessed 06 Dec 2024
22. Kunz, M., Dumke, R., Zenker, N.: Software metrics for agile software development. In: Proceedings of the Australian Conf. on Software Engineering, pp. 673–678 (2008). https://doi.org/10.1109/ASWEC.2008.4483261
23. Kupiainen, E., Mäntylä, M., Itkonen, J.: Why are industrial agile teams using metrics and how do they use them? In: Proceedings of the International Workshop on Emerging Trends in Software Metrics, pp. 23–29. ACM (2014). https://doi.org/10.1145/2593868.2593873
24. Kupiainen, E., Mäntylä, M., Itkonen, J.: Using metrics in agile and lean software development - a systematic literature review of industrial studies. Inf. Softw. Technol. **62**, 143–163 (2015). https://doi.org/10.1016/j.infsof.2015.02.005
25. lambdatest.com: Software testing metrics guide; definition, types & example (2023). https://www.lambdatest.com/learning-hub/software-testing-metrics. Accessed 08 Dec 2024

26. Lang, M.: Was sind story points und warum verwenden wir sie? (2018). https://agilescrumgroup.de/story-points/. Accessed 05 Dec 2024
27. Looks, H., Fangmann, J., Thomaschewski, J., Escalona, M.J., Schön, E.M.: Towards improving agility in public administration. Softw. Qual. J. **32**, 283–311 (2024). https://doi.org/10.1007/s11219-023-09657-x
28. López, L., et al.: Quality measurement in agile and rapid software development: a systematic mapping. J. Syst. Softw. **186**, 111187 (2022). https://doi.org/10.1016/j.jss.2021.111187
29. Maierhofer, S., Stelzmann, E., Kohlbacher, M., Fellner, B.: Requirement changes and project success: the moderating effects of agile approaches in system engineering projects. In: Riel, A., O'Connor, R., Tichkiewitch, S., Messnarz, R. (eds.) EuroSPI 2010. CCIS, vol. 99, pp. 60–70. Springer, Heidelberg (2010). https://doi.org/10.1007/978-3-642-15666-3_6
30. Mallidi, R., Sharma, M.: Study on agile story point estimation techniques and challenges. Int. J. Comput. Appl. **174**, 9–14 (2021). https://doi.org/10.5120/ijca2021921014
31. Mills, E.: Metrics in the software engineering curriculum. Ann. Softw. Eng. **6**, 181–200 (1998). https://doi.org/10.1023/A:1018909531948
32. Misra, S., Omorodion, M.: Survey on agile metrics and their inter-relationship with other traditional development metrics. ACM SIGSOFT Softw. Eng. Notes **36**, 1–3 (2011). https://doi.org/10.1145/2047414.2047430
33. Moløkken-Østvold, K., Haugen, N., Benestad, H.: Using planning poker for combining expert estimates in software projects. J. Syst. Softw. **81**, 2106–2117 (2008)
34. Münch, J., Armbrust, O., Kowalczyk, M., Soto, M.: Software Process Definition and Management. Springer, Heidelberg (2012). https://doi.org/10.1007/978-3-642-24291-5
35. Neumann, M., Schmid, K., Baumann, L.: Characterizing the impact of culture on agile methods: the moca model. In: Proceedings of the International Conference on Software and System Processes (2023)
36. Neumann, M.: Towards a taxonomy of agile methods: the tree of agile elements. In: Proceedings of the International Conference in Software Engineering Research and Innovation, pp. 79–87 (2021). https://doi.org/10.1109/CONISOFT52520.2021.00022
37. Neumann, M., Kuchel, T., Diebold, P., Schön, E.M.: Agile culture clash: unveiling challenges in cultivating an agile mindset in organizations. Comput. Sci. Inf. Syst. **21**(3), 1013–1031 (2024). https://doi.org/10.2298/CSIS230715029N
38. Ng, Y., Leśniewski, B., Marek, K., Neumann, M., Trzesicki, J.: Unlocking feedback in remote retrospectives: Games, anonymity, and continuous reflection in action. In: Proceedings of the International Conference on Information Systems Development. Springer, Cham (2024). https://doi.org/10.62036/ISD.2024.118
39. Nguyen, D., Tran, D.: A review of effort estimation studies in agile, iterative and incremental software development. In: Proceedings of the International Conference on Research Challenges in Information Science. IEEE (2013). https://doi.org/10.1109/RIVF.2013.6719861
40. Paetsch, F., Eberlein, D., Maurer, D.: Requirements engineering and agile software development (2003)
41. Panda, A., Satapathy, S., Rath, S.: Empirical validation of neural network models for agile software effort estimation based on story points. Procedia Comput. Sci. **57**, 772–781 (2015)
42. Paulish, D., Carleton, A.: Case studies of software-process-improvement measurement. Computer **27**, 50–57 (1994). https://doi.org/10.1109/2.312039

43. Pham, K.P.: Interview guideline for the focus groups (2024). https://doi.org/10.5281/zenodo.11206152
44. Pham, K.P.: Performance metrics repo documentation (2024). https://doi.org/10.5281/zenodo.11206133
45. Pham, K.P.: Rapid review protocol & documentation (2024). https://doi.org/10.5281/zenodo.12637754
46. Pham, K.P., Neumann, M.: How to measure performance in agile software development? A mixed-method study. In: Proceedings of the International Conference on Software Engineering and Advanced Applications (2024). https://doi.org/10.1109/SEAA64295.2024.00074
47. Pichler, M., Rumetshofer, H., Wahler, W.: Agile requirements engineering for a social insurance for occupational risks organization: a case study, pp. 246–251 (2006). https://doi.org/10.1109/RE.2006.8
48. Przybylek, A., Albecka, M., Springer, O., Kowalski, W.: Game-based sprint retrospectives: multiple action research. Empir. Softw. Eng. **27**(1), 1–56 (2022). https://doi.org/10.1007/s10664-021-10043-z
49. Ram, P., Rodriguez, P., Oivo, M.: Software process measurement and related challenges in agile software development: a multiple case study. In: Kuhrmann, M., et al. (eds.) PROFES 2018. LNCS, vol. 11271, pp. 272–287. Springer, Cham (2018). https://doi.org/10.1007/978-3-030-03673-7_20
50. Ram, P., Rodriguez, P., Oivo, M., Martinez-Fernandez, S.: Success factors for effective process metrics operationalization in agile software development: a multiple case study. In: Proceedings of the International Conference on Software and System Processes, pp. 14–23. IEEE (2019). https://doi.org/10.1109/ICSSP.2019.00013
51. Reichelt, D., Kühne, S., Hasselbring, W.: Automated identification of performance changes at code level (2023). https://doi.org/10.1109/QRS57517.2022.00096
52. Runeson, P., Höst, M.: Guidelines for conducting and reporting case study research in software engineering. Empir. Softw. Eng. **14**(2), 131–164 (2009). https://doi.org/10.1007/s10664-008-9102-8
53. Salido, M.G., Borrego, G., Palacio Cinco, R.R., Rodríguez, L.F.: Agile software engineers' affective states, their performance and software quality: a systematic mapping review. J. Syst. Softw. **204**, 111800 (2023). https://doi.org/10.1016/j.jss.2023.111800
54. Sidky, A., Arthur, J., Bohner, S.: A disciplined approach to adopting agile practices: the agile adoption framework. Innov. Syst. Softw. Eng. **3**(3), 203–216 (2007). https://doi.org/10.1007/s11334-007-0026-z
55. Soini, J.: A survey of metrics use in finnish software companies. In: Proceedings of the International Symposium on Empirical Software Engineering and Measurement, pp. 49–57. IEEE (2011). https://doi.org/10.1109/ESEM.2011.13
56. Son, H.: QA metrics in software testing: Definitions, types, formulas & examples (2023). https://www.testrail.com/qa-metrics/
57. Sonar: Sonarqube (2024). https://www.sonarsource.com/. Accessed 10 Dec 2024
58. Strauss, A., Corbin, J.: Open Coding. Sage (1990)
59. Tarhan, A., Yilmaz, S.: Systematic analyses and comparison of development performance and product quality of incremental process and agile process. Inf. Softw. Technol. **56**, 477–494 (2014). https://doi.org/10.1016/j.infsof.2013.12.002
60. Tobisch, F., Weigelt, K., Philipp, P., Matthes, F.: Investigating effort estimation in a large-scale agile ERP transformation program. In: Šmite, D., Guerra, E., Wang, X., Marchesi, M., Gregory, P. (eds.) XP 2024. LNBIP, vol. 512, pp. 70–86. Springer, Cham (2024). https://doi.org/10.1007/978-3-031-61154-4_5

61. Topp, J., Hille, J.H., Neumann, M., Mötefindt, D.: How a 4-day work week and remote work affect agile software development teams. In: Przybyłek, A., Jarzębowicz, A., Luković, I., Ng, Y.Y. (eds.) LASD 2022. LNBIP, vol. 438, pp. 61–77. Springer, Cham (2022). https://doi.org/10.1007/978-3-030-94238-0_4
62. Trzesicki, J., Marek, K., Przybylek, A.: Impact of the kanban maturity model on a team's agile transformation: tripling throughput and elevating quality in three months. In: Šmite, D., Guerra, E., Wang, X., Marchesi, M., Gregory, P. (eds.) XP 2024. LNBIP, vol. 512, pp. 107–116. Springer, Cham (2024). https://doi.org/10.1007/978-3-031-61154-4_7
63. Unadkat, J.: 7 common types of software bugs every tester should know (2023). https://www.browserstack.com/guide/types-of-software-bugs. Accessed 07 Dec 2024
64. Ungan, E., Cizmeli, N., Demirors, O.: Comparison of functional size based estimation and story points, based on effort estimation effectiveness in scrum projects. In: Proceedings of the International Conference on Software Engineering and Advanced Applications, pp. 77–80. IEEE, Verona (2014). https://doi.org/10.1109/SEAA.2014.83
65. Usman, M., Börstler, J., Petersen, K.: An effort estimation taxonomy for agile software development. Int. J. Softw. Eng. Knowl. Eng. **27**, 641–674 (2017). https://doi.org/10.1142/S0218194017500243
66. Usman, M., Mendes, E., Weidt, F., Britto, R.: Effort estimation in agile software development: a systematic literature review. In: Proceedings of the International Conference on Predictive Models in Software Engineering, pp. 82–91. ACM (2014). https://doi.org/10.1145/2639490.2639503
67. VersionOne, Collabnet: 17th annual state of agile survey (2023). stateofagile.com
68. Verwijs, C., Russo, D.: A theory of scrum team effectiveness. ACM Trans. Softw. Eng. Methodol. **32**(3) (2023). https://doi.org/10.1145/3571849
69. Verwijs, C., Russo, D.: Do agile scaling approaches make a difference? An empirical comparison of team effectiveness across popular scaling approaches. Empir. Softw. Eng. **29**(75) (2024). https://doi.org/10.1007/s10664-024-10481-5
70. Vyas, M., Hemrajani, N.: Predicting effort of agile software projects using linear regression, ridge regression and logistic regression. **13** (2021)
71. Williams, L.: Agile software development methodologies and practices. In: Advances in Computers, vol. 80, pp. 1–44. Academic Press (2010). https://doi.org/10.1016/S0065-2458(10)80001-4
72. Yin, R.K.: Case Study Research: Design and Methods, Applied Social Research Methods Series, vol. 5, 4th edn. Sage (2009)

Automatic Task Classification of Software Projects for Planning and Simulation

Włodzimierz Wysocki[1](✉) and Mirosław Ochodek[2]

[1] Faculty of Computer Science and Information Technology,
West Pomeranian University of Technology in Szczecin, Szczecin, Poland
`wwysocki@zut.edu.pl`
[2] Faculty of Computer Science and Telecommunications,
Poznan University of Technology, Poznan, Poland
`miroslaw.ochodek@cs.put.poznan.pl`

Abstract. Background: Information about project tasks stored in Issue tracking systems (ITS) can be used for project analytics or process simulation. However, such issues must be classified beforehand. Considering the number of tasks stored in ITS, this task shall be done automatically. **Aims:** Our research aims to build an automatic recurring Jira issue classification model based on types and textual descriptions to enable the practical application of the model for software project planning and management. **Method:** We study a dataset from six industrial projects containing 9.6K tasks and augment it with an additional dataset of 91K task descriptions from other industrial projects to upsample minority classes during training. We labeled the data using a semi-manual, active-learning-based method. We perform ten runs of 10-fold cross-validation for each project and evaluate classifiers using a set of state-of-the-art prediction quality metrics, i.e., Accuracy, Precision, Recall, F1-score, and MCC. Our machine-learning pipeline includes a Transformer-based sentence embedder ('mxbai-embed-large-v1') and an XGBoost classifier. We also study the impact of task-classification errors on project staffing issues. **Results:** The model automatically classifies software process tasks into 14 classes with MCCs ranging from 0.69 to 0.88. We built a confusion matrix that showed the most frequently confused task classes. We analyzed the consequences of classification errors. **Conclusions:** The study's results enable the practical application of the software process model to analyze, plan, and manage software development projects.

Keywords: Automatic Task Classification · Software Process Simulation · NLP · XGBoost

1 Introduction

Issue tracking systems (ITS) collect large amounts of data regarding project activities. Such data can be used for project analytics or as a basis for running process simulations to support project planning [20, 21]. Unfortunately, most ITS use simple categorization schemes allowing users to assign types to issues/tasks like stories, sub-tasks, bugs, etc. Such classification is shallow and does not reveal the true nature of the tasks. Consequently, using issue data for project analytics or simulation is limited. One could introduce a richer classification schema; however, it would cost team members more time to enter issues into a system. Another approach would be to augment the regular ITS issue classification with additional categories of issues automatically inferred from task descriptions, providing deeper insights.

ITS are no longer simple systems for tracking defects in software under development. They have been evolving into complex software project management for some time. They often can include plugins that extend their capabilities. Our work is moving in the direction of extending the capabilities of ITS both in the classification of task types and further in the direction of work and project team planning and verification of decisions using simulation. We intend to use the existing ability to extend ITS functions through the plugin system.

In our previous studies, we proposed a taxonomy of tasks in software projects that includes 21 types of tasks that are either stateful or recurring [22]. They take into account the nature of activities performed within a task. We have proposed an algorithm to classify stateful tasks [21]. However, classifying recurring tasks seems far more challenging.

Therefore, the study presented in this paper aims to investigate the possibility of employing machine learning (ML) algorithms to categorize recurring tasks into one of 14 classes defined in the taxonomy based on task descriptions and additional metadata stored in Jira ITS.

This is an extended version of the paper [19] presented at the SEAA 2024 conference. It significantly expands the section on automatic task classification in planning and simulation, giving a wider context. We have also included a quantitative and qualitative analysis and discussion of the consequences of classification errors on staffing issues in software projects. Thus, we show how abstract classification quality metrics, such as MCC, correspond to the practical impact of task misclassifications.

The remaining part of this paper is organized as follows. In Sect. 2, we compiled a review of papers on automatic classification in software projects. We presented their contributions and identified research gaps. In Sect. 3, we described the taxonomy of task classes in software projects and the applicability of task analysis for work planning and project team selection. We introduce the idea of simulation to test the consequences of decisions on the execution of work in a project. In Sect. 4 we pose the objectives and research questions, present the projects analyzed, and describe the heuristic labeling algorithm and training and validation of the task classification model. Section 5 presents the results obtained and discusses them. It details the practical implications of classification errors for the work of project teams. It gives recommendations on how to use the presented work in your applications and discusses threads of validity. Section 6 presents conclusions and considers further work.

2 Related Work

Bruegge et al. article [1] is one of the first papers on automatic task classification in software projects. They used machine learning methods to classify tasks according to activities in the Software Development Life Cycle. In their view, this is the basis for analyzing projects and determining metrics.

Santos et al. [14] classified tasks in terms of the APIs used while completing them. The automatic creation of such labels was supposed to allow developers to select a task for implementation in open-source projects.

Wu et al. [18] investigated with what accuracy different transformers classify the sentiment of project tasks.

The most popular branch of research is classifying bug reports from projects. One of the first articles on this topic [6] used the manual classification of more than 7,000 bug reports from open-source projects. The authors introduced six classes of bug reports to categorize the reports by type and the required response. Most of the articles in this stream describe the automatic classification of bug reports into bugs and other types [8,12,13,24]. The authors mostly use binary classifiers. In addition to their research results, some papers also provide tools to automatically classify the created notifications [8,24]. Meher et al. [10] described the most advanced research on bug classification. They developed a taxonomy of 8 bug classes, assigned keywords to them, heuristically labeled 1.35M bug reports from various open-source projects and checked the classification accuracy using four different transformers.

In addition to tasks and bug reports, the research includes the classification of commits - descriptions of code changes posted to the repository. Gharbi et al. [5] use multi-label classification to tag changes to make it easier for developers to track code changes. Shafiq et al. have published a review article [16] of research using machine learning in software engineering. The review orders the applications according to the software lifecycle. It does not include the applications mentioned above of classification models.

Table 1 shows the subject of the classification of the described papers. As we can see, only some papers focus on the classification of work in software projects due to the nature of the activities performed. The largest number of papers deals with bug classification. We have included them in this section due to their similarity in the subject matter and machine learning techniques. In summary, existing research does not exploit the potential of task classification in projects to analyze workflows and create a software development process model. Our research fills this gap by substantively extending the Bruegee [1] approach and enriching it with new classification techniques and a larger project dataset.

3 Task-Types Taxonomy; Stateful, Stateless and Recurring Tasks

In our analysis of the tasks carried out in software projects, we used data from six projects of the software industry from the financial sector (we provide the

Table 1. Subject of classification of related works

Subject of classification	Articles
Tasks	[1,14,18]
Bugs	[6,8,10,12,13,24]
Commits	[5]
Reviews	[16]

summary of these projects later in the paper—Sect. 4.2, Table 4). The project teams used the Jira ITS to define and manage tasks.

Jira provides a simple mechanism to categorize issues depending on their types. Figure 1 shows the frequency issues of different types in the considered projects. The most commonly used types by the projects' teams were 'Task' (with 'Sub-tasks') and 'Bug', which covered ca. 80% of all Jira issues in these projects.

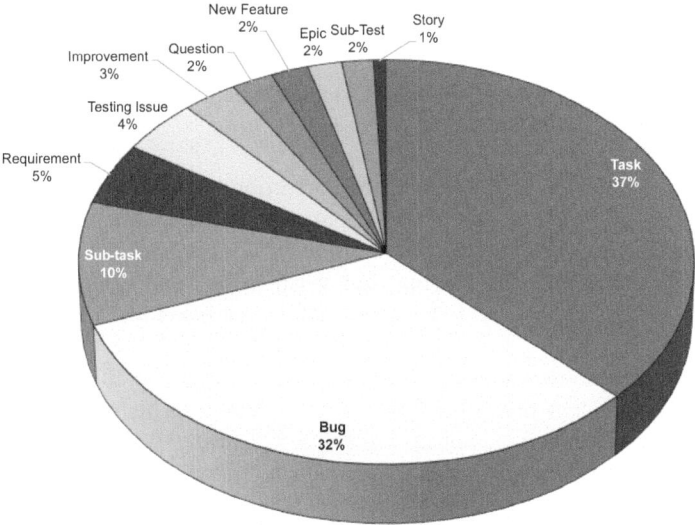

Fig. 1. Types of issue in the software industry projects studied

Although Jira issue categories, such as 'Task,' 'Bug,' and 'Sub-task,' are sufficient for everyday task management, they are too general to be used as a basis for performing deeper analyses, e.g., for effort estimation or process simulation. To understand the nature of the tasks, one must seek additional information in the summary or description of Jira issues or other meta-data, such as issue status.

The status of Jira issues changes as the issue traverses the workflow. Such workflow describes the possible transitions between the statutes. Figure 2 shows a simplified workflow used in the analyzed projects.

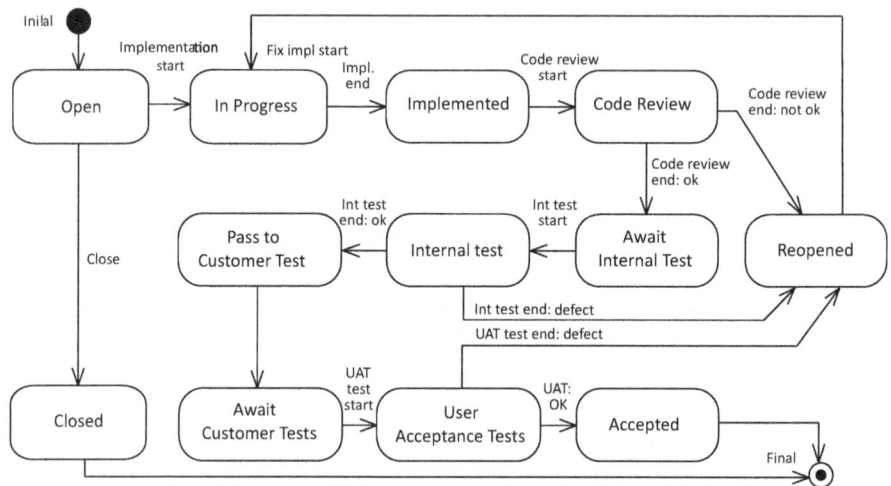

Fig. 2. The simplified workflow used in the software industry projects studied

The transitions between issue states correspond to the execution of basic activities in implementing new system features or fixing bugs. These include implementation, i.e., the creation of component source code, code review, creation of unit tests, function testing and verification, and acceptance testing. Each review or test can redirect the issue back to the developer to fix the defects found.

An interesting feature of the Jira system is storing a history of changes to the values of issue elements, including status. Storing the history supports issue execution tracking. However, not all issues use the state to track work progress. The Jira system allows staff to record working hours on an issue. In some activities, there is no need to track the change of states, as these works do not match the nature of the state flow diagram shown. Based on this feature, we divide project tasks into *stateful* and *stateless*.

Stateful Tasks. These are tasks in which the state changes according to the workflow. In our previous study, we proposed an algorithm to classify stateful tasks [22]. It divides tasks into subtasks and analyzes them according to the state diagram. These subtasks are programming, testing, code review, defect fixing, etc. Each subtask has an author, type, start date, and number of working hours. The algorithm analyzes tasks by looking at their state transition history. Many history records are difficult to interpret because users work with the Jira system differently. Some of them switch the issue to the appropriate state, perform the tasks, and immediately change the task status to the terminal state in the workflow "skipping" on some intermediate states. For example, a developer opens a task, switches the state to 'In progress', creates unit tests, implements a function, and finally switches the state to 'Implemented'. These tasks are easy to recognize. Other team members do the necessary work first and switch the value of the issue status field to 'Implemented' when finished. This working manner introduces some difficulties in interpretation. Besides, Jira enforces sequential state changes; you cannot jump directly to the correct state value. Sometimes, you have to click through sequential workflow states. The consequence is 'empty' state changes with no work completed or recorded hours in issue history. The algorithm must recognize and avoid these.

Stateless Tasks. Contrary to stateful tasks, stateless tasks do not require tracking their completion using workflows. As shown in Fig. 3, only around 27% of tasks in the considered projects were stateless. We also observed that such tasks, on average, require less effort. This observation is consistent with the fact that stateless tasks are small tasks that do not require verification and state tracking. In contrast, it is not fully consistent with identifying stateless tasks as cyclical tasks. Daily stand-up meetings within the project team accumulate large amounts of working hours. Figure 3 shows the quantities of tasks per project and their effort. We have learned that the work of the stateful tasks is related to implementing information systems functions. What is the stateless task purpose? The question is important because this can be a sizable part of the work in a project.

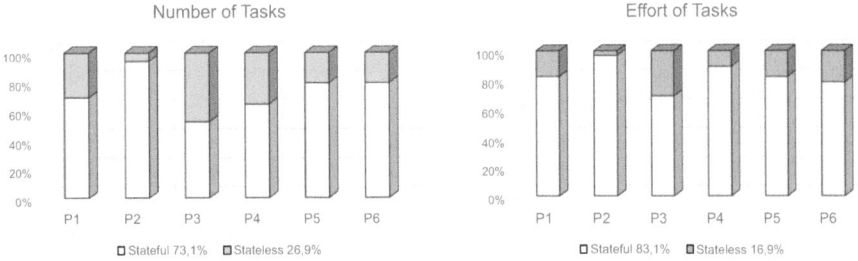

Fig. 3. Quantities and efforts of stateful and recurring tasks in the studied projects.

Recurring Tasks. When we looked at these single stateless tasks, we found that they belonged to more than a dozen classes. Stateless tasks related to managing hardware, network, or software infrastructure regularly occur and are executed as needed by the project. Writing and fixing scripts, creating new accounts for users, installing databases, and creating backups are all stateless tasks that belong to the group of administrative tasks. As a class of tasks, they become recurring because maintaining the software project environments consists of completing a certain number of these tasks monthly.

The situation is very similar for stateless testing tasks. Tasks involving testing components, system modules, or integration and manual testing are performed in each software development iteration when testers have completed verification of newly implemented features or when needed. These stateless tasks belong to the class of testing tasks. When we look at them this way, several testing tasks recur in an iteration.

Analyzing actual software projects allowed us to distinguish 14 classes of recurring tasks. Less emphasis on documenting is due to the concern for delivering working software to the client. Undoubtedly, the project team is very busy when developing a product. Hence, the idea is to support them with machine learning tools to deepen the semantics of the collected data. This article deals with *automatically classifying tasks as part of recurring issues*. These classes make it possible to relate the type of work carried out to the competencies of the people belonging to the development team. Table 2 provides a full list of them, with descriptions.

3.1 Task Classification as a Basis for Planning and Simulation

A detailed analysis of the completed tasks in the project is essential for planning the way forward. We used a multi-agent approach to build a project team model in earlier work [23]. Agents represented individuals from the project team with corresponding roles. These agents performed the project tasks and, thus, by the established methodology of the production process, created the project work plan. The multi-agent model works at the micro level. Agents perform atomic actions in the development process, such as requirements elicitation, creation of actors and use cases or user stories, design, test writing and code, and testing. The picture at the level of the whole project emerged emergently and showed the further course of the generation process.

In more recent work, we use a macro approach [20]. We consider aggregate (for an iteration or sprint) workflows and tasks. It is important to link the work done by project team members with specific roles and competencies to the project tasks. We have achieved this by dividing stateful tasks into subtasks of types determined by the team member's roles. The automatic classification of stateless tasks allows the transformation into recurring tasks whose class indicates the team member's role.

The flowchart in Fig. 4 presents the idea of using the model to plan the next stages of the software process based on completed iterations or a reference project. We discuss the elements of the model below. The analysis classifies the work done according to the tasks' types and the team members' roles. It divides tasks into stateful tasks, carried out according to the project's workflow, and recurring tasks, in which the task's state remains unchanged. Most recurring tasks, such as daily standups, are carried out regularly. However, some, such as manual testing of project areas, have been classified as recurring to simplify

Table 2. List of recurring task classes

Class	Description
ADM	Work performed by administrators to develop and maintain the technology infrastructure. Among other things, managing users, assigning and revoking access rights, installing new development, test, and production environments, including operating systems, utility applications, database servers and application servers. Analyzing server logs to detect the cause of errors, fixing faults, and installing software updates.
BLD	Managing the creation of new software versions, repairing and updating the scripts that build the release and deploy it to the servers, analyzing compilation and testing errors to detect the causes and overseeing the fixing of defects.
CFG	Creation of new plug-ins and their configuration. Configuration of software modules and customization to customer requirements. Creation of new reports and printouts. Create user accounts and user groups and manage access rights within the product under development.
CUST	Consultation with the customer, travel to the customer, technical support, meetings with customers, training courses, conferences, and generally assisting the customer with adapting to working with the new software.
DEV	Development work related to the analysis, design and implementation of the product's functional requirements.
DOC	Create and modify documentation and software help files.
EDU	Education, training and development of the development team.
MIGR	Work on migrating data from the client's previous IT system to the product under development.
MIT	Development team meetings: daily stand-up meetings, sprint planning, retrospectives, demo meetings, status meetings, introduction meetings, internal meetings, etc.
PM	Project management, project work planning, and issue management in Jira.
RQM	Preparation for requirements workshops and requirements workshops with the client. Requirements detailing, analysis, clarification, and client and user interviews.
RVW	Code, algorithms, documentation, requirements and script reviews.
TST	Testing work. Designing, executing, updating, automating exploratory, manual, automated, acceptance tests, etc.
BUG	Defect reporting from testers on the development team and defect reports from customers.

the model. The data collected support creating statistics and reports, allowing the project manager to understand the process better. The model assumes that tasks related to new features, functions, or defects are continuously created and modified.

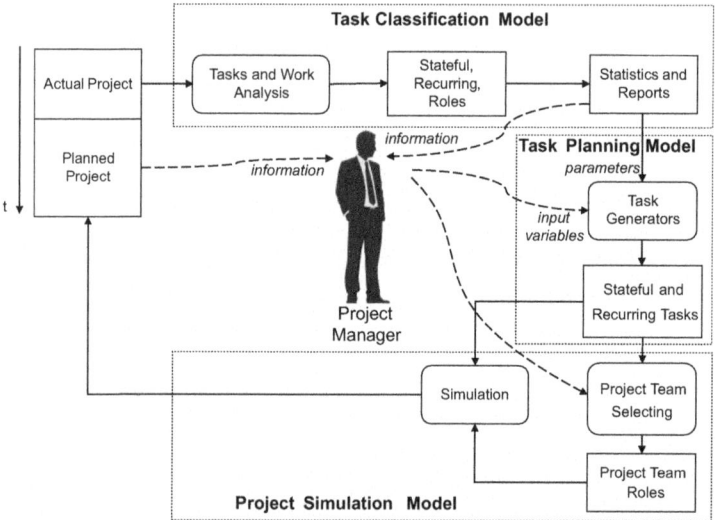

Fig. 4. Macrosimulation model idea. The project is analyzed and then aggregated according to task types and roles, which controls the task generator, which, once the project team is selected, is transformed through simulation into a project plan.

A dedicated generator creates tasks based on input parameters and analysis results in the model. Considering the monthly effort of tasks divided by type and class, the project manager selects the appropriate number of people to perform the necessary roles. Information about the tasks created, the roles assigned, and the number of employees goes into the simulation module, where the number of hours worked for each role is calculated and subtracted from the effort of recurring and stateful tasks. Work not completed in a given month is carried over to the next month. The data on tasks and work performed form the monthly element of the software development process plan (Work Plan).

Task Classification Model. The classification model consists of an algorithm that divides state tasks into subtasks and an algorithm that classifies stateless tasks. We described the idea of the stateful task partitioning algorithm above. For a detailed description, we refer you to the article [21]. The algorithm divides tasks into the following classes:

– DEV_PRG, DEV_TST - programming of new features, tester verification, defect fixes.

- BUG_DEV_PRG, BUG_DEV_TST - fixing defects reported by testers and verification by testers.
- BUG_DEV_PRG, BUG_DEV_TST - fixing defects reported by customers and their verification by testers.

This breakdown makes it possible to draw up monthly workflows for implementing new features, testing, and repairing defects, broken down into the work of developers and testers.

A model for classifying a stateless task is the subject of this article. In previous work, constructing a prototype for proof of concept, we classified stateless tasks manually, coarsely, and inaccurately. The resulting recurring task data allowed software projects to be reproduced and planned with sufficient accuracy. We proved our approach's reproductive and predictive capabilities by the experiments' results. The model outputs monthly project workflows of state tasks and recurring tasks in person-hours.

Task Planning Model. Task planning takes place separately for stateful and recurring tasks. The number of stateful tasks is dependent on the size of the project. The effort required for the recurring task is similar every month. We see an analogy with variable and fixed cost accounting in industrial production. Task generators are responsible for task planning.

Stateful Task Generator. In modern software development approaches, teams and clients create new tasks throughout the life of a project. This observation inspired us to create the concept of a stateful task generator. The input parameters of the generator are the number and effort of tasks and the parameters controlling the envelope of the generator. Figure 5 shows the concept of a stateful tasks generator.

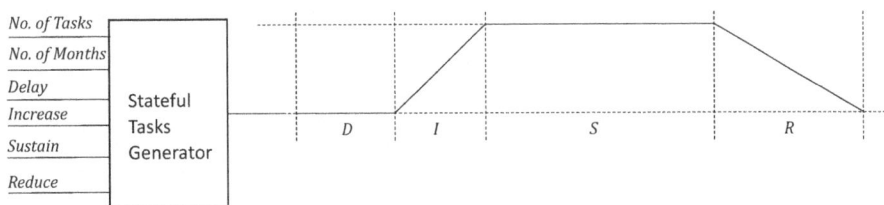

Fig. 5. Stateful task generator idea

In our previous articles, the project manager set the parameter values. Now we see the benefits of using a time series forecaster that, trained on similar projects and further trained on the current project, would plan stateful tasks.

Recurring Task Generator. The first idea for the cyclical task generator was to calculate the sum of tasks for each class for the entire project phase and then divide these sums by the phase number of months. This way, we obtained the effort of recurring tasks for all classes in the following months. Figure 6 shows the concept of a recurring tasks generator.

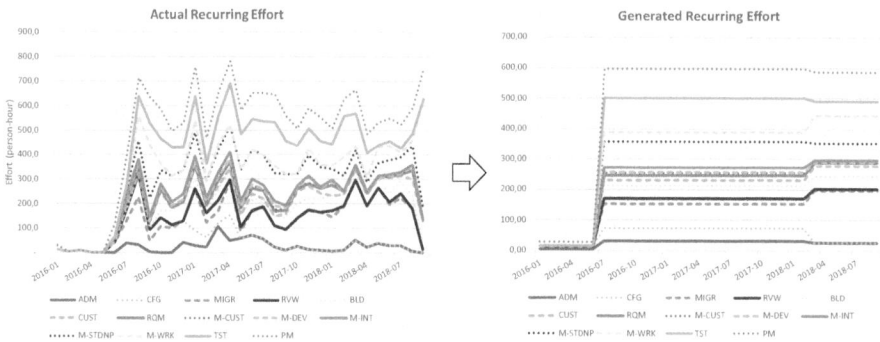

Fig. 6. Averaging operation of the recurring task generator.

We described generators of this type in the previous article [21] and verified the idea in the next article [20]. Despite the substantial differences between the actual and generated values, the simulation reproduced and predicted the work in the project. In hindsight and after gaining distance from the mentioned work, we see that time series forecasting could have performed better in this application.

Project Team. The project team model includes roles and the number of jobs assigned to each role, determined by project data analysis. An example is the role of the programmer. The model allows adding new roles and currently includes:

- ADM administrator,
- PRG programmer who is also involved in the design,
- PM team leader,
- SA System Analyst dealing with requirements gathering and analysis
- TST tester.

The number of jobs in the team is rounded up to a multiple of $\frac{1}{4}$ FTE. One FTE equals 165 person-hours per month, which can be modified. The project analysis takes into account the monthly effort by task class. This connection to task classes allows for the reconstruction of the team composition, which involves translating the number of person-days of work performed into roles and the number of FTEs. The roles of project team members are associated with the tasks performed by the members. Table 3 shows these associations. Programmers perform the largest number of task classes. All project team members perform the EDU and MIT tasks.

Table 3. Assigning recurring task classes to the roles of project team members

Role	Recurring task classes
ADM	ADM, EDU, MIT
PRG	BLD, CFG, DEV, DOC, EDU, MIGR, MIT, BUG, RVW
PM	PM, EDU, MIT
SA	CUST, RQM, EDU, MIT
TST	TST, EDU, MIT

Simulation. The simulation allows one to test the consequences of their decisions. It does not aim to plan the work precisely in a project team. It allows us to check, for example, what happens if two developers leave the team. The simulation requires the following input parameters:

- monthly effort of stateful tasks,
- monthly effort of recurring tasks,
- number of project team members with assigned roles,
- monthly salary by role.

The simulation of the monthly work of the project team first subtracts, taking into account the roles of the team members and the task classes, the effort of the recurring tasks in the month from the number of hours worked by the team. The simulation reports an understaffing error if the number of working hours runs out and the recurring tasks are not completed. The simulation then subtracts the effort of the state tasks from the remaining hours worked by the team, taking roles and classes into account. Simulation carries over state tasks not completed in the current month to the following months. Simulation signals overstaffing if the teamwork at the end of the current month remains greater than zero. Figure 7 shows the calculation diagram in the simulation. The result of the simulation is the workflow for the following months, i.e., the project plan. The simulation also calculates the planned cost of employing a project team based on the monthly salary by role and project team composition.

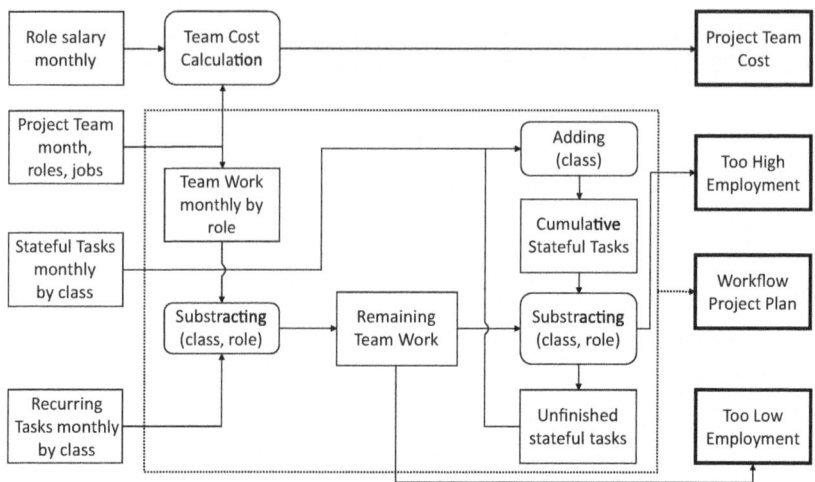

Fig. 7. Block diagram of the monthly teamwork simulation calculations.

4 Research Design

In this section, we describe the purpose of our article and pose our research questions. We then introduce the projects analyzed and describe the heuristic labeling algorithm. In the final section, we describe the training and validation of the task classification model.

4.1 Research Goal and Questions

The goal of our study is to investigate the possibility of automatically categorizing recurring tasks in software projects based on their description and metadata available in issue tracking systems (ITS). In particular, we aim to answer the following research questions:

- RQ1: Is it possible to automatically categorize recurring tasks in industrial IT projects based on the task description and additional metadata stored in ITS using machine-learning models?
- RQ2: Which types of recurring tasks are most often mutually miscategorized by a machine-learning-based model?

RQ1 is a central research question of our study. In [22], we proposed a taxonomy of software project tasks consisting of 21 types of tasks that are either stateful or recurring. In another study [21], we showed how one could use this taxonomy to support project planning using historical data from six software projects. However, a practical usage scenario would require project tasks to be automatically assigned to the categories. Therefore, we want to investigate whether it is possible to use machine-learning (ML) models to perform this task based on the descriptions and metadata of tasks stored in ITS. Since it is our first attempt to classify recurring tasks automatically, and we are also aware that the effectiveness of particular ML models might depend on the project context, we do not aim at performing a comprehensive comparison between ML algorithms but to apply a plausible ML pipeline to get first insights on this topic.

It is hard to expect the proposed ML-based model to categorize recurring tasks flawlessly. Therefore, it is crucial to investigate which types of recurring tasks are mutually miscategorized by the model (RQ2) to assess the potential impact of model inaccuracy on the practical use of the proposed taxonomy in project planning or project analytics.

The replication package for the study is available on GitHub[1]. Unfortunately, we were not allowed to publish the data due to confidentiality restrictions.

4.2 Industrial Dataset

We built the task-type classification model based on data analysis of actual software projects from the financial sector and managed the Jira ITS. Table 4 presents the main characteristics of these projects.

Table 4. Industrial project data

Project	Methodology	Number of Tasks			Project Duration (years)	Team Size (average)
		Stateful	Recurring	All		
P1	hybrid	7 455	3 318	10 773	8.0	14
P2	hybrid	2 545	160	2 705	3.6	12
P3	hybrid	4 102	3 717	7 819	3.2	19
P4	hybrid	782	430	1 212	2.6	8
P5	scrum	4 333	1 146	5 479	3.4	22
P6	scrum	3 128	821	3 949	1.9	23
Total		22 345	9 592	31 937	22.7	98

The software company was in the process of agile transformation while developing all projects. Therefore, In four projects (P1–P4), teams worked mainly according to "traditional" project-management methodologies with selected elements of agile approaches, while the two remaining project teams (P5 and P6) already modeled their development process using the Scrum framework. The total duration of the projects is about 22 years, meaning the project teams worked on most projects in parallel. The number of issues varies between the considered projects and ranges between ca. 1K and 11K. The total number of issues in all projects is 31K; however, only 30% of them are recurring tasks.

---

[1] https://github.com/zut-wwysocki/recurring-task-classification.git.

4.3 Dataset Labelling

Since we base our study on a historical dataset of issues retrieved from Jira ITS, we had to label each issue in projects P1–P6 according to the proposed taxonomy. Manual labeling of ca. 9.6K recurring issues would be infeasible. Therefore, we developed a semi-automatic, multi-stage, heuristic approach to issue labeling. Our approach is based on the analysis of how issues were authored in projects P1–P6, and it is not meant to be applicable to other project contexts.

In the first step, we decided to manually label a portion of the data to identify patterns in how issues were described in the projects under study. We started by labeling ca. 5% of the issues and supported this process with Active Learning (AL). AL is a machine-learning algorithm that iteratively trains and queries a classifier to select the potentially most informative unlabeled instances to be labeled by an oracle (e.g., a human annotator). Also, using AL allowed us to evaluate the consistency of the manual labeling process across the issues by observing the impact of providing new labeled instances on the accuracy of the AL classifier. The drop in accuracy usually meant that the annotator introduced some inconsistency in labeling resulting from changes in the perception of the taxonomy classes manifested in the issue descriptions. The response to this phenomenon was to extract, define, and consolidate the heuristics used by the author during the manual classification process. These heuristics assigned issues to classes based on their Jira metadata (mainly issue types) and *keywords* in their textual descriptions (issue summary and description).

Although Jira issue types (e.g., Task, Sub-task, Story, etc.) are general and do not reveal the true nature of tasks, we identified some consistent mappings between issue types in the projects and our taxonomy classes, presented in Table 5. In the case of issue-type Question, we also considered who was the creator of the issue. If a customer asked a question, we assigned it to class CUST (customer service). Otherwise, the issue was categorized as RQM (requirements work).

Table 5. Mapping between Jira issue types and our taxonomy classes.

Jira issue types	Task Class
Task, Sub-task, Epic, Story, Improvement, New Feature, Product Improvement, Quick Task, Request	DEV
Question created by customer	CUST
Question created by developer, Requirement, Wish, Suggestion	RQM
Test, Sub-Test, Testing Issue, UAT Test case	TST
Documentation	DOC
Technical task	ADM
Bug	BUG

Tasks classified as DEV in the first stage were later classified based on the keywords in their summary and text description.

We created the initial version of the keyword list by filtering project tasks in a spreadsheet and assigning the resulting task keywords. The priority was to derive groups of keywords that suggest a given issue to belong to a certain category. The keyword list contained groups of up to three keywords in the form of a subject, without a suffix, and their assigned task class. If a group consists of a single keyword only, that keyword must occur in the text. If the group includes two keywords (and the third is blank), both must be in the description text. For three words, the text must include three of them. One keyword gives one point to the class summary. Two words are two points, and three words are three points. Heuristic searches the entire list of keywords for each tagged assignment and sums the results for each class. The result is a list of classes with non-zero scores and the number of points.

For example, for the description: *"VPN reimplementation because of netmask change. We must extend our subnet. In the future we will use other address to access servers. So we must reconfigure. After change we will switch of the Juniper router."* we get the list of classes with scores: {'CFG': 4, 'ADM': 11}. Finally, we chose the class with the highest score, and if there was a tie, we chose the first in order. It is not a perfect method, but it is similar to manual marking using the AL method.

In the final step, we tested the effectiveness of a heuristic algorithm and a set of keywords using the procedure shown in Fig. 8. We manually compared the class match with the full task description for 10% of randomly selected tasks from each project. We used the outcome of manual verification to correct or add new keywords to the list used by the heuristic algorithm.

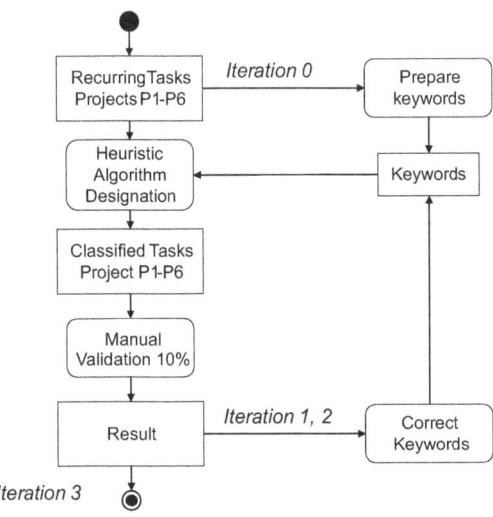

Fig. 8. Verification process for the heuristic algorithm and keyword selection

In total, we carried out three verification iterations, with each iteration correcting the keyword list two times and the last iteration checking accuracy. At each iteration, we observed improvement in accuracy, calculated as the percentage of correctly labeled tasks relative to the number of all tasks selected for validation. Table 6 shows the verification results for each project and, on average, for all successive iterations.

Table 6. Results of manual verification of the heuristic labelling algorithm correctness

	Iteration		
Project	1	2	3
P1	95.2%	96.1%	98.5%
P2	87.5%	100.0%	100.0%
P3	98.4%	97.0%	98.1%
P4	88.4%	97.6%	93.0%
P5	94.8%	94.8%	95.7%
P6	89.0%	93.9%	100.0%
Avg. accuracy	95.4%	96.2%	97.9%

The final version of the heuristic labeling algorithm was able to categorize issues with 93%–100% accuracy (mean 98%). Therefore, we assumed that the potential level of error in labeling is negligible from the practical perspective and applied the algorithm to label the entire dataset. The distribution of the number of recurring tasks in projects P1-P6 is presented in Fig. 9. The number of recurring tasks in the projects ranged from 160 to 3,717. The distribution of issues belonging to different taxonomy categories differs visibly between the projects.

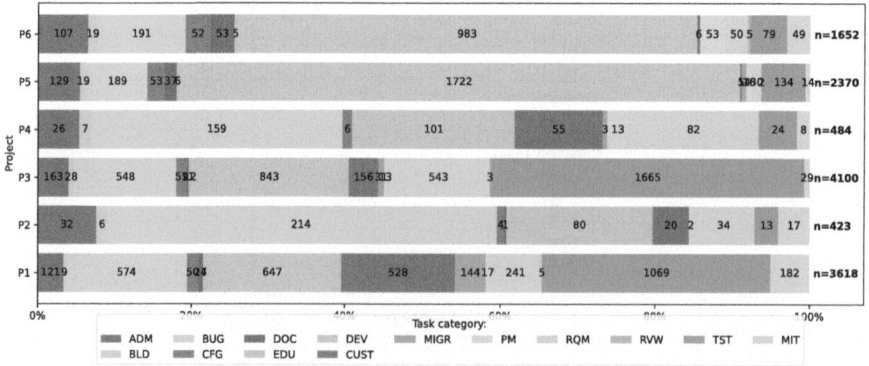

Fig. 9. The distribution of recurring task categories in the projects under study.

4.4 Training and Validation of Task Classification Model

There is a plethora of ML-based algorithms and pipelines that could be used for text classification. Since our goal is not to rank or evaluate each of them but rather to explore to what extent ML can be used to automatically categorize recurring tasks, we decided to choose and study a single, reasonable ML pipeline. The selected pipeline consists of two main components. The first is a pre-trained Transformer-based language model that we use to vectorize both summary and description of a task. We tried several pre-trained sentence embedding models and finally decided to use the 'mxbai-embed-large-v1' model published by mixedbread.ai [9,15]. As of March 2024, the 'mxbai-embed-large-v1' model archives SOTA performance for Bert-large sized models on MTEB [11] and matches the performance of much larger models commercial models. The model has a receptive field of 512 tokens. Therefore, longer texts have to be chunked, and the final embeddings are calculated as a vector-wise maximum of embedding vectors for the text chunks. Another option is to use the mean operation instead of the maximum. However, it could lead to "smoothing" the final embedding vector. Finally, the embedding vectors of issue summary and description (each consisting of 1024 numbers) are concatenated with additional features extracted from issue metadata presented in Table 7.

Table 7. List of Task Features prepared for classification

Feature	Type	Description
jira type	int 0/1 one-hot encoded	Jira type (Task, Bug, Test, ...)
creator	0 - customer, 1 - developer	Who is the author of the issue
assignee	0 - customer, 1 - developer	Who worked on the issue
summary	embeddings $n = 1024$	Sentence Transformer embeddings
description	embeddings $n = 1024$	Sentence Transformer embeddings

The second component is an XGBoost [3] classifier performing multi-class classification. We investigated several configurations, and our final set-up was 500 trees with a maximum height of 3 to mitigate the problem of overfitting (we have a relatively large number of features compared to the dataset size). As an alternative, we investigated the possibility of using the PCA algorithm to reduce the feature-vector dimensionality; however, we observed a drop in the model's accuracy and resigned from this idea.

We performed a separate computational experiment for each project using ten runs of 10-fold cross-validation. Unfortunately, as shown in Fig. 9, our dataset is strongly imbalanced, which could visibly influence the results of our study as only 90% of issues in a project are used for training in each iteration of the cross-validation procedure and in the worst-case scenario they might not even contain instances belonging to all task categories. There are several techniques to tackle the data-imbalance problem; among them are under-sampling, over-sampling [4] and SMOTE methods [2,7], however, the best possible option is to collect more data. Therefore, we decided to use an external database of issues collected from various industrial projects to up-sample minority classes in training subsets (up to the number of issues in the most represented category). Figure 10 shows the flow of the two stage validation procedure using the external issue. This dataset includes over 91K issues external to the projects under study. Unfortunately, we lack histories of changes and some metadata for most of these issues, so we could not include them directly in our study. However, after applying our heuristic labeling algorithm, we were able to use them to mitigate the problem of imbalance in the dataset.

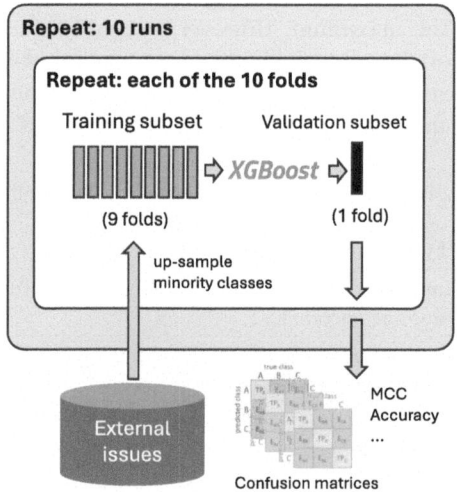

Fig. 10. Two stage validation procedure uses external issues to mitigate data imbalance problem.

Finally, we calculated a suite of classification quality measures, i.e., Accuracy, Precision, Recall, F1-score, and MCC. We also calculated confusion matrices that allow us to investigate which categories are mutually confounded by the model.

5 Results and Discussion

5.1 RQ1: Is it Possible to Automatically Categorize Recurring Tasks in Industrial IT Projects?

The results of performing project-wise ten runs of 10-fold cross-validation are presented in Table 8. The mean Accuracy of the trained classifiers ranged between 76% and 91% (depending on the project), which shows that most of the recurring issues were classified correctly. However, the accuracy measure is sensitive to class imbalance; therefore, the remaining ones are more informative in our case.

The calculated MCC was, on average, equal to 0.77, indicating a very high accuracy of the models. However, the average Precision, Recall, and F1-score show that the classifiers were often able to find instances of a given class (higher Recall) with the cost of the increased number of False Positives (lower Precision). Still, regular Precision, Recall, and F1-score measures are designed to be used for binary classification problems, and when applied to multi-class classification, they require some aggregation. Here, we use macro aggregation, which treats multi-class classification problems as multiple binary classification problems and averages the values of the measures across all the classes. This means that every class, independently of its cardinality, had the same impact on the final value of the measure.

Also, Table 8 presents standard deviations (across the runs) for each measure. As we can see, the prediction accuracy was remarkably stable between the runs, as the standard deviation for all measures did not exceed 0.03. This means that the results do not seem to depend on the composition and split of the dataset into training and validation parts.

We observed the highest prediction quality for the two largest projects—P1 (3316 tasks) and P3 (3717 tasks). The average MCC for these projects was equal to 0.87 and 0.88, respectively. It is an expected observation since using a larger (and possibly more coherent since it required less up-sampling from the external database) training dataset should lead to a better prediction model. However, another factor that could be important in this context is the project management methodology. We obtained the worst results for the two projects developed in Scrum—P5 (1146 tasks) and P6 (821 tasks). The average MCC was equal to 0.68 and 0.69, respectively. Interestingly, these projects were, size-wise, the third- and the fourth in the dataset. We could hypothesize that automatic task categorization in projects following a "traditional" approach to project management with visible project phases, centralized management, and repeatable process patterns might be easier than in dynamic, agile projects where the whole team manages the task backlog (there could be a higher variability in how the tasks are described).

Table 8. Prediction quality measures for recurring task classification (mean values across the runs and standard deviation).

Project	Accuracy	(macro) Recall	(macro) Precision	(macro) F1-score	MCC
P1	0.89 ± 0.00	0.92 ± 0.00	0.69 ± 0.01	0.75 ± 0.00	0.87 ± 0.00
P2	0.78 ± 0.02	0.74 ± 0.03	0.64 ± 0.02	0.64 ± 0.03	0.73 ± 0.02
P3	0.91 ± 0.00	0.70 ± 0.01	0.61 ± 0.01	0.64 ± 0.01	0.88 ± 0.00
P4	0.80 ± 0.01	0.59 ± 0.02	0.53 ± 0.01	0.54 ± 0.01	0.76 ± 0.01
P5	0.79 ± 0.00	0.91 ± 0.01	0.56 ± 0.02	0.65 ± 0.01	0.68 ± 0.01
P6	0.76 ± 0.01	0.76 ± 0.01	0.59 ± 0.02	0.64 ± 0.01	0.69 ± 0.01
Mean	0.82	0.77	0.60	0.64	0.77

5.2 RQ2: Which Types of Recurring Tasks are Most Often Mutually Miscategorized?

We calculated confusion matrices for each project (and averaged them across the runs) to analyze which task categories are the most difficult to classify and which of them are often mutually confused. The matrices for the projects are presented in Fig. 11, 12, 13, 14, 15 and 16.

Although misclassification of the categories differs between the projects, we identified some common patterns. For instance, DEV seems to be the most challenging class to categorize (True Positives: 24%–77%). It is mainly confused with ADM, BLD, CFG, and TST recurring tasks. All these types of tasks can also involve coding, e.g., maintaining administrative scripts, developing automated test cases, etc. And vice versa, the DEV task can also include activities like modifying configuration files, implementing unit-level tests, etc. Therefore, the descriptions of these tasks could sound similar; what matters is the proportion of different activities within a task and its primary intent (not always clearly stated). On the contrary, BUG is the easiest type of task to detect (True Positives: 100%) because it directly maps the Jira issue type and was consistently used by the project teams. The remaining types of recurring tasks are classified correctly for most of the projects; however, there is always at least one exception for each of them.

In order to show the practical significance of the number of misclassified tasks in a software project, we counted the errors in the number of tasks assigned to the roles of project team members according to Table 3. We used validation data from the confusion matrices shown in the figures. We entered the errors of the task classification model for each class $t_c^{p,r}$ for each project in a separate table. We assigned them to the respective roles of the project team members. Their values are sometimes positive and sometimes negative. As a result, they compensate each other. Validation adds up the misclassified numbers of tasks by repeating the procedure 10 times. Therefore, we divide the summed error by the number of repetitions $n_{fold} = 10$. The summation value $T^{p,r}$ is the error in planning the number of tasks for role r throughout project p.

$$T^{p,r} = \frac{1}{n_{fold}} \sum_{c \in C} t_c^{p,r} \qquad (1)$$

where:
n_{fold} - number of folds in validation procedure,
$t_c^{p,r}$ - number of misclassified tasks in project p, for role r, resulting from incorrect classification of class c tasks,
p - project $p \in \{P1, P2, P3, P4, P5, P6\}$,
r - role $r \in \{ADM, PRG, PM, SA, TST\}$,
c - recurring task class $c \in \{ADM, BLD, CFG, CUST, DEV, DOC, EDU, MIGR, MIT, PM, RQM, RVW, TST, BUG\}$.
$T^{p,r} > 0$ means that role r in project p has too many tasks planned, i.e., overstaffing may occur. Otherwise, if $T^{p,r} < 0$, role r has understaffing planned. As

a result, the people in this role in the team may not be able to keep up with the tasks in time.

We used the average effort of a recurring task and the length of the project in months to better demonstrate the practical significance of the number of misclassified tasks in a software project. Using RE^p of the average recurring task effort for project p, we can calculate the misplanned effort in the project calculated in person-hours.

$$E^{p,r} = T^{p,r} RE^p \qquad (2)$$

where:
RE^p - average recurring task effort of project p in person-hours.
Using L^p - project duration in months, we calculate the average number of inappropriately scheduled person-hours for role r in project p per month.

$$EM^{p,r} = \frac{E^{p,r}}{L^p} \qquad (3)$$

where:
L^p - project duration in months.
Continuing with the assumption that there is an average of 165 person-hours per month, we determine from the $EM^(p,r)$ figure the inappropriately planned number of people in role r in the p project team.

$$EJ^{p,r} = \frac{EM^{p,r}}{FTE} \qquad (4)$$

where:
FTE - 165 person-hours.

Project P1. Project P1 is the longest-running project among the industrial projects we analyzed. Its duration in months was $L^1 = 96.3$, the average effort of recurring tasks was $RE^1 = 3.56$. All 14 classes of recurring tasks occurred in it. Figure 11 shows a confusion matrix for classifying its recurring tasks. Table 9 shows the number of misclassified tasks for each class where errors occurred, and the assignment of these tasks to the roles of the team members project team members.

The model most frequently misclassified tasks of the DEV class (43.4% incorrect) and ADM (24.2% incorrect). In the remaining classes, the error rate was less than 10%. Due to model classification errors, tasks in the DEV class were assigned to administrators (ADM), overestimating the planned number of tasks for them and partly to system analysts. Incorrectly classified tasks of the ADM class were mainly assigned to programmers (PRG). Table 9 shows all misclassified tasks. We notice that most of the differences in the table compensate for each other. As the number of misassigned tasks assigned and the effort of these tasks is calculated for the entire project, and this is the longest project, the result is that the number of misassigned EM hours per month (1, r) is for each role r less than 30 person-hours. As a result, in the last row of the table, we can read that as a result of the errors recurring task classification:

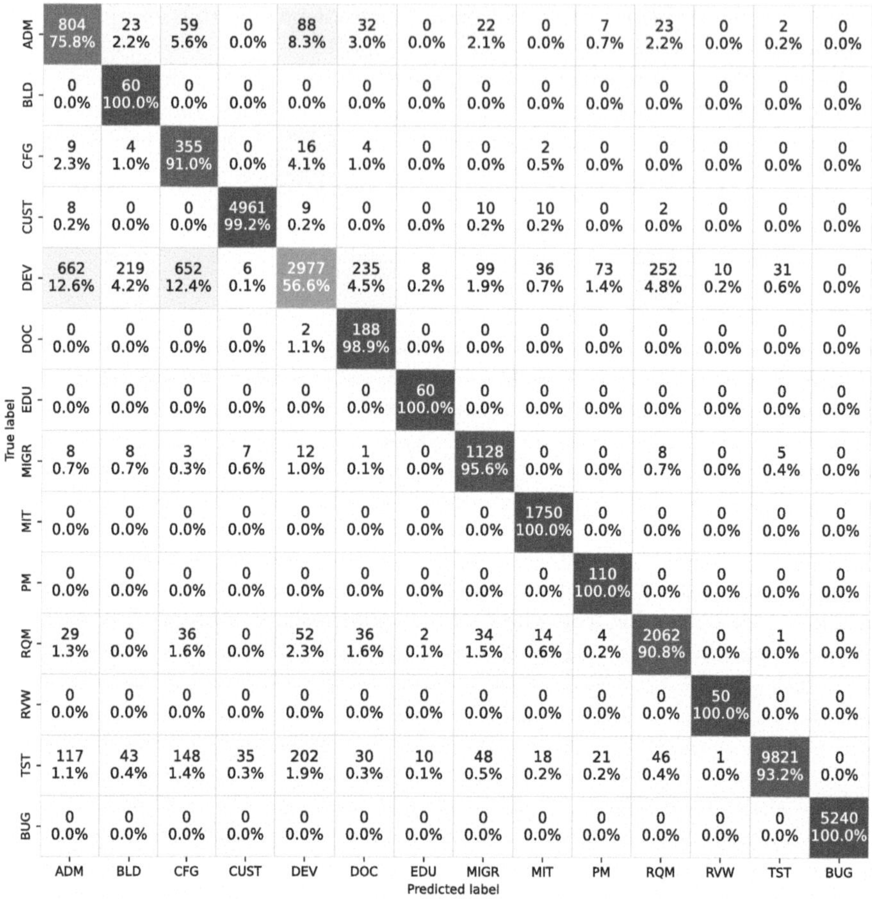

Fig. 11. Confusion matrix for project P1.

- Administrators (ADM) will have too many hours planned. In practice, there will be approximately 0.13 FTEs too many in the team for each month of the project,
- Testers (TST) will have too few hours planned. In practice, there will be approximately 0.15 FTEs too few in the team for each month of the project,
- programmers (PRG), project managers (PM), and system analysts (SA) have a planned number of hours within error (less than 5%).

Project P2. Project P2 was a moderately long project. Its duration in months was $L^2 = 43.6$ and the average effort of recurring tasks was $RE^2 = 3.23$. The project consisted of a small number of tasks (half of the average) and an even smaller number of recurring tasks. The five task classes CFG, DOC, EDU, MIGR, and RVW were absent. The absence of CFG class tasks may indicate using a

Table 9. Impact of P1 project classification errors on the planned project team

Recurring Tasks Classes	Roles of Team Members				
	ADM	PRG	PM	SA	TST
ADM	−256	224	7	23	2
CFG	9	−9	0	0	0
CUST	8	−10	0	2	0
DEV	662	−1018	73	252	31
MIGR	8	−21	0	8	5
PM	0		110	0	0
RQM	29	174	4	−208	1
TST	117	535	21	46	−719
Tasks $T^{P1,r}$	577	−125	215	123	−680
Effort $E^{P1,r}$	2056	−445	766	438	−2423
Monthly $EM^{P1,r}$	21	−5	8	5	−25
Jobs $EJ^{P1,r}$	0,13	−0,03	0,05	0,03	−0,15

specific naming convention for configuration tasks in the project. The absence of DOC class tasks may indicate the use of standard documentation. Lack of EDU tasks for non-participation of the team in training and coaching. Lack of MIGR tasks for developing a new project with no counterpart in the client organization, i.e., developing a new business activity. Lack of RVW tasks for not applying review and inspection practices. Figure 12 shows a confusion matrix for classifying its recurring tasks. The model most often incorrectly classified tasks in the DEV (81% incorrect), MIT (38% incorrect), TST (37% incorrect), RQM (34% incorrect), BLD (25% incorrect), and ADM (13% incorrect) classes. There were no errors in the other three classes: CUST, PM, and BUG. The number of recurring tasks is low, and the model's task classification errors compensate within roles. Consequently, the monthly effort error for the role is less than five person-hours. For project P2, we do not include the entire table of the impact of errors on project team composition as for project P1. We include the differences in the number of roles resulting from the errors in the summary Table 10.

Project P3. Project P3 was a medium-long project. Its duration in months was $L^3 = 37.9$ and the average effort of recurring tasks was $RE^3 = 3.47$. The project consisted of a large number of tasks (more than average) and a large number of recurring tasks (47.5%). Figure 13 shows a confusion matrix for classifying its recurring tasks. The model most often incorrectly classified tasks of class RVW (100% incorrect), PM (58% incorrect), BLD (43% incorrect), CFG (41% incorrect), DOC (38% incorrect), ADM (37% incorrect), EDU (29% incorrect), MIGR (23% incorrect), DEV (21% incorrect), MIT (12% incorrect) In the other four classes CUST, RQM, TST and BUG the error was less than 10%. Validation

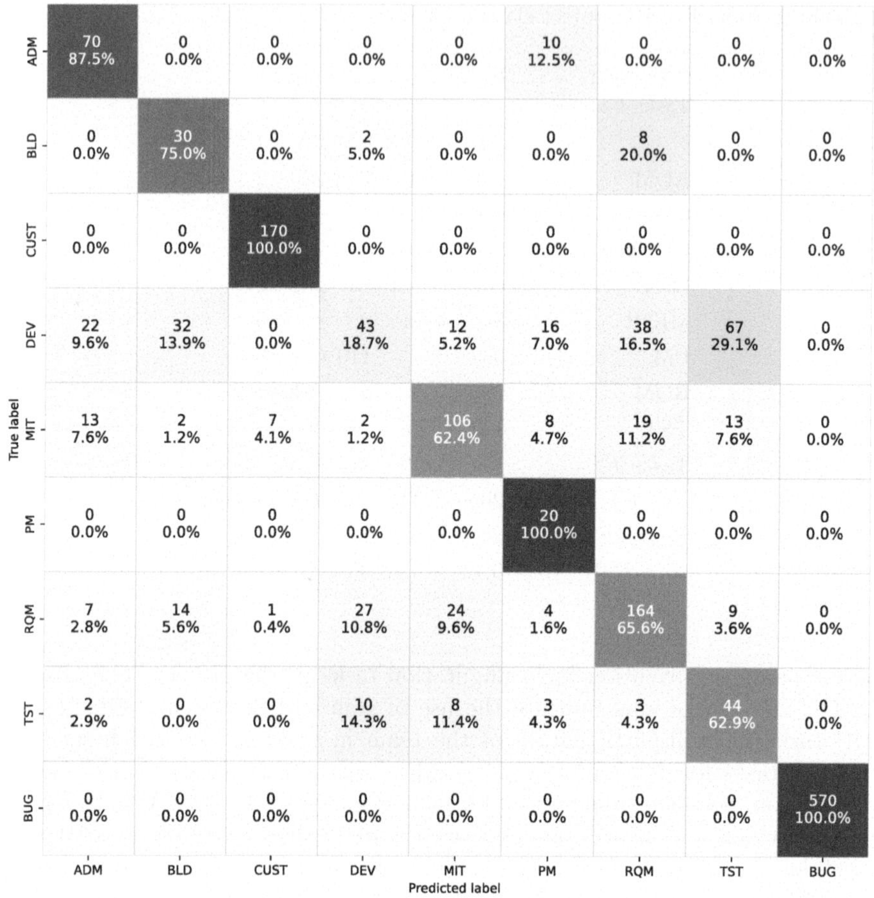

	ADM	BLD	CUST	DEV	MIT	PM	RQM	TST	BUG
ADM	70 / 87.5%	0 / 0.0%	0 / 0.0%	0 / 0.0%	0 / 0.0%	10 / 12.5%	0 / 0.0%	0 / 0.0%	0 / 0.0%
BLD	0 / 0.0%	30 / 75.0%	0 / 0.0%	2 / 5.0%	0 / 0.0%	0 / 0.0%	8 / 20.0%	0 / 0.0%	0 / 0.0%
CUST	0 / 0.0%	0 / 0.0%	170 / 100.0%	0 / 0.0%	0 / 0.0%	0 / 0.0%	0 / 0.0%	0 / 0.0%	0 / 0.0%
DEV	22 / 9.6%	32 / 13.9%	0 / 0.0%	43 / 18.7%	12 / 5.2%	16 / 7.0%	38 / 16.5%	67 / 29.1%	0 / 0.0%
MIT	13 / 7.6%	2 / 1.2%	7 / 4.1%	2 / 1.2%	106 / 62.4%	8 / 4.7%	19 / 11.2%	13 / 7.6%	0 / 0.0%
PM	0 / 0.0%	0 / 0.0%	0 / 0.0%	0 / 0.0%	0 / 0.0%	20 / 100.0%	0 / 0.0%	0 / 0.0%	0 / 0.0%
RQM	7 / 2.8%	14 / 5.6%	1 / 0.4%	27 / 10.8%	24 / 9.6%	4 / 1.6%	164 / 65.6%	9 / 3.6%	0 / 0.0%
TST	2 / 2.9%	0 / 0.0%	0 / 0.0%	10 / 14.3%	8 / 11.4%	3 / 4.3%	3 / 4.3%	44 / 62.9%	0 / 0.0%
BUG	0 / 0.0%	0 / 0.0%	0 / 0.0%	0 / 0.0%	0 / 0.0%	0 / 0.0%	0 / 0.0%	0 / 0.0%	570 / 100.0%

Fig. 12. Confusion matrix for project P2.

showed a high MCC = 0.88 for the project, the model's task classification errors compensating within roles. Consequently, the monthly effort error for the role is less than five person-hours. We include the differences in the number of P3 project roles in a summary Table 10. Planning too few 0.23 FTEs for testers may result in an excessive workload for them. Planning too many 0.12 FTE and 0.13 FTE for administrators and programmers may result in a shortage of tasks.

Project P4. The P4 project was short. Its duration in months was $L^4 = 30.6$ and the average effort of recurring tasks was $RE^4 = 1.87$. The project consisted of a small number of tasks and recurring tasks (35.5%). Figure 14 shows a confusion matrix for classifying its recurring tasks. The model most frequently misclassified tasks of class MIGR (100% incorrect), BLD (70% incorrect), TST (65% incorrect), DEV (58% incorrect), CFG (58% incorrect), ADM (40% incor-

	ADM	BLD	CFG	CUST	DEV	DOC	EDU	MIGR	MIT	PM	RQM	RVW	TST	BUG
ADM	871 62.7%	71 5.1%	77 5.5%	4 0.3%	306 22.0%	14 1.0%	1 0.1%	20 1.4%	10 0.7%	7 0.5%	8 0.6%	0 0.0%	1 0.1%	0 0.0%
BLD	38 16.5%	132 57.4%	12 5.2%	0 0.0%	40 17.4%	0 0.0%	0 0.0%	8 3.5%	0 0.0%	0 0.0%	0 0.0%	0 0.0%	0 0.0%	0 0.0%
CFG	58 12.9%	1 0.2%	264 58.7%	0 0.0%	105 23.3%	17 3.8%	0 0.0%	3 0.7%	0 0.0%	1 0.2%	1 0.2%	0 0.0%	0 0.0%	0 0.0%
CUST	10 0.7%	0 0.0%	35 2.4%	1423 96.1%	6 0.4%	3 0.2%	0 0.0%	0 0.0%	3 0.2%	0 0.0%	0 0.0%	0 0.0%	0 0.0%	0 0.0%
DEV	499 7.8%	53 0.8%	365 5.7%	47 0.7%	5053 78.6%	111 1.7%	20 0.3%	71 1.1%	46 0.7%	80 1.2%	60 0.9%	21 0.3%	4 0.1%	0 0.0%
DOC	0 0.0%	0 0.0%	0 0.0%	0 0.0%	20 25.0%	50 62.5%	0 0.0%	0 0.0%	5 6.2%	5 6.2%	0 0.0%	0 0.0%	0 0.0%	0 0.0%
EDU	0 0.0%	0 0.0%	0 0.0%	0 0.0%	19 19.0%	3 3.0%	71 71.0%	0 0.0%	0 0.0%	0 0.0%	7 7.0%	0 0.0%	0 0.0%	0 0.0%
MIGR	11 4.8%	0 0.0%	13 5.7%	1 0.4%	16 7.0%	2 0.9%	0 0.0%	177 77.0%	0 0.0%	7 3.0%	3 1.3%	0 0.0%	0 0.0%	0 0.0%
MIT	9 3.1%	0 0.0%	0 0.0%	0 0.0%	26 9.0%	1 0.3%	0 0.0%	0 0.0%	254 87.6%	0 0.0%	0 0.0%	0 0.0%	0 0.0%	0 0.0%
PM	5 4.5%	0 0.0%	7 6.4%	9 8.2%	13 11.8%	2 1.8%	0 0.0%	0 0.0%	0 0.0%	46 41.8%	21 19.1%	7 6.4%	0 0.0%	0 0.0%
RQM	21 0.4%	0 0.0%	22 0.4%	0 0.0%	83 1.6%	2 0.0%	9 0.2%	10 0.2%	28 0.5%	8 0.2%	5107 96.5%	0 0.0%	0 0.0%	0 0.0%
RVW	0 0.0%	9 30.0%	0 0.0%	0 0.0%	14 46.7%	1 3.3%	0 0.0%	0 0.0%	0 0.0%	5 16.7%	1 3.3%	0 0.0%	0 0.0%	0 0.0%
TST	165 1.0%	15 0.1%	72 0.4%	8 0.0%	249 1.5%	18 0.1%	9 0.1%	9 0.1%	0 0.0%	0 0.0%	4 0.0%	2 0.0%	15839 96.6%	0 0.0%
BUG	0 0.0%	0 0.0%	0 0.0%	0 0.0%	0 0.0%	0 0.0%	0 0.0%	0 0.0%	0 0.0%	0 0.0%	0 0.0%	0 0.0%	0 0.0%	4670 100.0%

Fig. 13. Confusion matrix for project P3.

rect) and MIT (20% incorrect). For the remaining classes PM, CUST, and RQM, the error was 4%. Validation showed an average MCC = 0.76 for the project. The model's task classification errors compensate within roles. Consequently, the monthly effort error for the role is less than one person hour. We include the differences in the number of P4 project roles in the summary Table 10. All values are within acceptable error, below 0.1 FTE.

Project P5. Project P5 was a medium-long project. Its duration in months was $L^5 = 40.9$ and the average effort of recurring tasks was $RE^5 = 8.52$, which is the highest among the projects analyzed. The project consisted of an average number of tasks and a small number of recurring tasks (20.9). Figure 15 shows a confusion matrix for classifying its recurring tasks. The model most often incorrectly classified tasks in the classes CUST (100% incorrect), RQM (52%

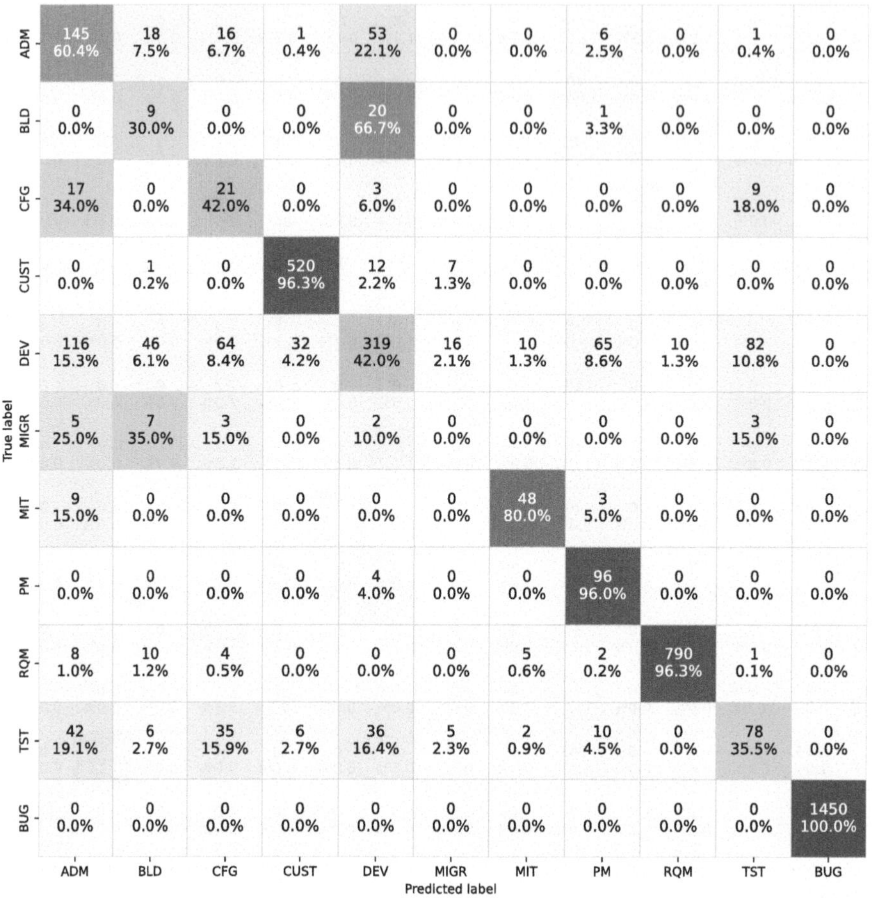

Fig. 14. Confusion matrix for project P4.

incorrect), TST (25% incorrect), DEV (24% incorrect), ADM (21% incorrect), and CFG (20% incorrect). In the remaining eight classes, the model correctly classified all tasks. The project validation obtained the lowest MCC value = 0.68. The model's task classification errors compensate within roles. Consequently, the monthly effort error for the role is less than one person-hour. We include the differences in the number of P5 project roles in the summary Table 10. All values are within acceptable error, less than 0.1 FTE.

Project P6. Project P6 was the shortest project. Its duration in months was $L^6 = 22.8$ and the average effort of recurring tasks was high $RE^6 = 7.15$. The project consisted of an average number of tasks and a small number of recurring tasks (20.8%). The two task classes, MIGR and RVW, were not present. Figure 16 shows a confusion matrix for classifying its recurring tasks. The model most often

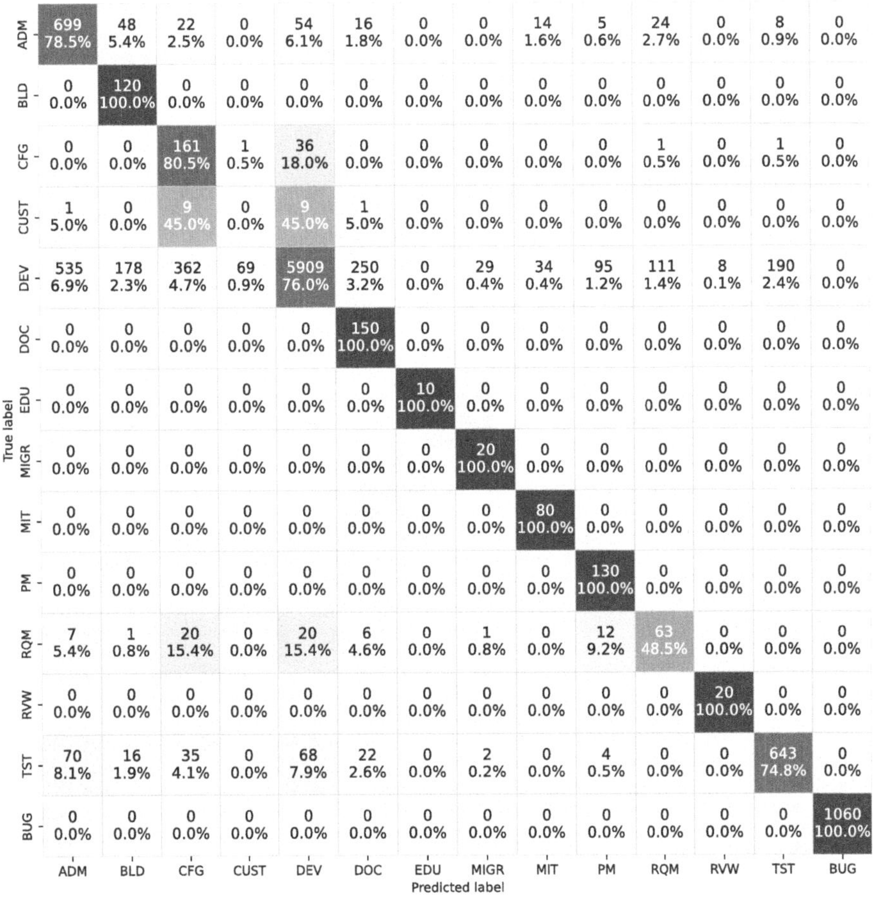

True label	ADM	BLD	CFG	CUST	DEV	DOC	EDU	MIGR	MIT	PM	RQM	RVW	TST	BUG
ADM	**699** / 78.5%	48 / 5.4%	22 / 2.5%	0 / 0.0%	54 / 6.1%	16 / 1.8%	0 / 0.0%	0 / 0.0%	14 / 1.6%	5 / 0.6%	24 / 2.7%	0 / 0.0%	8 / 0.9%	0 / 0.0%
BLD	0 / 0.0%	**120** / 100.0%	0 / 0.0%	0 / 0.0%	0 / 0.0%	0 / 0.0%	0 / 0.0%	0 / 0.0%	0 / 0.0%	0 / 0.0%	0 / 0.0%	0 / 0.0%	0 / 0.0%	0 / 0.0%
CFG	0 / 0.0%	0 / 0.0%	**161** / 80.5%	1 / 0.5%	36 / 18.0%	0 / 0.0%	0 / 0.0%	0 / 0.0%	0 / 0.0%	0 / 0.0%	1 / 0.5%	0 / 0.0%	1 / 0.5%	0 / 0.0%
CUST	1 / 5.0%	0 / 0.0%	**9** / 45.0%	0 / 0.0%	**9** / 45.0%	1 / 5.0%	0 / 0.0%	0 / 0.0%	0 / 0.0%	0 / 0.0%	0 / 0.0%	0 / 0.0%	0 / 0.0%	0 / 0.0%
DEV	535 / 6.9%	178 / 2.3%	362 / 4.7%	69 / 0.9%	**5909** / 76.0%	250 / 3.2%	0 / 0.0%	29 / 0.4%	34 / 0.4%	95 / 1.2%	111 / 1.4%	8 / 0.1%	190 / 2.4%	0 / 0.0%
DOC	0 / 0.0%	0 / 0.0%	0 / 0.0%	0 / 0.0%	0 / 0.0%	**150** / 100.0%	0 / 0.0%	0 / 0.0%	0 / 0.0%	0 / 0.0%	0 / 0.0%	0 / 0.0%	0 / 0.0%	0 / 0.0%
EDU	0 / 0.0%	0 / 0.0%	0 / 0.0%	0 / 0.0%	0 / 0.0%	0 / 0.0%	**10** / 100.0%	0 / 0.0%	0 / 0.0%	0 / 0.0%	0 / 0.0%	0 / 0.0%	0 / 0.0%	0 / 0.0%
MIGR	0 / 0.0%	0 / 0.0%	0 / 0.0%	0 / 0.0%	0 / 0.0%	0 / 0.0%	0 / 0.0%	**20** / 100.0%	0 / 0.0%	0 / 0.0%	0 / 0.0%	0 / 0.0%	0 / 0.0%	0 / 0.0%
MIT	0 / 0.0%	0 / 0.0%	0 / 0.0%	0 / 0.0%	0 / 0.0%	0 / 0.0%	0 / 0.0%	0 / 0.0%	**80** / 100.0%	0 / 0.0%	0 / 0.0%	0 / 0.0%	0 / 0.0%	0 / 0.0%
PM	0 / 0.0%	0 / 0.0%	0 / 0.0%	0 / 0.0%	0 / 0.0%	0 / 0.0%	0 / 0.0%	0 / 0.0%	0 / 0.0%	**130** / 100.0%	0 / 0.0%	0 / 0.0%	0 / 0.0%	0 / 0.0%
RQM	7 / 5.4%	1 / 0.8%	20 / 15.4%	0 / 0.0%	20 / 15.4%	6 / 4.6%	0 / 0.0%	1 / 0.8%	0 / 0.0%	12 / 9.2%	**63** / 48.5%	0 / 0.0%	0 / 0.0%	0 / 0.0%
RVW	0 / 0.0%	0 / 0.0%	0 / 0.0%	0 / 0.0%	0 / 0.0%	0 / 0.0%	0 / 0.0%	0 / 0.0%	0 / 0.0%	0 / 0.0%	0 / 0.0%	**20** / 100.0%	0 / 0.0%	0 / 0.0%
TST	70 / 8.1%	16 / 1.9%	35 / 4.1%	0 / 0.0%	68 / 7.9%	22 / 2.6%	0 / 0.0%	2 / 0.2%	0 / 0.0%	4 / 0.5%	0 / 0.0%	0 / 0.0%	**643** / 74.8%	0 / 0.0%
BUG	0 / 0.0%	0 / 0.0%	0 / 0.0%	0 / 0.0%	0 / 0.0%	0 / 0.0%	0 / 0.0%	0 / 0.0%	0 / 0.0%	0 / 0.0%	0 / 0.0%	0 / 0.0%	0 / 0.0%	**1060** / 100.0%

Predicted label

Fig. 15. Confusion matrix for project P5.

incorrectly classified tasks of the classes CUST (48% incorrect), RQM (44% incorrect), CFG (43% incorrect), TST (37% incorrect), ADM (36% incorrect), DEV (31% incorrect), BLD (22% incorrect), MIT (7% incorrect), DOC (6% incorrect) and PM (6% incorrect). In the remaining three classes, the model correctly classified all tasks. The project validation achieved a low MCC value = 0.69. We include the differences in the number of P6 project roles in the summary Table 10. Planning too few 0.61 FTEs for programmers, the largest error for all projects may result in an excessive workload for them. Planning too much 0.24 FTE, 0.19 FTE, and 0.13 FTE for admins, project managers, and system analysts may result in too little workload.

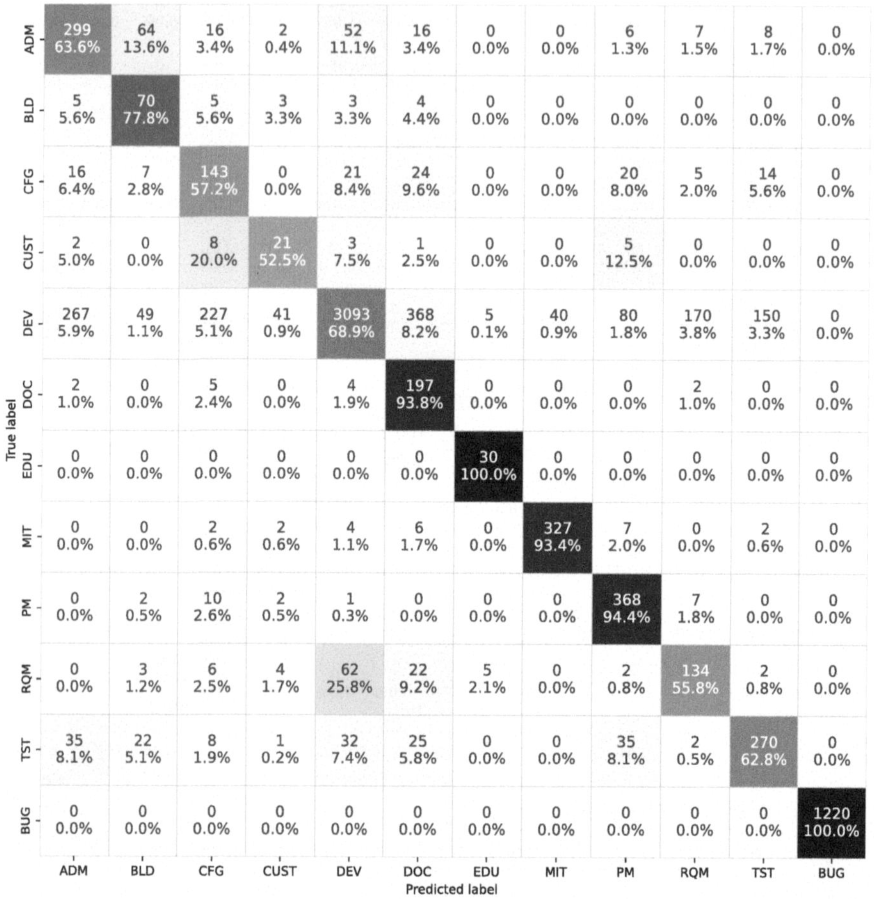

Fig. 16. Confusion matrix for project P6.

Table 10. Impact of projects classification errors on the planned project team

Jobs $EJ^{P1,r}$ for Project	Roles of Team Members				
	ADM	PRG	PM	SA	TST
P1	0,13	−0,03	0,05	0,03	−0,15
P2	0,01	−0,03	0,02	−0,01	0,02
P3	0,02	0,15	0,02	−0,04	−0,25
P4	0,03	−0,04	0,03	−0,01	−0,01
P5	0,05	−0,08	0,01	0,01	0,00
P6	0,24	−0,61	0,19	0,13	0,01

5.3 Recommendations on How to Train/adapt the Classifier

The results of our study show that ML algorithms can be used to train effective task classification models. However, from the practical perspective, it is important to consider how to implement such models in a project-specific context.

Based on lessons learned from our study, we recommend two approaches to training/adapting a task classifier:

1. Re-use the model presented in this study—our replication package includes an instance of a classification model trained on the whole dataset. One can consider using it directly if no data for training is available. The text feature extraction is based on a pre-trained language model, so it seems possible that the task classifier might provide satisfactory results for other projects that use different vocabularies or language structures.
2. Train a proprietary model—another option is to follow the same procedure as in our study to train a model based on intra-organization data from ITS. We recommend labeling a small portion of data and then adapting provided heuristic labelers with keywords better suited for a particular organization. Once the heuristic provides satisfactory results, we recommend applying it to label the existing data and train a classifier.

5.4 Threats to Validity

In our study, we have adopted the proposed framework by Wohlin et al. [17] for addressing potential threats to validity.

The main threat to construct validity concerns the taxonomy and how specific classes manifest in task descriptions. Although the definitions of the taxonomy classes are precise and mature since the taxonomy was designed and used in some previous studies, it can be challenging, even for a human annotator, to categorize some particular tasks based on their descriptions. We introduced a multi-stage process of labeling the dataset according to the taxonomy and employed Active Learning to assess the consistency of the human annotator in labeling the task. With every drop in accuracy, we reflected on the potential cause and corrective actions (e.g., enhancing definitions of taxonomy classes).

The next threat is related to the previous one and regards both construction and internal validity. Since the dataset included more than 9.6K recurring issues, we had to introduce a semi-automatic approach to its labeling. We developed heuristic keyword-based algorithms that could introduce some systematic bias into the labeling. To mitigate this threat, we introduced additional validation steps based on manual labeling (15% of the dataset) and monitored the accuracy of labeling algorithms based on the manually labeled samples. To compensate for errors caused by unbalanced data, we used a set of 91K issues from external software projects. Unfortunately, we did not examine this data set for imbalance. For its classification, we used heuristics adapted and verified using the P1-P6 project tasks. We are not sure whether the heuristics correctly classified the additional 91K issues.

Finally, our heuristic labeling algorithm assigned a single taxonomy class to each task (multi-class classification); however, we can imagine that some of the tasks could belong to many classes simultaneously (multi-label classification). We did not control this threat; however, we believe that its impact is minor since it works against the proposed automatic classifier, artificially raising the number of False Positives.

The main threat to external validity regards the possibility of using the same or similar approach to categorize recurring tasks in other projects. Considering a small sample of studied projects, we would be cautious in generalizing our findings. However, we introduced several elements to our study design to increase the generalizability of our classification model and the study's outcomes. First, we used a foundation, pre-trained language model for feature extraction. The embedding spaces of such models capture the semantics of the language. Therefore, the model might be able to categorize tasks that use slightly different language in task descriptions. We also used an external dataset of tasks to augment the training datasets and increase the diversity of tasks used for training the models.

6 Conclusion

The goal of our study was to investigate the possibility of applying machine learning (ML) algorithms to train a model capable of automatic categorization of recurring tasks in software development projects. We use a taxonomy of project tasks proposed in our previous studies [20–22], which includes 14 types of such tasks.

We conducted a simulation study on the dataset from six industrial projects containing 9,589 tasks and augmented it with an additional dataset of 91,145 task descriptions from other industrial projects to up-sample minority classes during training. We performed ten runs of 10-fold cross-validation for each project and evaluated the classifier using a set of state-of-the-art prediction quality metrics, i.e., Accuracy, Precision, Recall, F1-score, and MCC. Our ML pipeline included a Transformer-based sentence embedder ('mxbai-embed-large-v1') and XGBoost classifier.

The Accuracy of the automatic task classifiers ranged between 0.76 and 0.91 (mean: 0.82), with MCC between 0.69 and 0.88 (mean: 0.77). The measures were stable across the runs, as the standard deviation ranged between 0.00 and 0.03. We observed higher prediction quality for the largest projects in the dataset and those managed according to "traditional" project management methodologies.

We also analyzed which task categories are most difficult to categorize and often mutually confusing by analyzing confusion matrices. The most difficult class is DEV (development tasks), as such tasks are often confused by classifiers with other categories involving coding activities (ADM, BLD, CFG, and TST). We found the largest errors in team composition planning in project P6 (0.61 FTE too few for the programmer role, 0.24 FTE too many for the administrator role) and project P3 (0.25 FTE too few for the tester role). It is worth noting that this is only an estimated error calculated under several assumptions. The main assumption is to take the project's average labor intensity of recurring tasks. We can see that between the projects, this value can vary several times ($RE^4 = 1.87$, $RE^5 = 8.52$). Similarly, different classes of tasks can have different efforts within a project.

Finally, we provided a replication package that includes analysis code and trained models that can be used by practitioners or researchers.

6.1 Future Work

Planning. As we mentioned in Sect. 3.1, we are considering using time series forecasting to schedule stateful and recurring tasks in the project. The actual project workflows are variable and periodic. Our early work using multi-agent simulation did not reproduce this phenomenon. A possible reason for this is the multi-competent composition of modern project teams. Looking at the problem from this perspective, one can see people switching between tasks. When they finish a certain part of the implementation, it is time to detail and clarify further requirements. This problem is difficult to model and later to verify. Machine learning models may not give us insight into how these processes work, but they will allow us to simulate real data more closely.

Additional Dataset. To compensate for errors caused by unbalanced data, we used a set of 91,000 tasks from external software projects. Unfortunately, we could not share this data due to its confidentiality. We did not analyze this data and adapt the heuristics and keywords created for the P1-P6 projects to it. We intend to verify some of these tasks to extend our knowledge of classified tasks and find their classes and patterns.

Standalone Model. In recent years, we have analyzed many software projects and their tasks. We have noticed many regularities, patterns, and dependencies. We intend to build a model that automatically classifies tasks without needing an external dataset. We aim to use our knowledge to build a large, balanced dataset to build a model that automatically classifies project tasks.

References

1. Bruegge, B., David, J., Helming, J., Koegel, M.: Classification of tasks using machine learning. In: Proceedings of the 5th International Conference on Predictor Models in Software Engineering, pp. 1–11. ACM. https://doi.org/10.1145/1540438.1540455. https://dl.acm.org/doi/10.1145/1540438.1540455
2. Chawla, N.V., Bowyer, K.W., Hall, L.O., Kegelmeyer, W.P.: SMOTE: synthetic minority over-sampling technique. **16**, 321–357. https://doi.org/10.1613/jair.953. https://www.jair.org/index.php/jair/article/view/10302
3. Chen, T., Guestrin, C.: XGBoost: a scalable tree boosting system. In: Proceedings of the 22nd ACM SIGKDD International Conference on Knowledge Discovery and Data Mining, pp. 785–794 (2016)

4. Cohen, G., Hilario, M., Sax, H., Hugonnet, S., Geissbuhler, A.: Learning from imbalanced data in surveillance of nosocomial infection. **37**(1), 7–18. https://doi.org/10.1016/j.artmed.2005.03.002. https://www.sciencedirect.com/science/article/pii/S0933365705000850
5. Gharbi, S., Mkaouer, M.W., Jenhani, I., Messaoud, M.B.: On the classification of software change messages using multi-label active learning. In: Proceedings of the 34th ACM/SIGAPP Symposium on Applied Computing, pp. 1760–1767. ACM. https://doi.org/10.1145/3297280.3297452
6. Herzig, K., Just, S., Zeller, A.: It's not a bug, it's a feature: how misclassification impacts bug prediction. In: 2013 35th International Conference on Software Engineering (ICSE), pp. 392–401. IEEE. https://doi.org/10.1109/ICSE.2013.6606585. http://ieeexplore.ieee.org/document/6606585/
7. Hu, S., Liang, Y., Ma, L., He, Y.: MSMOTE: improving classification performance when training data is imbalanced. In: 2009 Second International Workshop on Computer Science and Engineering, vol. 2, pp. 13–17. https://doi.org/10.1109/WCSE.2009.756. https://ieeexplore.ieee.org/abstract/document/5403368
8. Kallis, R., Di Sorbo, A., Canfora, G., Panichella, S.: Ticket tagger: machine learning driven issue classification. In: 2019 IEEE International Conference on Software Maintenance and Evolution (ICSME), pp. 406–409. IEEE. https://doi.org/10.1109/ICSME.2019.00070. https://ieeexplore.ieee.org/document/8918993/
9. Li, X., Li, J.: Angle-optimized text embeddings. arXiv preprint arXiv:2309.12871 (2023)
10. Meher, J.P., Biswas, S., Mall, R.: Deep learning-based software bug classification. **166**, 107350. https://doi.org/10.1016/j.infsof.2023.107350. https://linkinghub.elsevier.com/retrieve/pii/S0950584923002057
11. Muennighoff, N., Tazi, N., Magne, L., Reimers, N.: MTEB: massive text embedding benchmark. arXiv preprint arXiv:2210.07316 (2022)
12. Otoom, A.F., Al-jdaeh, S., Hammad, M.: Automated classification of software bug reports. In: Proceedings of the 9th International Conference on Information Communication and Management, pp. 17–21. ACM. https://doi.org/10.1145/3357419.3357424. https://dl.acm.org/doi/10.1145/3357419.3357424
13. Pandey, N., Sanyal, D.K., Hudait, A., Sen, A.: Automated classification of software issue reports using machine learning techniques: an empirical study. **13**(4), 279–297. https://doi.org/10.1007/s11334-017-0294-1. http://link.springer.com/10.1007/s11334-017-0294-1
14. Santos, F.: Supporting the task-driven skill identification in open source project issue tracking systems. **48**(1), 54–58. https://doi.org/10.1145/3573074.3573088. https://dl.acm.org/doi/10.1145/3573074.3573088
15. Lee, S., Shakir, A., Koenig, D., Lipp, J.: Open source strikes bread - new fluffy embeddings model (2024). https://www.mixedbread.ai/blog/mxbai-embed-large-v1
16. Shafiq, S., Mashkoor, A., Mayr-Dorn, C., Egyed, A.: A literature review of using machine learning in software development life cycle stages. **9**, 140896–140920. https://doi.org/10.1109/ACCESS.2021.3119746. https://ieeexplore.ieee.org/document/9568959/
17. Wohlin, C., Runeson, P., Höst, M., Ohlsson, M.C., Regnell, B., Wesslén, A.: Experimentation in Software Engineering. Springer, Cham (2012)
18. Wu, J., Ye, C., Zhou, H.: BERT for sentiment classification in software engineering. In: 2021 International Conference on Service Science (ICSS), pp. 115–121. IEEE. https://doi.org/10.1109/ICSS53362.2021.00026. https://ieeexplore.ieee.org/document/9492202/

19. Wysocki, W., Ochodek, M.: Automatic classification of recurring tasks in software development project. In: Proceedings of the International Conference on Software Engineering and Advanced Applications (2024). https://doi.org/10.1109/SEAA64295.2024.00076
20. Wysocki, W.: Macrosimulation model of software development process. Procedia Comput. Sci. **225**, 746–755. https://doi.org/10.1016/j.procs.2023.10.061. https://linkinghub.elsevier.com/retrieve/pii/S187705092301219X
21. Wysocki, W.: Task planning model of software process. Procedia Comput. Sci. **225**, 736–745. https://doi.org/10.1016/j.procs.2023.10.060. https://linkinghub.elsevier.com/retrieve/pii/S1877050923012188
22. Wysocki, W., Miciuła, I., Mastalerz, M.: Classification of task types in software development projects. Electronics **11**(22), 3827 (2022)
23. Wysocki, W., Orłowski, C.: A multi-agent model for planning hybrid software processes. Procedia Comput. Sci. **159**, 1688–1697 (2019)
24. Zhou, Y., Tong, Y., Gu, R., Gall, H.: Combining text mining and data mining for bug report classification: combining text mining and data mining for bug report classification. **28**(3), 150–176. https://doi.org/10.1002/smr.1770. https://onlinelibrary.wiley.com/doi/10.1002/smr.1770

LogGenST: A Framework for Synthetic Log Generation Using LLMs for Smart-Troubleshooting

Sania Partovian[1,2](✉), Francesco Flammini[1], Alessio Bucaioni[1], and Johan Thornadtsson[2]

[1] School of Innovation, Design and Engineering, Mälardalen University, Västerås, Sweden
{sania.partovian,francesco.flammini,alessio.bucaioni}@mdu.se
[2] Sigma Technology Information, Stockholm, Sweden
johan.thornadtsson@sigmatechnology.com

Abstract. Log files are essential for monitoring, diagnosing, and troubleshooting smart systems, capturing critical operational events. However, privacy concerns and limited access to real-world log datasets hinder the development and evaluation of anomaly detection techniques. Synthetic log generation has emerged as a viable solution to this challenge, enabling researchers to create diverse datasets that include both normal and fault-related logs. In this paper, we introduce novel methodologies for generating synthetic log files using Generative Adversarial Networks and Large Language Models. First, we propose a GAN-based approach, leveraging different GAN implementations to produce high-quality synthetic logs. A comprehensive evaluation reveals that CTGAN outperforms other models in generating realistic and varied log entries. Building on these findings, we present LogGenST, an innovative synthetic log generation framework that employs three LLMs in an adversarial setup. Unlike traditional GAN-based methods, LogGenST features a unique Prompt Engineer LLM that refines prompts based on feedback from generator and discriminator LLMs. This approach ensures temporal consistency, logical coherence, and domain-specific patterns without requiring extensive model training. Comparative analysis shows that LogGenST significantly enhances log authenticity, pattern consistency, and fault representation, supporting advanced smart-troubleshooting experimentation in industrial cyber-physical systems and the Internet of Things.

Keywords: Generative Adversarial Network · Synthetic Data · Log Files · Industry 4.0 · Smart-Troubleshooting · Large Language Models

1 Introduction

As technology rapidly advances, systems and applications become increasingly complex, resulting in a diverse array of anomalies that include faults, errors, and failures [1]. Faults refer to defects in a system that may cause errors, errors are deviations from expected behavior, and failures occur when a system's intended function is not performed. Anomalies are challenging for humans to detect because of system complexity, large data volumes, and dynamic environments [2]. Smart-troubleshooting is a method that involves collecting critical data from various interconnected devices, analyzing this data for anomaly detection and prediction, and integrating it with troubleshooting guidelines and software solutions [3]. Compared to traditional troubleshooting, which often relies on manual diagnostics and is reactive in nature, smart-troubleshooting offers a more proactive and automated approach, significantly enhancing the speed and accuracy of problem resolution [3]. Log files are central to smart-troubleshooting, as they play a crucial role in tracing the status of systems, applications, or devices and recording critical events. This data assists administrators in effectively diagnosing anomalies, including system bugs, failures, and errors [4]. There exists a multitude of anomaly detection techniques grounded in the analysis of log files. The utilization of log files for anomaly detection is often hindered by several issues, including the followings. First, the presence of sensitive information within them [5]. Due to privacy concerns and data protection regulations, many companies are reluctant to share log file data publicly [6]. Additionally, despite numerous systems generating large amounts of log data, there are very few publicly available log files labeled with error or failure information [7]. The lack of publicly available and usable datasets of log files makes new anomaly detection methodologies grounded in the analysis of log files less reliable due to a lack of proper validation. Specifically, the absence of large-scale benchmark datasets for software engineering research is a well-known problem, as highlighted in several studies [8].

In previous paper [9], the problem of generating synthetic log files was tackled using Generative Adversarial Networks (GANs). The proposed methodology utilized GANs, including VanillaGAN, CTGAN (Conditional Tabular GAN), and SeqGAN (Sequential GAN), to generate realistic synthetic logs tailored for troubleshooting in Industry 4.0. These GAN-based approaches ensured that the generated logs mirrored the statistical properties and patterns of real-world logs. Specifically, VanillaGAN served as a baseline model, CTGAN was optimized for tabular data generation, and SeqGAN targeted the sequential characteristics of log data. The study also provided a comparative analysis of these GAN architectures and demonstrated their applicability in generating high-quality synthetic logs. To foster transparency and reproducibility, a replication package was made publicly available, enabling further validation by the research community.

Building on the foundation established in previous research, this work extends the synthetic log generation methodology by introducing LogGenST, a novel approach that addresses key limitations of GAN-based methods. Traditional GAN models often rely on extensive training data or predefined templates, which limit their adaptability and scalability in diverse industrial scenarios. LogGenST overcomes these challenges by incorporating a Large Language Model (LLM)-based adversarial framework into the log generation pipeline.

LogGenST integrates three specialized LLMs into its architecture: the Generator LLM (G-LLM), which produces synthetic logs, and the Discriminator LLM (D-LLM), which evaluates the authenticity of the generated logs. This adversarial framework eliminates the need for conventional training processes or predefined templates, ensuring scalable and adaptable log generation with minimal setup. By leveraging the advancements in LLMs, LogGenST achieves high-quality log generation that goes beyond the capabilities of GAN-based systems, offering a more flexible and efficient solution for synthetic log generation in Industry 4.0.

This paper introduces a novel extension to prior work by unifying GANs and LLMs into a cohesive framework for synthetic log generation. While GANs laid a solid foundation for generating realistic logs in previous work [9], the integration of LLMs in LogGenST represents a significant advancement, enhancing both the scalability and adaptability of the log generation process. This innovative hybrid approach not only improves the quality and efficiency of generated logs but also addresses key limitations of traditional methods, marking a substantial contribution to the state-of-the-art in smart troubleshooting methodologies.

2 Preliminaries and Related Work

In this section, we provide background information to support the context of our paper, including foundational concepts and relevant studies. Additionally, we discuss related work to offer a comprehensive understanding of the current state of research in topics relevant to our study.

2.1 Log Files

There is a wide range of formats for different systems that generate and utilize log files. The created content depends on the specific domain that a system or application is built for. The diversity in log file types is crucial for generating synthetic log files, as it ensures that the synthetic data can accurately reflect the variety of real-world scenarios and patterns [10]. Some common types of log files include the following. *System logs* record events related to the operating system, such as startup/shutdown sequences, hardware errors, and system resource usage [11]. *Application logs* are generated by software applications, which capture information about all user interactions, containing errors, warnings, and other relevant events within the application [12]. *Access logs* record all requests made by the system or user, accessing individual files, in connection to a request from a system [13]. *Security logs* document the status of a system and significant security events. These logs assist security experts in identifying intrusions and compromises, providing valuable insights into the overall system status [14]. *Server logs* files, or sets of files, are automatically generated and maintained records of the activities performed by a server. An example of this is the web server, which keeps a history of page requests [15].

2.2 Generative Adversarial Networks

Synthetic data generation creates artificial datasets to address challenges in obtaining real data, such as privacy concerns or data scarcity just like lack of public log files. Traditional methods cannot often replicate key statistical properties of the original data. Machine Learning (ML) and Deep Learning (DL) offer innovative approaches by automatically learning patterns from existing data. ML and DL models can capture distribution, patterns, and correlations, providing statistical fidelity to the original dataset. They require fewer user-defined rules, are flexible across domains, scalable for large datasets, and aid in privacy preservation e.g. in the case of customer data. However, challenges like over-fitting and data diversity need consideration in implementing ML and DL for synthetic data generation [16]. A productive method for acquiring knowledge about generative models involves utilizing the GANs framework, proposed by Goodfellow et al. in 2014 [17]. GAN functions essentially as follows: the underlying data distribution is modeled by a generative model, represented by G. On the other hand, a discriminative model, represented by the letter D, is responsible for determining the probability that a particular sample comes from the training data rather than from G. G is trained by maximizing the likelihood that D will classify samples incorrectly. This framework can be thought of as a two-player minimax game until it reaches Nash equilibrium [17]. The loss function for a GAN consists of two components: the generator loss ($\mathcal{L}_G$) and the discriminator loss ($\mathcal{L}_D$). The loss function for the generator can be formulated as:

$$\mathcal{L}_G = -\mathbb{E}_{z \sim p(z)}[\log D(G(z))]$$

where:

- z is a random noise vector sampled from a prior distribution $p(z)$.
- $G(z)$ represents the generated data by the generator.
- $D(G(z))$ is the discriminator's output when fed with the generated data.

The loss function for the discriminator can be formulated as:

$$\mathcal{L}_D = -\mathbb{E}_{x \sim p_{\text{data}}(x)}[\log D(x)] - \mathbb{E}_{z \sim p(z)}[\log(1 - D(G(z)))]$$

where:

- x represents real data samples.
- $D(x)$ is the discriminator's output when fed with real data.

The discriminator aims to maximize $\mathcal{L}_D$, while the generator aims to minimize $\mathcal{L}_G$.

Basic GAN, CTGAN [18], and SeqGAN (GRU-based) [19] were chosen for their ability to address the unique aspects of log data. Basic GANs offer a fundamental approach, making them valuable for establishing a baseline understanding. CTGAN excels in processing tabular and categorical data, making it highly suitable for structured datasets. SeqGAN, enhanced with GRU, is specifically tailored for managing sequential data. Although other variants such as WGAN-GP or StyleGAN may provide additional advantages, we selected these models for their comprehensive capability to meet the diverse needs of log data generation, particularly their proficiency in handling both categorical and sequential data types. While the use of GANs in our project came with higher CPU and memory costs during the training phase, the investment was justified by the superior quality and realism of the synthetic data generated. The inference phase of GANs was relatively efficient, making them practical for generating large amounts of synthetic data once trained. By balancing the computational costs with the quality of synthetic data, our choice of GANs provided significant advantages, especially given the complexity and diversity of the data types we were working with. This approach ensured that we could generate realistic and high-quality synthetic data, which was crucial for achieving our research's objectives.

2.3 Large Language Models

Large Language Models (LLMs) have revolutionized the field of natural language processing (NLP) by demonstrating remarkable capabilities in tasks such as text generation, classification, summarization, and question answering. These models, often comprising billions of parameters, leverage extensive pre-training on diverse datasets to capture linguistic patterns and contextual semantics [20]. Their capability to produce coherent and contextually relevant text has facilitated applications spanning conversational agents, content creation, data synthesis, and augmentation. Recent research has investigated the use of LLMs to generate synthetic datasets for training smaller, task-specific models, enhancing data and computational efficiency in resource-constrained environments [20]. For example, iterative data synthesis approaches reduce the distribution gap between synthetic and real-world data by dynamically refining datasets based on model feedback, leading to improved performance [20].

Furthermore, approaches utilizing federated learning and differential privacy have enabled the deployment of LLMs in privacy-sensitive applications, such as mobile keyboards, while preserving user data confidentiality [21]. These advancements underline the potential of LLMs to enhance both data quality and model performance, making them integral to modern artificial intelligence pipelines. Despite their strengths, LLMs face challenges related to distribution mismatches, bias, and noise in synthetic data, which can affect model reliability [20]. Addressing these issues often involves prompt engineering, filtering mechanisms, and iterative refinement strategies to ensure high-quality data synthesis and adaptation to target domains [20]. As research progresses, novel methodologies combining synthetic data generation, error extrapolation, and privacy-preserving mechanisms continue to enhance the performance and usability of LLMs across diverse domains. These advancements not only improve data efficiency but also demonstrate the broader potential of LLMs as foundational tools for modern artificial intelligence systems [21].

2.4 Related Work

The state-of-the-art methods in synthetic log file generation are either based on systematic approaches or generative models. The first method involves systematically generating synthetic log data that replicates the behavior of linear program execution logs, incorporating both normal operations and various types of anomalies to create a comprehensive dataset for testing anomaly detection algorithms. For example, a method is proposed to synthetically generate a log dataset that mimics the behavior of a linear program execution log file, including both normal and anomalous behaviors. The method involves simulating multiple program executions of a machine, with each execution consisting of a sequence of steps and possible errors [22]. However, a drawback of this approach is that synthetic data may not capture all the complexities and unpredictabilities of real-world data, potentially limiting the generalizability of research findings based on this dataset. The use of Generative models to generate synthetic log files is another innovative method that tackles the issue of insufficient labeled log data for training anomaly detection models. For instance, in a research, a generative model was used to create adversarial log files with subtle modifications designed to evade anomaly detection systems. The primary goal of employing this generative model is to demonstrate the vulnerabilities in current log parsing tools and show how adversaries can manipulate logs to avoid detection, thereby compromising the security and reliability of system log analysis [7]. Its focus is on log parsing and log structure rather than on the dataset itself.

In a research conducted by Kim et al., a Deep Neural Network (DNN) model was utilized to generate synthetic density log data for wells in the Golden field, Alberta, Canada. The primary purpose of employing this generative model is to address the data shortage problem commonly faced in reservoir modeling due to the high costs and logistical challenges of acquiring well log data through drilling [23]. Wurzenberger et al. employed a generative model to create synthetic log files by utilizing log line clustering and Markov chain simulation. This model generates Network Event Sequence (NES) data that accurately reflects actual system behavior by using a small set of real network data as input. The main purpose of this approach is to produce realistic synthetic log data for evaluating and testing security and network analysis tools offline, ensuring these tools can manage the complexities of real-world data without compromising the integrity of a live network [24]. While Markov chains are useful for certain types of synthetic data generation, especially when the system has simple and well-defined transitions, they are less powerful compared to GANs for handling complex data [25].

Regarding the use of GANs in this research area, Chen et al. propose a framework using GAN to address the imbalance problem in network threat detection datasets, particularly those with few-shot samples. The method involves generating synthetic samples through GANs to augment the small number of malicious logs, network traffic data, and other cyber threat-related data [26]. Compared to the research discussed, our work focuses on generating synthetic logs for a broader range of applications, including system monitoring and operational analysis, rather than being confined to security threats. Therefore, our approach extends beyond addressing few-shot problems and specific security scenarios.

Generally, prior work in synthetic log generation has focused on several approaches:

1. Traditional Methods: Traditional methods for log generation have relied on predefined rules and structured frameworks. Rule-based generation systems operate by defining explicit conditions and rules to create logs based on domain-specific requirements. These systems are straightforward but often lack flexibility when dealing with complex patterns or anomalies. Template-based approaches extend this concept by using predefined templates that incorporate placeholders, enabling faster log generation with minimal customization. However, they struggle to capture the diversity and variability found in real-world logs. Statistical modeling methods, such as Hidden Markov Models (HMMs) and n-grams, leverage probabilistic techniques to simulate patterns observed in log data. While these methods provide some adaptability, they are often limited by the need for large training datasets and may fail to generalize effectively in dynamic environments.
2. Machine Learning Approaches: Modern machine learning methods have significantly advanced log generation by capturing complex dependencies and patterns. GAN-based architectures use a generator-discriminator framework to produce synthetic logs that closely resemble real data, leveraging adversarial training to improve authenticity. Sequence-to-sequence models, including recurrent neural networks (RNNs) and transformers, generate logs by learning sequential dependencies, making them effective for capturing time-series patterns and contextual information. Variational autoencoders (VAEs) offer another powerful approach, encoding input data into a latent space and generating outputs by decoding sampled latent variables, thus supporting diverse and flexible log synthesis. These techniques address many limitations of traditional methods, providing higher adaptability and scalability.
3. Recent LLM Applications:
Recent advancements in large language models (LLMs) have further revolutionized log generation by leveraging pre-trained models capable of understanding and generating human-like text. Single LLM generation approaches use powerful models such as GPT to generate logs directly, reducing the need for extensive training on task-specific data. Prompt engineering techniques enhance the performance of LLMs by designing input prompts that guide the model to generate logs with specific structures and characteristics, enabling customization for different scenarios. Fine-tuning approaches adapt pre-trained LLMs to domain-specific tasks by updating model weights with task-relevant datasets, ensuring greater accuracy and contextual relevance. These methods provide scalable and flexible solutions for generating logs that closely mimic real-world data, making them particularly suitable for modern troubleshooting and diagnostic applications. This evolution from traditional systems to advanced LLM-based approaches highlights the increasing

sophistication of log generation methods, enabling more accurate, diverse, and scalable solutions for complex systems.

3 Methodology

In this section, we explained methodology proposed to this purpose. The sequence diagram in Fig. 1 illustrates the process of log generation, verification, and refinement involving multiple components: the user, LogSynthesizer, LogVerifier, Hadoop, and Metrics. The process begins when the user initiates log generation, prompting the LogSynthesizer to fetch data from Hadoop via the LogVerifier. After receiving a response, the LogSynthesizer generates logs, which enter a feedback loop for refinement. During this loop, logs are iteratively refined based on feedback from the LogVerifier until they meet the required standards. Once the logs are finalized, they are sent to both the Metrics and Hadoop systems for evaluation and comparison with real data. Metrics processing occurs in parallel, analyzing generated logs against real data to validate performance and accuracy. The process concludes when the logs are verified, and the results are communicated back to the user, ensuring iterative improvements and high-quality log synthesis.

Overview LogGenST consists of three main components working in an adversarial setup:

3.1 Component Roles

Generator LLM (G-LLM): G-LLM plays a critical role in the log generation process by handling multiple key responsibilities. It receives refined prompts from the Prompt Engineering LLM (PE-LLM) to guide the generation of synthetic log entries. G-LLM ensures that the generated logs maintain temporal and causal relationships, preserving logical sequences and dependencies within the data. Additionally, it incorporates system-specific patterns, aligning the synthetic logs with the structural and contextual characteristics of real-world data, thereby enhancing authenticity and usability.

Discriminator LLM (D-LLM): D-LLM serves as a critical evaluation component in the log generation process, ensuring the quality and authenticity of synthetic logs. Its primary functions include analyzing the generated logs by comparing them against real examples to assess their accuracy and consistency. The D-LLM provides detailed feedback on authenticity, highlighting specific issues and suggesting improvements to refine the logs further. Additionally, it identifies patterns or anomalies that may deviate from real-world data and assigns quality scores to the generated logs, enabling continuous enhancements and ensuring high standards in log generation.

Prompt Engineer LLM (PE-LLM): PE-LLM plays a pivotal role in optimizing the log generation process by facilitating effective communication between the Generator LLM (G-LLM) and the Discriminator LLM (D-LLM). Its core responsibilities include analyzing feedback provided by the D-LLM to identify areas for

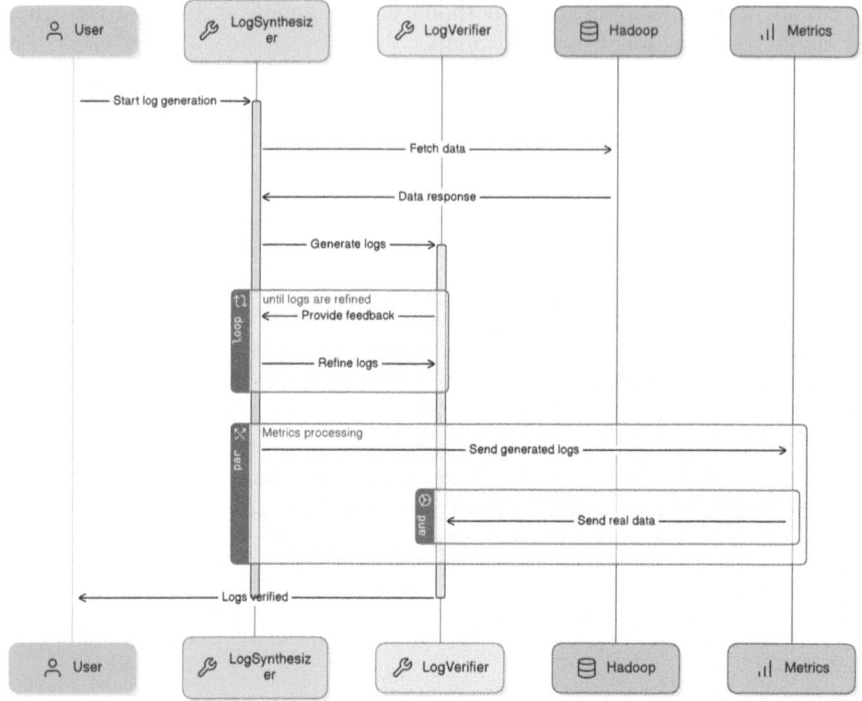

Fig. 1. Overview of proposed LogGenSt process

improvement in the generated logs. Based on this analysis, the PE-LLM refines prompts for the G-LLM, ensuring they are tailored to produce more accurate and authentic outputs. It maintains the quality of prompts by iteratively enhancing their structure and content, promoting consistency and relevance. Additionally, the PE-LLM drives continuous improvement, enabling adaptive refinements to achieve higher standards in log generation over successive iterations.

3.2 System Architecture

Adversarial Process: The project relies on several Python libraries to implement its functionality and evaluation processes. The replicate library is used to interface with the Replicate API, enabling seamless integration with large language models (LLMs). For data visualization, matplotlib is employed to create graphical representations of performance metrics, providing clear insights into trends and improvements. Additionally, sklearn is utilized to compute key evaluation metrics, including precision, recall, and F1 score, ensuring robust performance assessment throughout the log generation and validation process.

Figure 2 demonstrates the initial setup required for a Python script to perform log generation and evaluation using machine learning techniques. It begins by importing essential libraries, including os for environment variable management, replicate for interfacing with the Replicate API to access LLMs, random for generating random numbers, and matplotlib.pyplot for data visualization. Additionally, it imports precision, recall, and F1 score metrics from sklearn.metrics, which are critical for evaluating model performance. The snippet also sets the environment variable REPLICATE with a placeholder API token, enabling secure authentication with the Replicate service. This setup ensures seamless integration with external APIs and provides the tools necessary for generating, visualizing, and assessing synthetic logs.

```
import os
import replicate
import random
import matplotlib.pyplot as plt
from sklearn.metrics import precision_score,
recall_score, f1_score

os.environ["REPLICATE_API_TOKEN"] = "your_api_token_here"
```

Fig. 2. Key Setup Code

4 Log Generation

Figure 3 defines a function called call generator replicate, which interacts with the Replicate API to generate synthetic logs using a large language model (LLM). The function initializes a client connection to the Replicate service by retrieving the API token from the environment variable REPLICATE API TOKEN. It then sends a request to the specified LLM model, meta/meta-llama-3-8b-instruct, with the provided prompt as input. The response from the API is processed by concatenating all parts into a single text string. Finally, the function filters and returns non-empty lines from the generated response after stripping any whitespace. This implementation effectively utilizes the Replicate API for dynamic log generation, enabling seamless integration with advanced language models to produce structured and contextually relevant synthetic logs.

5 Log Validation

Figure 4 defines a function, analyze logs with discriminator, designed to validate and analyze generated logs using a discriminator model. It constructs a detailed prompt by combining a predefined DISCRIMINATOR PROMPT with the provided logs, ensuring context for analysis. The function initializes a connection to the Replicate API using an API token stored in the environment variable REPLICATE API TOKEN. It then sends the constructed prompt to the meta/meta-llama-3-8b-instruct model for processing. The response, which

```
def call_generator_replicate(prompt):
    api = replicate.Client(api_token=os.environ
    ["REPLICATE_API_TOKEN"])
    response = api.run(
    "meta/meta-llama-3-8b-instruct",
    input={"prompt": prompt}
    )
    response_text = " ".join(response)
    return [line.strip() for line in
    response_text.split('\n') if line.strip()]
```

Fig. 3. Log Generation Code

contains the analysis results, is returned as a concatenated string. This approach leverages the discriminator's capabilities to evaluate log authenticity, highlight anomalies, and provide feedback for improving log quality.

```
def analyze_logs_with_discriminator(generated_logs):
    prompt = f"{DISCRIMINATOR_PROMPT}\n\nAnalyze this
    log:\n" + "\n".join(generated_logs)
    api = replicate.Client(api_token=os.environ
    ["REPLICATE_API_TOKEN"])
    response = api.run(
    "meta/meta-llama-3-8b-instruct",
    input={"prompt": prompt}
    )
    return " ".join(response)
```

Fig. 4. Log Validation Code

4 Experimental Setup

We chose two datasets of real log files from various sources to serve as the training data for our GAN models. These log files include a variety of faults, errors, and failure patterns typical of industrial applications. The dataset was preprocessed to standardize the log formats. Then, three GAN models were selected for this study and tailored for log file generation to meet our specific requirements.

These models were then trained using adversarial methods, where the generator and discriminator networks were iteratively refined to achieve the desired quality of synthetic log files. This training process ensured that the generated logs closely mimicked the characteristics and patterns of the real log data. In the next step, we evaluated our results using these metrics: Generator Loss, Discriminator Loss, F1 score, precision, recall and Cumulative Sum (Cumsum) Plots. Generator Loss assessed the quality of the synthetic log entries, while Discriminator Loss evaluated the accuracy of distinguishing real from synthetic logs, with balanced discriminator losses being desirable. Cumsum Plots provided a visual comparison of the distributions of real and synthetic log data, helping to identify any discrepancies.

4.1 Dataset

We used publicly available dataset as input to our GANs. The logs include data from various systems such as Hadoop Distributed File System (HDFS)[1] and ZooKeeper[2]. Apache Spark

4.2 Architecture of Proposed GANs

In this subsection, we will define the architecture of our customized GAN models.

Vanilla GAN: First, we customize the GAN for our dataset as it is shown in Table 1. Both the Discriminator and Generator models utilize a series of dense layers with ReLU activation for the intermediate layers to ensure non-linearity. For the output layers, we use specialized activation functions (Tanh for the Generator and Sigmoid for the Discriminator)to suit their specific tasks within the GAN framework.

Table 1. Vanilla GAN Generator, Discriminator Model Architecture

	Layer Type	Units	Input Shape	Activation
Generator	Dense	128	(input_dim,)	relu
	Dense	64	(128,)	relu
	Dense	32	(64,)	relu
	Dense	output_dim	(32,)	relu
Discriminator	Dense	128	(input_dim,)	relu
	Dense	64	(128,)	relu
	Dense	32	(64,)	relu
	Dense	1	(32,)	sigmoid

---

[1] https://github.com/logpai/loghub/tree/master/Hadoop.
[2] https://github.com/logpai/loghub.

CTGAN: The table 2 describes the CTGAN architecture. The Generator starts with an input layer for the latent vector, followed by dense layers with 256 and 128 units using ReLU activation, interspersed with batch normalization and dropout layers. The final layer uses Tanh activation to produce the output. The Discriminator begins with an input layer, followed by dense layers with 256 and 128 units using ReLU activation, and dropout layers to prevent overfitting. The final layer uses Sigmoid activation to output a probability score, distinguishing real from generated data.

Table 2. CTGAN Generator, Discriminator Model Architecture

	Layer Type	Units	Output Shape	Activation
Generator	Input	–	(latent_dim,)	–
	Dense	256	(256,)	relu
	BatchNormalization	–	(256,)	–
	Dropout	–	(256,)	–
	Dense	128	(128,)	relu
	BatchNormalization	–	(128,)	–
	Dropout	–	(128,)	–
	Dense	output_dim	(output_dim,)	tanh
Discriminator	Input	–	(input_dim,)	–
	Dense	256	(256,)	relu
	Dropout	–	(256,)	–
	Dense	128	(128,)	relu
	Dropout	–	(128,)	–
	Dense	1	(1,)	sigmoid

SeqGAN: Table 3 describes the SeqGAN model architecture for both the Generator and Discriminator. The Generator starts with an input layer followed by GRU layers with units decreasing from 256 to 32, each with batch normalization, LeakyReLU activation, and dropout layers. The final layer uses Tanh activation for output. The Discriminator also begins with an input layer, followed by GRU layers with units decreasing from 256 to 32, with LeakyReLU activation and dropout layers. The final dense layer uses Sigmoid activation to output a probability score. This architecture uses GRU layers for sequential data, with activation and regularization techniques to improve performance and robustness.

The a priori hypothesis is that CTGAN would perform well due to its specific design for handling tabular and categorical data, which aligns well with log data characteristics. SeqGAN (GRU-based) was expected to capture the sequential dependencies effectively. These approaches were selected based on their compatibility with the nature of log data, aiming to leverage their strengths in modeling the unique properties of log datasets.

Table 3. SeqGAN Generator, Discriminator Model Architecture

Layer Type	Units	Output Shape	Activation
Input	–	(input_dim, 1)	–
GRU	256	(input_dim, 256)	–
BatchNormalization	–	(input_dim, 256)	–
LeakyReLU	–	(input_dim, 256)	–
Dropout	–	(input_dim, 256)	–
GRU	128	(input_dim, 128)	–
BatchNormalization	–	(input_dim, 128)	–
LeakyReLU	–	(input_dim, 128)	–
Dropout	–	(input_dim, 128)	–
GRU	64	(input_dim, 64)	–
BatchNormalization	–	(input_dim, 64)	–
LeakyReLU	–	(input_dim, 64)	–
Dropout	–	(input_dim, 64)	–
GRU	32	(32)	–
BatchNormalization	–	(32)	–
LeakyReLU	–	(32)	–
Dropout	–	(32)	–
Dense(Generator*)	output_dim	(output_dim)	tanh
Dense(Discriminator*)	1	(1)	sigmoid

5 Results

This section highlights the performance trends observed during the iterative rounds of log generation and classification. The analysis distinguishes between real logs, sourced from authentic Hadoop datasets, and synthetic logs, synthesized by G-LLM and classified using D-LLM. Figure 5 illustrates the performance metrics-Precision, Recall, and F1 Score-evaluated over five rounds of log generation and refinement. The Recall metric consistently achieves the highest values, peaking at approximately 0.95 in the second round before slightly declining but remaining above 0.91. The F1 Score follows a similar trend, reaching its maximum around 0.91 in the second round and then fluctuating slightly in subsequent rounds. Precision, while starting lower, peaks near 0.88 in the second round and experiences moderate variations across the remaining rounds. These trends highlight the system's ability to refine logs iteratively, achieving significant improvements early in the process and stabilizing performance over time. The variations also emphasize the need for continued optimization to maintain consistency and maximize overall performance across all metrics.

Figure 6 visualizes the performance metrics-Precision, Recall, and F1 Score-across five rounds of log generation and refinement. Each cell displays the numer-

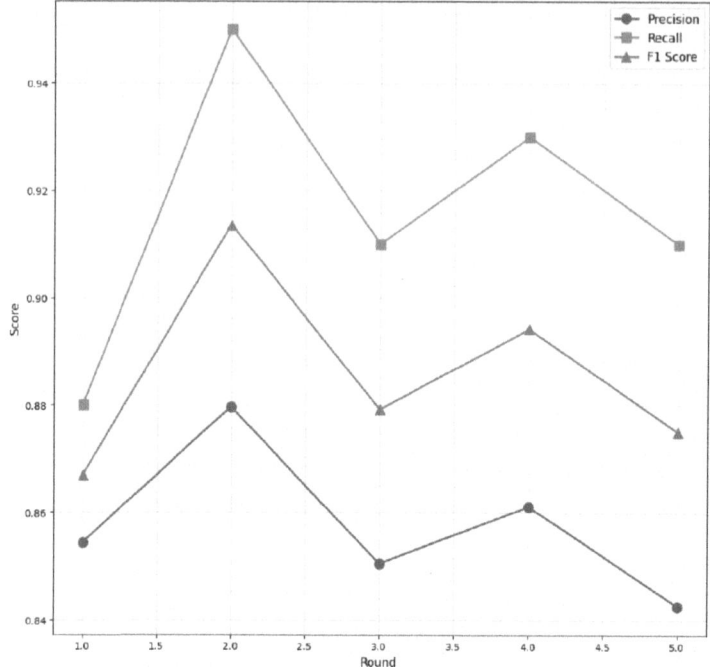

Fig. 5. Classification Metrics Over Time

ical value of the respective metric, with colors representing the score intensity based on the accompanying color bar. Darker shades indicate higher scores, while lighter shades correspond to lower values. Notably, Recall consistently achieves higher scores compared to Precision and F1 Score, peaking at 0.950 in Round 2 and maintaining high values throughout the iterations. F1 Scores also follow a similar trend, reflecting improvements in balancing precision and recall, reaching 0.913 in Round 2 and stabilizing in subsequent rounds. This visualization highlights the iterative refinement process, demonstrating enhanced log quality early on, followed by slight fluctuations, which emphasize the need for further optimization to maintain consistency across rounds.

5.1 Evaluation Metrics

Each round of log generation and validation evaluates system performance by producing predictions and calculating key metrics. precision measures the proportion of correctly identified real logs out of all predicted real logs, while recall assesses the proportion of correctly identified real logs relative to all actual real logs. To balance these measures, the F1 Score, which represents the harmonic mean of precision and recall, is also computed. These metrics are tracked and visualized across multiple rounds, enabling the monitoring of performance trends and improvements as the system undergoes iterative refinements. The visualiza-

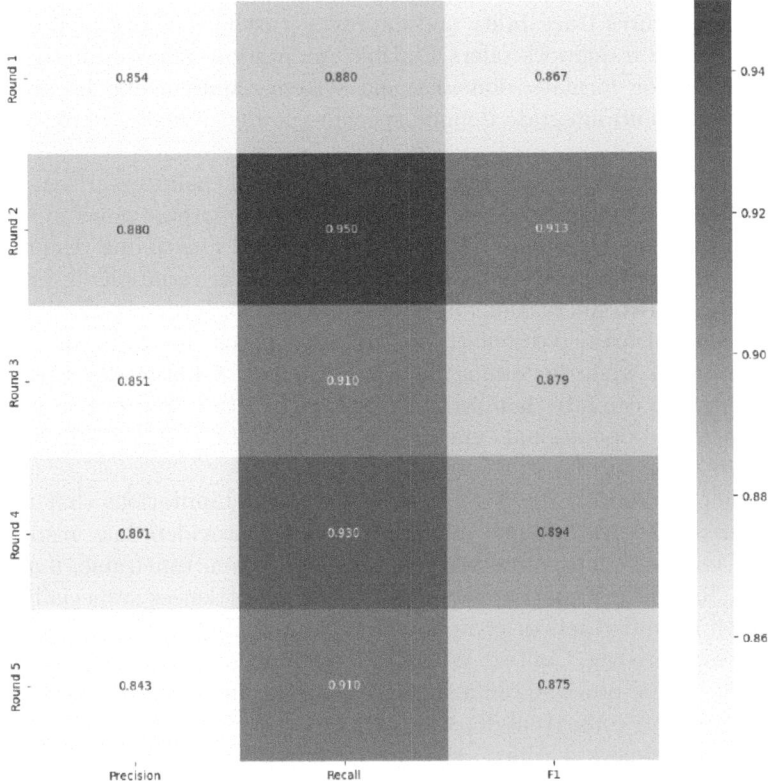

Fig. 6. Metrics Heatmap by Round

tions provide insights into the model's ability to generate and classify logs more accurately over time, showcasing its adaptability and effectiveness in handling log authenticity tasks.

6 Discussion

The proposed framework for synthetic log generation and validation demonstrates several advantages, yet it also presents challenges and limitations that need to be addressed for broader applicability.

One of the key strengths of the framework is Automated Prompt Refinement, which leverages iterative feedback loops to dynamically adjust prompts based on discriminator evaluations. This automation reduces manual intervention, ensuring that logs are continuously refined and improved. Additionally, the framework supports Continuous Quality Improvement by integrating evaluation metrics, enabling it to adapt and evolve over multiple iterations to produce more accurate and realistic logs. Another important feature is Explainable Changes, which provide transparency by highlighting specific refinements made during the process. This ensures traceability and improves trust in the generated outputs. Furthermore, the framework offers Flexible Adaptation, allowing it to accommodate diverse log formats, domains, and system requirements. Its ability to modify prompts and integrate domain-specific knowledge makes it versatile for different use cases.

Despite these strengths, the framework faces several challenges. Prompt Convergence can be a complex task, as ensuring that prompts converge to optimal configurations may require multiple iterations and fine-tuning. Maintaining Quality Consistency across logs is another challenge, as variations in inputs or prompts can lead to fluctuations in output quality. Performance Optimization remains a critical area, particularly for reducing processing time and computational overhead while sustaining high performance. Additionally, Cost Management must be carefully handled, as frequent API calls and evaluations can result in increased operational expenses, making scalability a concern for larger deployments.

Alongside challenges, the framework has inherent Limitations that need to be considered. API Rate Limits imposed by service providers may restrict the number of requests that can be processed within a given timeframe, impacting scalability. Response Time Latency can also be a bottleneck, especially when dealing with large datasets or complex prompts, potentially delaying the refinement process. Moreover, Context Window Constraints in LLMs limit the amount of data that can be processed in a single prompt, posing difficulties in handling logs with extensive contextual dependencies or multi-step sequences.

While the framework offers significant advantages through automation, adaptability, and continuous improvement, it also faces challenges related to performance and cost optimization. Furthermore, limitations like API constraints and latency highlight areas for future enhancement. Addressing these challenges and limitations will be essential to ensure broader adoption and scalability of the framework in real-world applications.

7 Conclusions and Future Work

In our previous work, we addressed the challenge of public log data scarcity from heterogeneous interconnected devices by leveraging GANs to synthesize realistic log files. This approach was particularly valuable for generating log data tailored for smart-troubleshooting, ensuring the synthetic logs captured faults, errors, and failures in patterns resembling real-world scenarios. Specifically, we employed Vanilla GAN, CTGAN, and SeqGAN to generate synthetic logs, with CTGAN demonstrating the highest performance in producing high-quality data. This work laid a solid foundation for enhancing the reliability and efficiency of synthetic log generation, paving the way for scalable and effective diagnostics in industrial applications. Despite these promising results, challenges such as improving data accuracy, ensuring fairness, and addressing privacy concerns remained key areas for further development.

Building upon this foundation, we developed LogGenST, an advanced and adaptable framework for synthetic log generation that integrates LLMs to overcome some of these challenges. LogGenST employs a novel approach by combining generator and discriminator LLMs with iterative prompt engineering, achieving high authenticity without requiring extensive model training. This method significantly reduces the computational overhead while maintaining the quality and contextual relevance of the generated logs. Through this approach, LogGenST provides a flexible and scalable solution for generating logs across various domains, facilitating improvements in software testing and development processes.

The iterative prompt engineering used in LogGenST enables dynamic refinement of synthetic logs, allowing the system to adapt to different error scenarios and data formats. By leveraging LLMs, LogGenST captures complex patterns and anomalies in logs, closely mimicking real-world data distributions. This adaptability makes it particularly suitable for scenarios where data diversity and authenticity are critical, such as testing distributed systems and debugging software pipelines.

Future work will focus on expanding support for multi-system log formats, incorporating domain-specific knowledge for error simulation, and automating feedback analysis through advanced prompt engineering techniques. Further enhancements will address scalability, privacy, and fairness concerns, ensuring the generated logs maintain high quality and relevance across diverse scenarios. By exploring reinforcement learning and real-time log generation, LogGenST aims to become a more versatile tool for modern log generation and troubleshooting challenges.

References

1. Singh, P., et al.: Using log analytics and process mining to enable self-healing in the internet of things. Environ. Syst. Decis. **42**(2), 234–250 (2022)
2. Caporuscio, M., Flammini, F., Khakpour, N., Singh, P., Thornadtsson, J.: Smart-troubleshooting connected devices: concept, challenges and opportunities. Futur. Gener. Comput. Syst. **111**, 681–697 (2020)
3. Partovian, S., Bucaioni, A., Flammini, F., Thornadtsson, J.: Analysis of log files to enable smart-troubleshooting in industry 4.0: a systematic mapping study. IEEE Access 1 (2023)
4. Xia, B., Bai, Y., Yin, J., Li, Y., Xu, J.: LogGAN: a log-level generative adversarial network for anomaly detection using permutation event modeling. Inf. Syst. Front. **23**, 285–298 (2021)
5. Baruh, L., Secinti, E., Cemalcilar, Z.: Online privacy concerns and privacy management: a meta-analytical review. J. Commun. **67**, 26–53 (2017)
6. Zahid, M., Bucaioni, A., Flammini, F.: Model-based trustworthiness evaluation of autonomous cyber-physical production systems: a systematic mapping study. ACM Comput. Surv. **56** (2024)
7. Sun, J., Liu, B., Hong, Y.: Logbug: generating adversarial system logs in real time. In: Proceedings of the 29th ACM International Conference on Information & Knowledge Management, CIKM '20, (New York, NY, USA), pp. 2229–2232, Association for Computing Machinery, 2020

8. Bozyigit, F., et al.: Generating domain models from natural language text using nlp: a benchmark dataset and experimental comparison of tools. Softw. Syst. Model. 1–19 (2024)
9. Partovian, S., Flammini, F., Bucaioni, A.: Leveraging gans to generate synthetic log files for smart-troubleshooting in industry 4.0. In: 2024 50th Euromicro Conference on Software Engineering and Advanced Applications (SEAA), pp. 1–8, 2024
10. Kim, S., Kim, K.H., Min, B., Lim, J., Lee, K.: Generation of synthetic density log data using deep learning algorithm at the golden field in Alberta, Canada. Geofluids **2020** (2020)
11. Tomono, A., Uehara, M., Shimada, Y.: Improvement and evaluation of a method to manage multiple types of logs. In: 2011 IEEE Workshops of International Conference on Advanced Information Networking and Applications, pp. 601–606, 2011
12. Stuike, B., Amannejad, Y.: Pairwise application log classification. In: 2023 IEEE International Conference on Big Data and Smart Computing (BigComp), pp. 349–350, 2023
13. Karimi, L., Aldairi, M., Joshi, J., Abdelhakim, M.: An automatic attribute-based access control policy extraction from access logs. IEEE Trans. Dependable Secure Comput. **19**(4), 2304–2317 (2022)
14. Xu, A., Chen, L., Jiang, Y., Lv, H., Yang, H., Li, B.: Finding gold in the sand: identifying anomaly indicators though huge amount security logs. In: 2020 IEEE 6th Intl Conference on Big Data Security on Cloud (BigDataSecurity), IEEE Intl Conference on High Performance and Smart Computing, (HPSC) and IEEE Intl Conference on Intelligent Data and Security (IDS), pp. 140–144, 2020
15. Sharma, P., Yadav, S., Bohra, B.: A review study of server log formats for efficient web mining. In: 2015 International Conference on Green Computing and Internet of Things (ICGCIoT), pp. 1373–1377, 2015
16. Garcia Torres, D.: Generation of Synthetic Data with Generative Adversarial Networks. PhD thesis, KTH ROYAL INSTITUTE OF TECHNOLOGY, October 2018
17. Goodfellow, I.J., et al.: Generative adversarial networks, 2014
18. Xu, L., Skoularidou, M., Cuesta-Infante, A., Veeramachaneni, K.: Modeling Tabular Data Using Conditional GAN, pp. 7335–7345. Curran Associates Inc., Red Hook, NY, USA, 2019
19. Yu, L., Zhang, W., Wang, J., Yu, Y.: Seqgan: sequence generative adversarial nets with policy gradient. In: Proceedings of the Thirty-First AAAI Conference on Artificial Intelligence, AAAI'17, pp. 2852–2858, AAAI Press, 2017
20. Wang, R., Zhou, W., Sachan, M.: Let's synthesize step by step: Iterative dataset synthesis with large language models by extrapolating errors from small models. In: Bouamor, H., Pino, J., Bali, K. (eds.), Findings of the Association for Computational Linguistics: EMNLP 2023 (Singapore), pp. 11817–11831, Association for Computational Linguistics, December 2023
21. Wu, S., Xu, Z., Zhang, Y., Zhang, Y., Ramage, D.: Prompt Public Large Language Models to Synthesize Data for Private On-device Applications, arXiv e-prints, p. arXiv:2404.04360, April 2024
22. Luftensteiner, S., Praher, P.: A synthetic dataset for anomaly detection of machine behavior. In: Kotsis, G., et al. (eds.),Database and Expert Systems Applications - DEXA 2022 Workshops, pp. 424–431. Springer, Cham (2022)
23. S. Kim, K. H. Kim, B. Min, J. Lim, and K. Lee, "Generation of synthetic density log data using deep learning algorithm at the golden field in alberta, canada," *Geofluids*, vol. 2020, pp. Article ID 5387183, 26 pages, 2020

24. Wurzenberger, M., Skopik, F., Settanni, G., Scherrer, W.: Complex log file synthesis for rapid sandbox-benchmarking of security- and computer network analysis tools. Inf. Syst. **60**, 13–33 (2016)
25. Figueira, A., Vaz, B.: Survey on synthetic data generation, evaluation methods and gans. Mathematics **10**(15) (2022)
26. Chen, L., Song, Y., Chen, J.: A framework for few-shot network threats based on generative adversarial networks. In: 2023 IEEE Symposium on Computers and Communications (ISCC), pp. 1–6, 2023

Software, System, and Service Engineering (S3E'24)

Blockchain for Public Transportation: Digital Identity and Transaction Verification Architecture

Hidayet Burak Saritas[1,2](✉) and Geylani Kardas[1]

[1] Ege University International Computer Institute, 35100 Bornova, Izmir, Turkey
geylani.kardas@ege.edu.tr
[2] Kentkart Teknoloji AŞ, Ege Teknopark, Ege University, 35100 Bornova, Izmir, Turkey
burak.saritas@kentkart.com

Abstract. Blockchain technology has emerged as a promising solution to address key challenges in public transport, such as interoperability, privacy and transaction transparency. Despite these advances, the lack of a unified platform for integrating different transport modes and the diversity of ticketing solutions across operators remain significant barriers to seamless collaboration and interoperability. This paper proposes a blockchain-based architecture for transaction verification and digital identity management in multimodal public transport systems. The approach ensures secure co-payment, reliable data validation and trust among diverse operators by leveraging private blockchain networks, where operators act as verification nodes through consensus-based transaction approval without a central authority. The system incorporates standardized data formats, advanced algorithms for operator data integration, and a comprehensive model for managing operators, assets, and transactions. To protect user privacy, Zero-Knowledge Proof (ZKP) techniques enable secure authentication without revealing sensitive information. This study shows how blockchain technology can improve interoperability, ensure fair revenue sharing, and provide a secure, decentralized infrastructure for efficient and privacy-preserving collaboration in public transport networks.

Keywords: Blockchain Technology · Public Transportation · Co-payment Systems · Data Verification · Interoperability · Transaction Security · Decentralized Networks · Zero-Knowledge Proofs · Standardized Data Format · Privacy Preservation

1 Introduction

With advancements in technology, the public transportation sector is expanding and offering a variety of options to a wider audience. In addition to the traditional methods, new alternatives like shared vehicles, scooters, and app-controlled taxis are becoming more popular [1]. Regulations in this field set limits to prevent unfair competition and encourage cooperation. Mobility partners have the freedom to make their own decisions. Various public transport providers need to work together on a common platform to manage this diversity and deliver an enhanced user experience [2]. This can improve users' transportation experiences and reduce private vehicle usage. However, actors who offer different transportation methods have their own ticketing solutions. This may pose a significant challenge in the development process of a unified platform [3]. These actors include ABT Kentkart [4], STIB-MIVB [5], MVV [6], and Whim [7]. Users need to adapt to various ticketing solutions, and each actor needs to offer features such as payment, personalization, and usability [8, 9]. Therefore, creating a unified and accessible platform within the public transportation ecosystem is considered a significant innovation and challenge for the sector [10].

It is not easy to combine different actors of the public transportation industry. But it can be made simpler and efficient with following solutions like a single application, account management and a single card. To combine services and share profits, researchers are constantly exploring easy integration methods to create a common language that all transportation solution providers can use [11]. They are also working to establish a method for verifying every user transaction [10]. To solve these problems, this study proposes developing a blockchain-based solution that processes and verifies data produced by different transportation actors. Blockchain is a distributed ledger system that operates without central authority, ensuring data security and transparency [12]. In essence, Distributed Ledger Technology (DLT) is a secure and decentralized database that records transactions in an immutable manner, providing a trusted environment for data exchange [13]. It enables trust in transactions between two parties and eliminates the need for a central intermediary to provide this service. This allows for the secure transfer of unique assets, such as money, title deeds, and identification information, without intermediaries. Two users can conduct a financial transaction without the need for an intermediary institution [14]. They can communicate directly without any trust issues [15].

This study extends our previous conference paper on a blockchain-based transaction verification infrastructure [16], by focusing on the detailed architecture of digital identity and transaction verification in public transportation systems. The earlier work primarily focused on a standardized message format, transaction verification on Hyperledger Fabric among transportation companies, and privacy through Zero-Knowledge Proofs (ZKPs). In contrast, the current study extends adoption of these technologies significantly by providing a detailed technical architecture with explicit roles and interactions of components, implementing smart contracts and an API gateway, as well as enhancing digital wallet functionality for managing Decentralized Identifiers (DIDs) and Verifiable Credentials (VCs). Additionally, a dual-chain architecture is introduced, integrating both private and public blockchains to achieve greater scalability, interoperability, and privacy preservation. These advancements collectively contribute to a more robust and practical blockchain architecture for public transportation.

The standard message package format was developed on a private blockchain network. This format creates an environment where transportation operators can add data. The study considered parameters such as speed and assets that validating operators must have. This way, different operators in the public transportation sector can use blockchain technology to integrate with each other, trust each other, and query all transactions created with standard message format. Creating a trustworthy environment is crucial and can be achieved through a consensus mechanism and blockchain structure to confirm transactions. All businesses can join the blockchain network as validators, and data produced by any business can be added to the network after being approved by all nodes. The data added to the network in standard message format is trusted by everyone. To achieve this, a common data format and extensible approval mechanism have been created for the public transportation sector.

The rest of the paper is organized as follows: Sect. 2 reviews related work on blockchain applications in similar transportation sectors. In Sect. 3, we introduce the foundational elements and components of a blockchain environment optimized for public transportation. This section covers the architecture, roles, and interactions of transactions, as well as detailed descriptions of nodes, assets, and standardized message formats. In Sect. 4, we look at how to use decentralized technologies to keep people's information safe in public transportation. These technologies let people manage their digital identities without revealing sensitive information, which helps enhance people's privacy. We also look at how these technologies can be used with a single blockchain-based transaction verification system to verify user credentials. In Sect. 5, we summarize the contributions and implications of our blockchain-based architecture tailored for the public transportation sector.

2 Related Work

To address the outlined challenges, several studies have explored blockchain applications in public transportation. This section reviews key works in this area and highlights their relevance to our study. Some notable research has been done on using blockchain for public transportation. Jayalath et al. [17] propose a micro-transaction model based on blockchain to improve service in Sri Lanka's public transportation sector. They focus on a ticketing system using an Ethereum-based blockchain to reduce transaction fees and improve service quality. This approach creates QR-based tickets for users to make micro-payments without third-party intermediaries.

Wang et al. [18] introduce "InterTrust," an interoperable blockchain architecture to enhance interoperability and reliability across various blockchain systems. The InterTrust model is for communication and interoperability among existing blockchain systems, which is a broader scope. However, our study aims at providing a specialized blockchain network for the public transportation domain.

Yang et al. [19] suggest a blockchain and Edge Computing-based communication system for maritime transportation. Their work uses blockchain and Edge Computing to improve Internet of Things (IoT) device performance and security in maritime environments. This is different from our work, which focuses on public transportation.

Enescu et al. [20] discuss a blockchain application to promote ecological transportation and reduce traffic congestion. They imagine a system where blockchain records transactions and gives users digital currencies, which helps the environment and makes public transportation more popular.

Jabbar et al. [21] review blockchain applications in Intelligent Transportation Systems (ITS). They show how blockchain can improve transactional trust and efficiency. This supports various functionalities including automatic parking and fee payments.

Ganzha et al. [22] introduces a framework combining Blockchain-based Self-Sovereign Identity (SSI) and registry proof smart contracts to provide privacy-preserving solutions for Inter-Organizational Business Processes (IOBP). This approach effectively addresses the challenges of data sharing across organizations due to regulatory restrictions like the General Data Protection Regulation (GDPR) and demonstrates its applicability through a pharmaceutical supply chain case study on the Ethereum Blockchain.

Karataş et al. [23] propose a Self-Sovereign Identity (SSI)-based e-petition scheme utilizing the Sovrin blockchain. Their approach employs decentralized identifiers (DIDs) and verifiable credentials to ensure user privacy and anonymity while participating in e-petitions. This method addresses privacy concerns by enabling secure citizen engagement without revealing sensitive personal information.

Lastly, Chen et al. [24] describe a "Full-Spectrum Blockchain as a Service" (FSBaaS) approach with "Blockchain Lite" and "Hyperledger Fabric," focusing on providing blockchain services that cater to both centralized and decentralized frameworks. This study shows the flexibility needed in blockchain adoption.

Our study is different from the above-mentioned noteworthy efforts by providing a mechanism for public transportation operators to establish mutual trust. Each operator can independently verify and validate data transactions without relying on a central authority or intermediary. This ensures the accuracy of data and consistency of messages across the network, fostering seamless collaboration among operators. It facilitates collaboration among operators without dependence on a single authority. Additionally, this study improves privacy and security in public transportation systems by using DIDs, VCs, ZKPs explained in later sections. It supports user privacy by authenticating users and transactions without exposing sensitive personal information. This approach not only safeguards digital identities and transactions but also sets a precedent for incorporating privacy-preserving technologies in public transportation. The proposed framework introduces a standard message format and private blockchain network tailored for the public transportation sector. By utilizing consensus mechanisms and decentralized identifiers, the system ensures accurate transaction validation, secure data sharing, and enhanced privacy for users. This research aims to enable seamless integration among operators, establish trust, and set a precedent for privacy-preserving technologies in public transportation.

3 Key Elements and Core Components of the Blockchain Model

In this section, we present a detailed overview of the main model elements and foundational components of a blockchain-based transaction verification system specifically designed for public transportation. This includes an exploration of the core building blocks, the interactions between various system elements, and the overall architecture that facilitates secure, efficient, and transparent transaction processing across multiple transportation operators.

3.1 High-Level Overview of the Model in a Public Transportation Network

This section provides a conceptual view of the proposed blockchain-based transaction verification system for public transportation. The model integrates various transportation actors, enabling secure and transparent transactions while ensuring data privacy. Figure 1 illustrates the high-level design of the system, highlighting key components and their interactions within the network.

Core Concept of the Model. At the heart of the system, there exist the transactions, representing user actions such as ticket purchases or payments made across multiple transportation modes, including buses, scooters, and cars. These transactions are routed through the blockchain network, where a consensus mechanism ensures their validity and integrity. Participating businesses, acting as network nodes, collaboratively verify transactions without relying on a central authority. This decentralized approach fosters trust and reduces reliance on intermediaries.

Blockchain Environment and Consensus Mechanism. The system is built on the Hyperledger Fabric blockchain environment, which is tailored to enterprise-level applications [25]. Hyperledger Fabric provides:

Enhanced Transaction Control. Organizations can define private channels to restrict the visibility of specific transactions and data, ensuring privacy among participants.

Scalable Consensus. The system utilizes the Raft consensus algorithm, known for its ability to efficiently handle high transaction volumes with minimal latency [26]. Raft's practical fault tolerance makes it ideal for the dynamic and high-demand operations in public transportation [27]. Organizations (businesses) on the network verify transaction accuracy through a consensus mechanism [28].

Ensuring User Data Privacy. To safeguard user data, the system leverages advanced cryptographic techniques such as ZKPs:

1. Sensitive information like user identity or payment details is never directly revealed on the blockchain.
2. Instead, cryptographic proofs are included in transactions, allowing validators to confirm the authenticity of the transaction without accessing private data.
3. This mechanism ensures that only the essential details required for verification are shared, maintaining the integrity of the system while protecting user privacy.

Role of Smart Contracts. Hyperledger Fabric smart contracts (chaincodes) define the business logic of the system and automate transaction processing. These chaincodes:

1. Validate and enforce transaction rules.
2. Enable operations such as ticket issuance, membership validation, and fee payments.
3. Once validated, transactions are added to the blockchain ledger, which serves as a secure, immutable, and transparent record of all operations.

Visualization and Monitoring with Blockchain Explorer. To enhance transparency and monitoring:

1. A blockchain explorer is incorporated, allowing stakeholders to visualize, query, and track transactions and blocks.

2. This tool provides critical functionalities for auditing, reporting, and system monitoring, ensuring accountability across all participants.

Role of Network Participants

1. Businesses (Organizations): Act as nodes within the blockchain network, validating transactions and managing data related to their services.
2. Users: Initiate transactions (e.g., purchasing a ticket) via client applications that interact with the blockchain network.
3. Interconnected Nodes: Collaborate to validate transactions, ensuring decentralized governance and efficient data management.

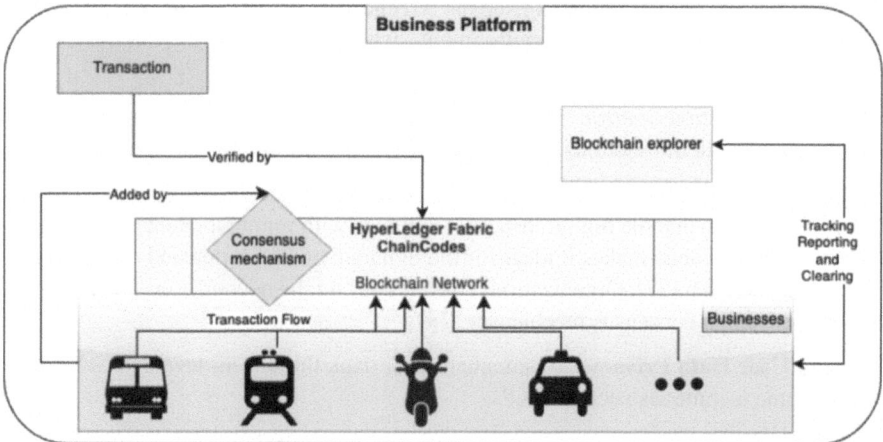

Fig. 1. High Level System Design

This high-level architecture provides the conceptual framework for secure and efficient transaction verification, while the underlying infrastructure ensures its seamless operation. It integrates privacy-preserving technologies, decentralized collaboration, and transparent data management, enabling seamless operations across diverse transportation operators while safeguarding user information.

3.2 Detailed Technical Architecture of the Blockchain Model

This section dives into the technical details of the proposed blockchain-based system, focusing on the roles, functionalities, and interactions of individual components. The system leverages Hyperledger Fabric's modular architecture and privacy features to meet the specific needs of public transportation. Figure 2 depicts the technical architecture, which ensures secure, decentralized, and efficient transaction processing.

Key Technical Components

User. This is the end-user of the public transportation network. Users interact with the system via client applications to undertake actions such as purchasing tickets, validating them, and making enquiries regarding their balance.

Client Applications. These comprise mobile and web applications that serve as the principal interface through which users interact with the blockchain network. The applications process user requests and relay them to the blockchain infrastructure via the client gateway.

Client Gateway. Serves as an intermediary between client applications and the blockchain network. The gateway validates incoming requests and routes them to the appropriate network services, thereby ensuring secure communication.

Businesses. Refers to the various transportation operators or stakeholders that are participants in the blockchain network. Each organization has its own set of peers, the responsibility of which is to validate transactions and maintain the ledger.

Peers. Nodes within the blockchain network that validate transactions, execute smart contracts, and maintain a copy of the ledger. Each organization is represented by multiple peers to ensure redundancy and reliability.

REST APIs. Facilitate interaction between external systems and applications and the blockchain network. The APIs facilitate integration with third-party systems, including those providing payment services or reporting tools.

The Ordering Service. It is responsible for ensuring the proper sequencing of transactions across the network. It aggregates transactions into blocks and transmits them to peers for validation and incorporation into the ledger.

Ledger. An immutable, distributed database that records all transactions and state changes within the network. It functions as the definitive source of information for all participants.

Chaincode (Smart Contracts). Serves to define the business logic of the network. It processes incoming transactions, enforces the established rules, and executes the required operations in a secure and automatic manner.

Ticket Engine. A specialized module for the administration of ticket-related functionalities, including the issuance, validation, and revocation of tickets. It interacts with the ledger and chain code to guarantee accurate and secure processing.

Kafka Cluster. Provides messaging and event streaming capabilities for the network, ensuring efficient communication between components and handling event-driven processes, such as notifications.

Notification Manager. Manages alerts and updates for users and system operators, ensuring timely communication of critical information, such as transaction statuses.

Organization Registration Module (ORM). It functions as a network manager designed to streamline the process of adding organizations and peers to the blockchain network. The network manager leverages automated services and scripts to manage network expansion securely and efficiently.

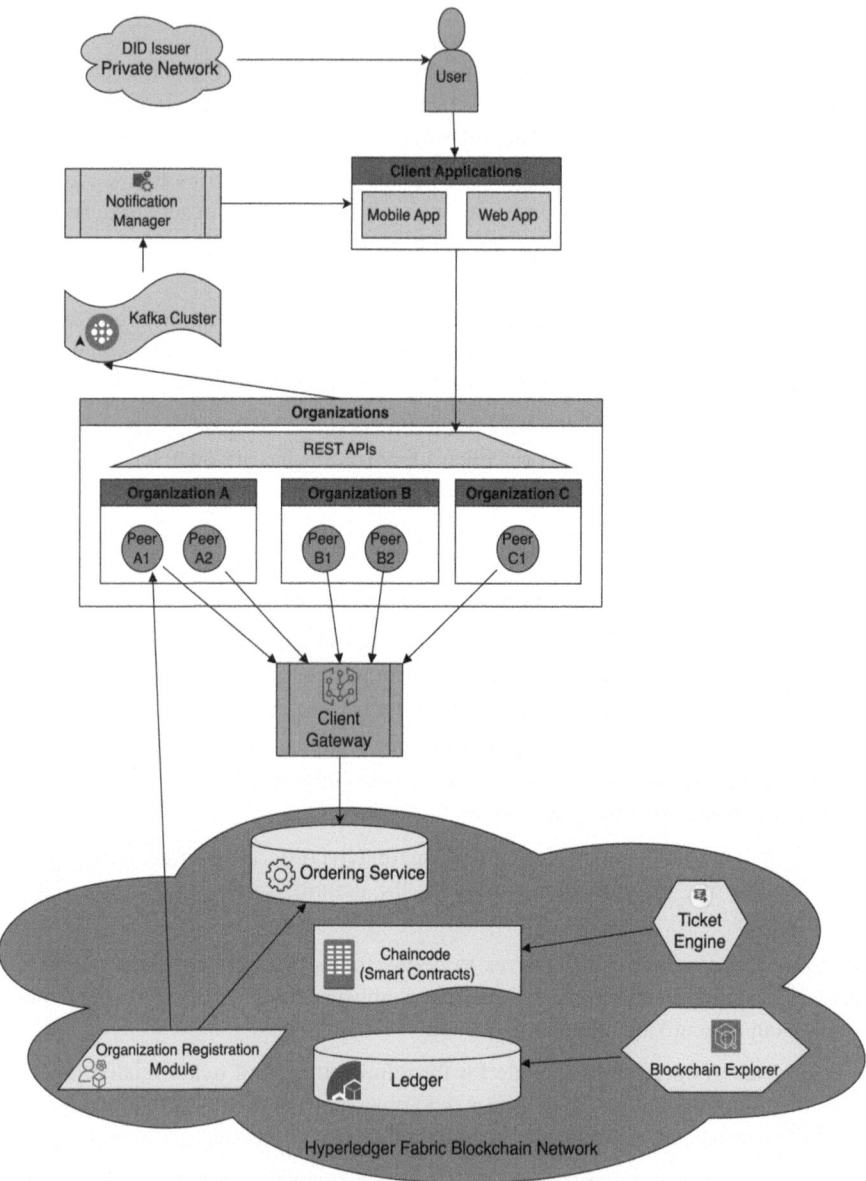

Fig. 2. Technical Architecture of the Blockchain-Based Public Transportation System

Transaction Flow in the Architecture

1. DID Retrieval (Optional): A user retrieves their DID and corresponding VCs from the issuer network. This process ensures that the user possesses a cryptographically

secure and self-sovereign identity that can be used for transactions within the public transportation ecosystem.
2. Membership Creation: During membership creation, one of the verifiers (e.g., a transportation operator) adds the user's transaction information (e.g., membership ID, validity, or privileges) to the blockchain network. This information is linked to the user's DID but does not expose sensitive personal data, ensuring privacy.
3. A user initiates a transaction (e.g., ticket purchase) through a client application.
4. The client gateway receives the request, validates it, and forwards it to the blockchain network.
5. The transaction is processed by the ordering service, which organizes it into a block and distributes it to peers for validation.
6. Peers execute the relevant chaincode (smart contract) to validate the transaction and apply the business rules.
7. Once validated, the transaction is added to the ledger and becomes part of the blockchain's immutable history.
8. The blockchain explorer allows stakeholders to query and visualize the transaction, ensuring transparency and accountability.

By combining these components, the proposed system provides a scalable, secure, and privacy-preserving solution for managing transactions in public transportation networks.

3.3 Definitions and Contents of Model Elements

This section describes the model elements and their roles that form the basis of a private blockchain environment customized for public transportation. The structures used clearly demonstrate how nodes, entities, and transactions on the blockchain are identified, processed, verified, and integrated into the public transportation system.

The diagram in Fig. 3 shows the defined classes for the fundamental components of the blockchain-based transaction verification system. The diagram demonstrates how a blockchain network is structured and how different components interact with each other. For example, a transaction executed by a node can trigger a smart contract, resulting in the addition of a block to the blockchain. Nodes communicates using different data formats and messaging protocols. This plays a crucial role in maintaining the security and integrity of the blockchain network.

Nodes (Businesses). Each node in the blockchain network represents a business or organization. These nodes manage various transportation services, such as buses, trams, and scooters, and perform critical roles in the system, including:

Transaction Management. Nodes initiate, process, and approve transactions on the network.

Consensus Participation. Nodes contribute to the consensus mechanism, ensuring the integrity and security of the blockchain.

Data Sharing. Nodes communicate using standardized data formats and messaging protocols, enabling seamless collaboration between businesses.

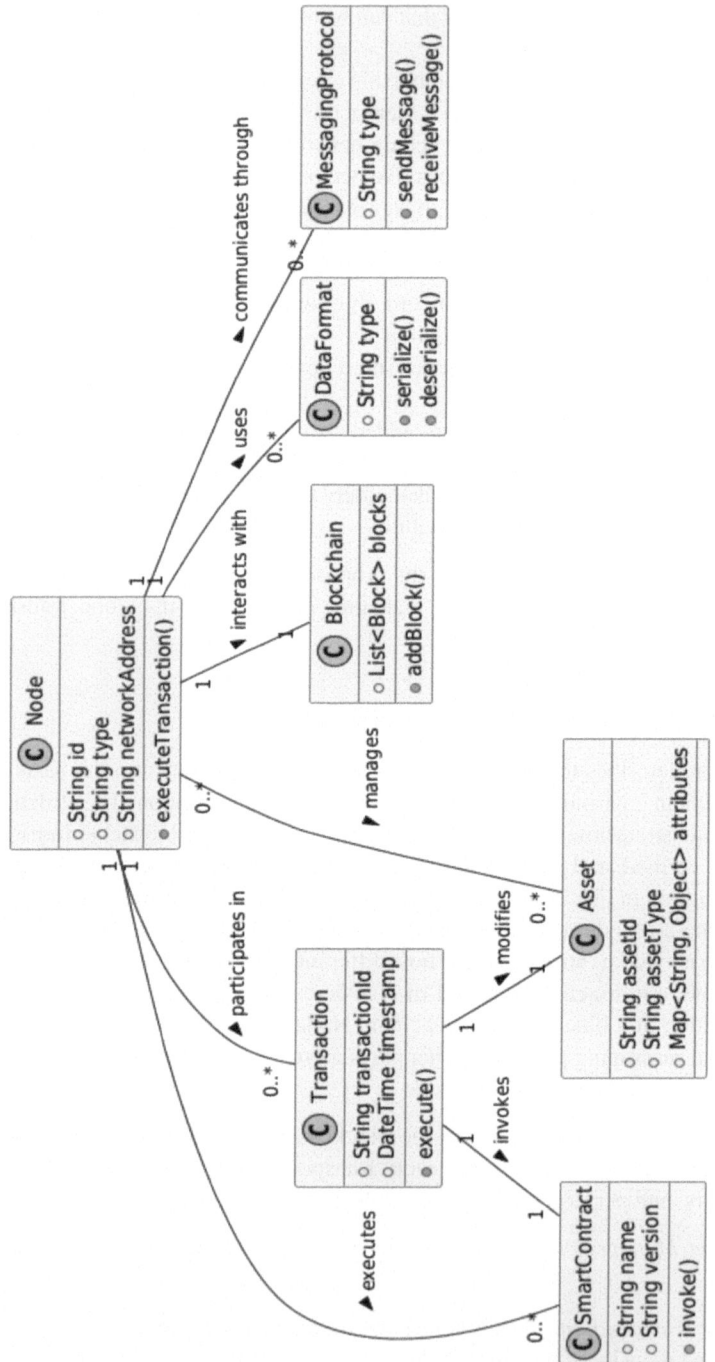

Fig. 3. Interactions between Components of Blockchain-based Transaction Verification System

For instance, a transportation operator (e.g., a bus company) acts as a node, issuing tickets and validating user transactions. When a user purchases a ticket, the node records the transaction, which is verified by other nodes before being added to the blockchain.

Assets. Assets represent physical or digital items such as tickets, memberships, or payment records. For example, a ticket sales transaction creates an asset, while a boarding transaction represents the use of a ticket asset. An asset can be any item defined on the blockchain. Each entity has its own attributes, such as those given in the Table 1 defining the attributes of the Assets model element. Each asset has an Asset ID and Asset Type, along with other predefined or optional attributes. Additional attributes may include time information, journey details, or any definition attributes necessary for verifying operations.

Table 1. Message Structure of Assets Model Element

Attribute Name	Attribute Detail
Asset ID (assetId)	Each asset has a unique identifier
Asset Type (assetType)	The category into which the asset is classified (for example, 'ticket', 'membership')
Other Attributes	Other information that defines the properties of the asset (for example, validity period, price)

Assets are stored on the blockchain in a JSON-like structure, allowing for extensibility. For example, a ticket asset can include details such as route, validity, and pricing, as shown in Listing 1.

Listing 1. Message Structure of Assets Model Element

```
{
  "assetId": "123456",
  "assetType": "ticket",
  "attributes": {
    "issueDate": "2024-11-05 12:00:00",
    "expiryDate": "2024-12-05 12:00:00",
    "passengerId": "21412",
    "journeyDetails": {
      "origin": "Station A",
      "destination": "Station B",
      "departureTime": "2024-11-05 15:00:00"
    }
  }
}
```

Example Scenario. When a user purchases a monthly pass, the system creates an asset with attributes such as the pass ID, validity dates, and user association. This ensures that the pass can be validated without exposing sensitive user data.

Transactions: Transactions are defined as actions that create a change in the state of assets. Transaction types can include creating, updating, and deleting assets. Attributes of the Transactions model element are defined in Table 2.

Transactions record all movements that users and businesses make on the network. Every transaction must be verified by other nodes in the network. Any unique transaction must contain the Transaction ID, which is a unique identifier, the timestamp of the transaction, and the type of transaction.

Table 2. Message Structure of Transactions Model Element

Attribute Name	Attribute Detail
Transaction ID (transactionId)	Each transaction has a unique identifier
Timestamp	Indicates the time when the transaction took place
Operation Type	Indicates what type of action the operation is (for example, 'create', 'update', 'delete')

With the transaction examples given in Listing 2, it can be explained in detail how a transaction is initiated, how it progresses on the network and how it is concluded. For example, scenarios such as purchasing a ticket and boarding can be handled this way.

Listing 2. Message Structure of Transactions Model Element

```
{
  "transactionId": "tx123456789",
  "timestamp": "2024-11-05 12:00:00",
  "operation": "create",
  "transactionDetails": {
      "assetId": "123456",
      "assetType": "ticket",
      "attributes": {
          // Detailed information about the asset
      }
  },
  "signature": "DigitalSignatureOfTheUser"
}
```

Examples of transaction-specific data (payload) to be added to the message for different transactions in the standard message format to be sent over the network are given below. Listing 3 shows the ticket creation process, Listing 4 shows the membership update process, and Listing 5 shows sample "payload" information for fee payment.

These payload samples represent the information required for various public transportation operations and can be customized according to the needs of the transaction. Payload content may vary depending on the transaction type and the characteristics of the asset being processed.

Payload Examples

Listing 3. Payload of Ticket Creation Process

```
"payload": {
  "ticketNumber": "1234567890",
  "issueDate": "2024-11-01 10:00:00",
  "expiryDate": "2024-11-02 10:00:00",
  "passengerName": "Hakan Demir",
  "journeyDetails": {
    "origin": "Station A",
    "destination": "Station B",
    "departureTime": "2024-11-01 11:00:00"
  }
}
```

Listing 4. Payload of Membership Update Process

```
"payload": {
  "membershipId": "MEMB1234567",
  "memberName": "Hakan Demir",
  "validFrom": "2024-11-01",
  "validTo": "2024-11-01",
  "membershipType": "Gold",
  "additionalBenefits": ["Extra Luggage", "Priority Boarding"]
}
```

Listing 5. Payload of Fee Payment

```
"payload": {
  "fareId": "FARE12345",
  "amountPaid": "15.00",
  "currency": "USD",
  "paymentMethod": "Credit Card",
  "transactionDate": "2024-11-01 12:30:00",
  "serviceType": "Tram"
}
```

These payloads define the necessary data for various public transportation operations. The content can be customized based on the type of transaction and the asset being processed.

3.4 Standardized General Message Format

It is necessary to determine a general message format to use all the message contents that we defined specifically for assets and transactions in the previous headings on the network. In this way, messages sent on the network can be standardized by using a common message format to produce transaction-specific data. Sample JSON structure and descriptions for the standard message format that can be used among all models in public transportation is defined as in Listing 6.

This format is designed to encapsulate all necessary details for executing and verifying transactions, such as payments or asset transfers. It standardizes data for all parties involved in the transaction and maintains the system's integrity and reliability. Moreover, it supports various transportation modes and is versatile in different scenarios. The message's key components are detailed below.

Transaction Metadata

- transactionType: Specifies the type of transaction (e.g., Payment, Asset Transfer).
- transactionId: A unique identifier for the transaction, ensuring traceability.
- invokedBy: Identifies the initiator of the transaction, which can be a UserID (for individual transactions) or BusinessID (for operator-initiated actions).

Transportation Details

This section captures all transport-related information:

- modeOfTransport: Specifies the transport type (e.g., bus, tram, metro).
- startLocation and endLocation: Define the journey's starting and ending points.

Membership Details

This section securely encodes membership-specific information for users who are eligible for benefits such as discounts:

- membershipId: A unique identifier for the user's membership (e.g., student, elder, or disabled).
- proofOfDID: An optional field containing the ZKP generated from the user's DID.

Transaction Details

This section details the specific asset being acted upon and the nature of the transaction:

- assetId: The unique identifier of the asset (e.g., a ticket ID, membership ID).
- assetType: The type of asset (e.g., ticket, membership).
- journeyDetails: Includes origin, destination, and departure time.

Listing 6. Standardized General Message Format

```
{
"transactionType": "PaymentorAssetTransfer",
   "transactionId": "UniqueTransactionID",
   "timestamp": "2024-12-01 12:00:00",
   "invokedBy": "UserIDorBusinessID",
   "transportationDetails": {
      "modeOfTransport": "bus/tram/scooter/minibus/metro",
      "routeId": "RouteID",
      "startLocation": "StartingLocation",
      "endLocation": "EndLocation",
      "fare": {
        "amount": "Amount",
        "currency": "Currency"
      },
      "membershipDetails": {
        "membershipId": "MembershipID",
        "validity": "MembershipValidity"
        "proofOfDID": "ZKPProofofUser" (Optional)
        "proofOwnerDID": "DIDofProofOwner" (Optional)
        "verifierDID": "DIDOfVerifier" (Optional)
      }
   },
   "transactionDetails": {
      "assetId": "AssetID",
      "assetType": "AssetType",
      "operation": "create/update/delete",
      "payload": {
        // Customized data fields
        "journeyDetails": {
           "origin": "Station A",
           "destination": "Station B",
           "departureTime": "2024-05-05 15:00:00"
        },
        "fareDetails": {},
        "seatAllocation": {},
      }
   },
   "signature": "DigitalSignatureOfTheUser",
   "consensusDetails": {
      "endorsedBy": ["NodeID1", "NodeID2"],
      "consensusTimestamp": "2024-01-01 12:00:10",
      "consensusAlgorithm": "ConsensusAlgorithmUsed"
   }
}
```

3.5 Practical Implementation

This section outlines the development details of the blockchain-based transaction verification system, including implemented smart contracts and API gateways. It provides process of adding organizations and peers.

Adding New Nodes and Peers. Organization Registration Module (ORM) is responsible for adding new peers and organizations (nodes) to the network. The ORM includes a network manager that processes new requests using dedicated services and scripts. Organization and Peer Controllers validate certificates and execute the necessary code to integrate the new entities into the blockchain channel seamlessly.

Application Gateway (API Gateway). The Application Gateway bridges external client applications and the blockchain network by providing RESTful APIs. The gateway supports operations such as initializing the ledger, submitting transactions, and retrieving data securely. In Listing 7 is an example of how the gateway initializes services and connects to the blockchain. This code snippet is written in JavaScript and runs in a Node.js environment. The gateway uses the fabric-gateway library to interact with the blockchain network securely and efficiently.

Listing 7. API Gateway Services

```
async function startServer() {
  try {
    // Establish connection to the blockchain network
    await blockchainService.connectGateway();

    // Inject the blockchain contract into the ticketService
    ticketService.setContract(blockchainService.contract);

    // Initialize the ledger (e.g., preload data)
    await ticketService.initLedger();

    // Start the Express server
    app.listen(PORT, () => {
      console.log(`Server is running on port ${PORT}`);
    });
  } catch (error) {
    console.error(`Failed to start the application: ${error}`);
    process.exit(1);
  }
}
```

Key functionalities provided with the implementation given in Listing 7 can be summarized as below:

1. Blockchain Connection:
   a. Establishes a secure connection to the Hyperledger Fabric blockchain network using the blockchainService.connectGateway() method.
2. Service Initialization:
   a. Injects the blockchain contract into a ticketService for managing blockchain transactions.
   b. Calls the ticketService.initLedger() method to initialize the blockchain ledger, potentially preloading essential data.
3. Server Setup:
   a. Starts an Express.js server to provide a RESTful API for external applications. The server listens on the specified port (PORT) and serves as the entry point for client requests.

Ticket Creation Using Standard Message Format. This process involves generating a new ticket asset on the blockchain network using a standardized message format. The example provided in Listing 8 highlights the practical use of these standardized methods to generate new ticket and membership assets securely, ensuring the blockchain ledger's integrity and immutability. This code snippet is written in TypeScript and is designed to run on the Hyperledger Fabric blockchain platform. It demonstrates the implementation of ticket creation and membership management using a standardized message format within a smart contract. The standardized format ensures consistent communication and interoperability between blockchain nodes, service providers, and client applications in the public transportation ecosystem.

Key functionalities provided with the implementation given in Listing 8 can be summarized as below:

1. Transaction Creation:
   a. The createTransaction function accepts transaction data, parses it into a TransactionRecord object, and validates its uniqueness by checking the blockchain ledger for existing transaction IDs.
   b. If the transaction ID is unique, it stores the transaction data on the blockchain ledger using ctx.stub.putState.
2. Membership Creation:
   a. The createMembership function allows the creation of a new membership for a user.
   b. It checks if a membership already exists for the provided user ID using the membershipExists method. If it does, an error is thrown to prevent duplication.
   c. The new membership data is saved to the blockchain ledger for future validation and use.

Importance of Standardized Message Format. The use of a standardized message format simplifies communication between various components of the system by:

- Ensuring uniform data structures for transactions and memberships.
- Reducing the complexity of data exchange between operators, service providers, and client applications.
- Supporting seamless integration and scalability across diverse public transportation scenarios.

Listing 8. Example Smart Contract Code for Transaction and Membership Creation

```
@Transaction()public async createTransaction(ctx: Context, transactionData: string): Promise<void> {
    // Parse transaction data from input
    const transaction: TransactionRecord = JSON.parse(transactionData);
    // Ensure transaction ID is unique before storing
    const exists = await ctx.stub.getState(transaction.transactionId);
    if (exists && exists.length > 0) {
        throw new Error(`Transaction with ID ${transaction.transactionId} already exists`);
    }
    // Save transaction data to the ledger
    await ctx.stub.putState(transaction.transactionId, Buffer.from(stringify(transaction)));
}

@Transaction()public async createMembership(ctx: Context, userID: string, membershipStatus: string): Promise<void> {
    // Create a new membership entry for a user
    const membership = new Membership(userID, membershipStatus);
    // Verify membership uniqueness
    const exists = await this.membershipExists(ctx, userID);
    if (exists) {
        throw new Error(`Membership for user ${userID} already exists`);
    }
    // Store membership in the ledger
    await ctx.stub.putState(userID, Buffer.from(JSON.stringify(membership)));
}
```

4 Privacy-Preserving Digital Identities for Public Transportation

This section explains how decentralized technologies can help protect user privacy in public transportation. It also looks at the challenges in digital systems that affect personal data security and how blockchain technology can help protect user privacy. This study provides how these technologies can be used to improve privacy in public transportation.

4.1 Privacy Challenges in the Digital Era

In today's world, it is crucial to securely store and process personal data due to the significant impact of social media and digitalization. Despite existing laws and regulations to protect user data, data breaches still occur, highlighting significant vulnerabilities. Storing personal data on company or institution servers is often the main cause of security breaches [22]. This is because central storage of personal data can be vulnerable to attacks and single point of failure can make it susceptible to cyber-attacks and unauthorized access. Personal data must be stored securely, and access should be restricted to authorized personnel only.

4.2 Emerging Solutions for Data Protection

To tackle the challenges addressed in Sect. 4.1, digital identity solutions have been developed. These include the DID protocol [29], VC [30], and ZKP [31]. These technologies promote secure and digital storage of user data on individuals' devices, departing from traditional centralized systems. The DID protocol enables users to create and manage their digital identities without relying on central authorities. Verifiable Credentials enhance the dependability of digital identities and claims presented by users. They only include necessary data for a transaction. ZKP enables mathematical verification of information while maintaining privacy by not revealing personal details. The system is designed to utilize Polygon public chain nodes for issuing credentials and decentralized verification [32], integrating user wallet applications and verifier nodes to enable seamless, privacy-centric interactions.

4.3 Application in Public Transportation Systems

A unified architecture allows users to securely access various public transportation services. The proposed study is different from conventional systems because users do not have to repeatedly share sensitive personal information with each service provider. Instead, it uses Verifiable Credentials stored in digital wallets, backed by the DID protocol. The claim information is stored in a data structure called the Sparse Merkle Tree [33]. This ensures data integrity by updating the root hash value, which is critical for verifying proofs. The root hash value is stored immutably on the blockchain.

4.4 Implementing a Privacy-Preserving Approach

Users prove their eligibility to service providers by presenting ZKP-generated proofs alongside their credential information. These proofs can demonstrate eligibility as a student, teacher, elderly person, or person with a disability. Personal information is not required to be disclosed. Service providers verify these claims by referencing the proof and the root hash value on the blockchain. This model promotes a secure environment that minimizes personal data exposure and prioritizes privacy. Figure 4 shows how users can manage their digital identities securely and provide verification to service providers without revealing personal information. This is done by using technologies such as DID, VC, ZKP, and blockchain and explained step-by-step below.

Step-by-Step Process

1. DID Creation:
   - Users generate a unique DID through their wallet application.
2. Credential Issuance:
   - The user requests a credential from an issuer (e.g., proof of student status).
   - The issuer validates the claim, generates a VC, and signs it.
3. Membership Creation:
   - A transport network node verifies the user's eligibility (e.g., student or elder discount) during membership registration.
   - The user's digital wallet generates a ZKP for the credential and shares it with the verifier, who is typically a transportation operator.
   - Proof of credential is stored in membership creation transaction in Hyperledger blockchain
4 Proof Verification:
   - The operator (verifier) requests proof of claim, DID and retrieves the current state from the blockchain to validate the transaction.
   - It cross-checks the root hash stored on the blockchain to validate the proof.
   - If valid, the transaction proceeds and is recorded on the blockchain.

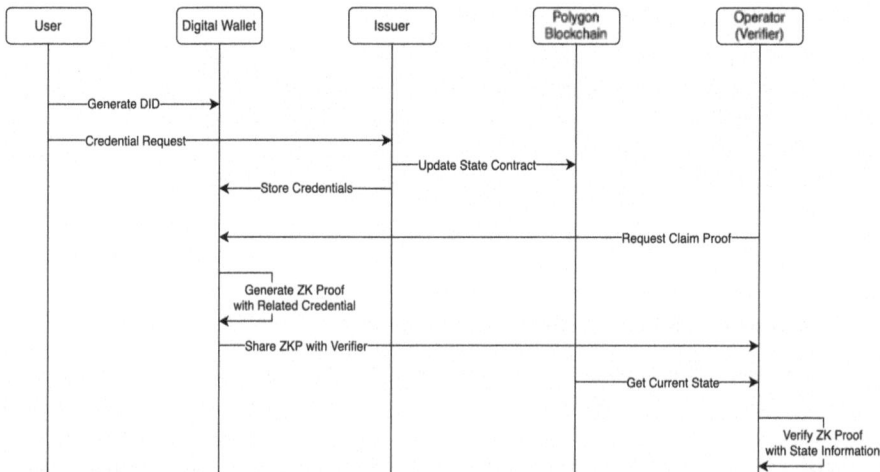

Fig. 4. User Privacy Protection in a Blockchain-Enabled Public Transportation System

4.5 A Sample Implementation: Proof Generation and Membership Creation

This section demonstrates a practical implementation of proof generation and membership creation processes within a blockchain-enabled public transportation network. The examples are implemented using TypeScript and leverage Hyperledger Fabric and Polygon for decentralized identity verification and transaction management.

Proof Generation on Digital Wallet. In the first step, a user's digital wallet generates a ZKP based on their credentials. This proof is used to validate claims (e.g., student or elder status) without exposing sensitive personal information. The implementation of proof generation is shown in Listing 9.

Key Highlights

- The generateProof function:
  - Encodes credential data (cred_data) using Base64 for secure transport.
  - Retrieves the user's stored credentials and parses their DID.
  - Authenticates the user and generates a ZKP.

- The generated proof is returned as a secure object for use in the next steps.

Listing 9. Identity Controller Sample Code for Proof Generation on Digital Wallet

```typescript
import {Base64} from 'js-base64';
import { DID } from '@iden3/js-iden3-core';

export default class IdentityController {
generateProof = async (cred_data) => {
  try {
    const url_param = Base64.encode(JSON.stringify(cred_data))
    const credentials = await this.credentialWallet.list();
    const _did = DID.parse(this.identityDID);
    const msgBytes = base64ToBytes(url_param);
    const authRes = await this.AuthHandler.handleAuthorizationRequest(_did, msgBytes);
    return new ReturnObj(ReturnObj.OK, 'Proof Generated Successfully', authRes);
  } catch (error) {
    return new ReturnObj(ReturnObj.ERR, error, null);
  }
}
}
```

Membership Creation with User Proof

Once the proof is generated, it is used during the membership creation process. The transportation network node verifies the user's eligibility using their ZKP and stores the validated membership details in the blockchain ledger. The membership record is structured using a standardized message format, as shown in Listing 10.

Key Highlights

- The membershipDetails object contains:
  - A unique membershipId.
  - The validity period (validity).
  - Proof of Decentralized Identity (proofOfDID) from the user.
  - The DIDs of both the proof owner and the verifying node.

- The record is securely stored on the Hyperledger Fabric ledger for use in future verifications.

Listing 10. Membership Creation with User Proof

```
"membershipDetails": {
  "membershipId": "MembershipID",
  "validity": "MembershipValidity"
  "proofOfDID": "eyJhbGciOiJncm90aDE2IiwiY2lyY3VpdElkI-
joiYXV0aFYyIiwiY3JpdCI6WyJjaXJjdWl0SWQiXSwidHl-
wIjoiYXBwbGljYXRpb2..."
  "proofOwnerDID": "did:iden3:poly-
gon:amoy:x6x5sor7zpyAJu49Nch4Lixzawxlqd95sjtwnb2Uf"
  "verifierDID": "did:iden3:poly-
gon:amoy:2qa3Ni16rkJ4BSvK4M3u8FMmjcMyKbqn7kNNKSjeMs"
}
```

4.6 Outlook for Privacy Enhancement

The adoption of DIDs, VCs, and ZKPs represents a significant step forward in personal data protection and privacy. Self-Sovereign Identity (SSI) frameworks powered by blockchain have the potential to decentralize control of digital identities, empowering individuals to manage their data securely and privately without reliance on centralized authorities [34].

This study highlights the importance of these technologies within the system's architecture, supported by an infrastructure that ensures secure verification of credentials without exposing sensitive user information. By adopting open standards such as W3C's Verifiable Credentials and Decentralized Identifiers, the system ensures interoperability across networks while maintaining user privacy. The development of SSI systems will require collaboration between technologists, policymakers, and industry stakeholders. This collaboration is essential to address challenges such as governance models, usability, and wider adoption. The integration of privacy-preserving technologies like ZKPs into the public transportation infrastructure lays the groundwork for a user-centric ecosystem.

5 Conclusion

5.1 Summary of Contributions

This paper presents a blockchain-based infrastructure designed to address key challenges in the public transportation sector, including interoperability, privacy, and transactional transparency. By leveraging a private blockchain, the system facilitates seamless integration of diverse transportation providers, ensuring secure and efficient transaction processing through consensus mechanisms. Transportation providers participate as network nodes, enabling decentralized collaboration and trust.

Key aspects of the proposed infrastructure include:

1. Interoperability: A standardized message format ensures that diverse providers can operate on a unified platform, reducing complexity for both users and operators.
2. Privacy Protection: The integration of ZKPs and DIDs protects sensitive user information while enabling secure and verifiable transactions.
3. Smart Contract Automation: APIs and smart contracts enable autonomous agreements, extending functionality to include real-time fare adjustments, ticket management, and membership validations across the network.

Use of Dual-Chain Architecture. The system employs a hybrid dual-chain architecture by integrating a private Hyperledger Fabric blockchain with a public blockchain. The private blockchain enhances transaction processing speed and efficiency, making it suitable for the operational needs of transportation networks. Meanwhile, the public blockchain ensures privacy-preserving functionalities, such as credential verification across multiple issuers, enabling secure and decentralized identity management. This combination leverages the strengths of both blockchain types to create a robust and efficient system.

5.2 Planned Improvements

Future development efforts will focus on real-world testing by utilizing large datasets that simulate various transportation scenarios, such as buses, trams, and scooters, to evaluate system performance under increased transaction volumes and diverse network conditions. A dedicated revenue distribution report tool will be developed to facilitate fair profit-sharing among operators based on blockchain-stored transaction data. Additionally, the user wallet will be enhanced to improve usability and security, integrating DIDs, VCs, and ZKP generation for privacy-preserving transactions. To support broader interoperability, the development of issuer nodes on a public blockchain, such as Polygon, will be prioritized, enabling distributed credential issuance and efficient verification. Furthermore, we aim at benefitting from the results of our previous research (e.g. [35, 36]) on model-driven engineering of public transportation systems to supporting the design and implementation of the public transportation applications considering the digital identity and transaction verification architecture introduced in this paper.

Acknowledgments. Special acknowledgment is due to Kentkart A.Ş. Company for their generous support and guidance during the preparation of this paper.

References

1. Oeschger, G., Carroll, P., Caulfield, B.: Micromobility and public transport integration: the current state of knowledge. Transp. Res. Part D: Transp. Environ. (2020). https://doi.org/10.1016/j.trd.2020.102628
2. Arslan, S., Kardas, G.: Modeling Internet of Things software for public transformation. J. Intell. Transp. Syst. Appl. **6**(2), 425–445 (2023). https://doi.org/10.51513/jitsa.1328020
3. Aydin, M.B., Oz, C., Cetin Tulazoglu, D., Kardas, G.: Development of an ITxPT compliant information system for public transportation vehicles. J. Intell. Transp. Syst. Appl. **2**(2), 1–13 (2019)
4. ABT Kentkart: Automated fare collection system. Kentkart (2022). https://www.kentkart.com/fare-collection-system. Accessed 14 Dec 2024
5. STIB-MIVB: Ticket information. STIB-MIVB Ticket (2022). https://www.stib-mivb.be/article.html?l=en&_guid=80bb5be7-429c-3810-a795-dfe836d62585. Accessed 14 Dec 2024
6. MVV: Online and handy ticket. MVV Ticketing (2022). https://www.mvv-muenchen.de/en/tickets-and-fares/online-und-handyticket/index.html. Accessed 14 Dec 2024
7. Whim: MaaS Global, Whim (2019). https://maasification.com/applications/by-application/whim-maas-global/. Accessed 14 Dec 2024
8. Kazi, S., Bagasrawala, M., Shaikh, F., Sayyed, A.: Smart e-ticketing system for public transport bus. In: Proceedings of the 2018 International Conference on Smart City and Emerging Technology (ICSCET), pp. 1–7 (2018). https://doi.org/10.1109/ICSCET.2018.8537302
9. Khedekar, T., Jamdar, V., Waghmare, S., Dhore, M.L.: FID automatic bus ticketing system. In: Proceedings of the 2021 International Conference on Artificial Intelligence and Machine Vision (AIMV), pp. 1–6 (2021). https://doi.org/10.1109/AIMV53313.2021.9670957
10. Pasquale, G.D., Bie, J.D., Singh, J.: Ticketing in mobility as a service. In: International Association of Public Transport (UITP) (2022). https://cms.uitp.org/wp/wp-content/uploads/2022/07/Report-Ticketing-MaaS-JULY2022-web.pdf. Accessed 14 Dec 2024
11. Arslan, S., Kardas, G., Alfraihi, H.: On the usability of a modeling language for IoT-based public transportation systems. Appl. Sci. **14**(13), 5619, 1–30 (2024). https://doi.org/10.3390/app14135619
12. Nakamoto, S.: Bitcoin: a peer-to-peer electronic cash system. Technical report (2008). https://bitcoin.org/bitcoin.pdf. Accessed 14 Dec 2024
13. Kakavand, H., Kost De Sevres, N., Chilton, B.: The blockchain revolution: an analysis of regulation and technology related to distributed ledger technologies. SSRN Electron. J. (2016). https://doi.org/10.2139/ssrn.2849251
14. Nath, I.: Data exchange platform to fight insurance fraud on blockchain. In: Proceedings of the 2016 IEEE 16th International Conference on Data Mining Workshops (ICDMW), pp. 821–825 (2016)
15. Gupta, S., Sinha, S., Bhushan, B.: Emergence of blockchain technology: fundamentals, working and its various implementations. In: Proceedings of the International Conference on Innovative Computing & Communications (ICICC) (2020). https://doi.org/10.2139/ssrn.3569577

16. Saritas, H.B., Kardas, G.: A blockchain-based transaction verification infrastructure in public transportation. In: 2024 19th Conference on Computer Science and Intelligence Systems (FedCSIS), Belgrade, Serbia, pp. 169–176 (2024). https://doi.org/10.15439/2024F5274
17. Jayalath, S.A., Rajapakse, C., Senanayake, J.M.D.: A micro-transaction model based on blockchain technology to improve service levels in the public transport sector in Sri Lanka. In: Proceedings of the 2020 International Research Conference on Smart Computing and Systems Engineering (SCSE), pp. 82–89 (2020). https://doi.org/10.1109/SCSE49731.2020.9313037
18. Wang, G., Nixon, M.: InterTrust: towards an efficient blockchain interoperability architecture with trusted services. In: Proceedings of the 2021 IEEE International Conference on Blockchain, Melbourne, Australia, pp. 150–159 (2021). https://doi.org/10.1109/Blockchain53845.2021.00029
19. Yang, T., Cui, Z., Alshehri, A.H., Wang, M., Gao, K., Yu, K.: Distributed maritime transport communication system with reliability and safety based on blockchain and edge computing. IEEE Trans. Intell. Transp. Syst. (2022). https://doi.org/10.1109/TITS.2022.3157858
20. Enescu, F.M., Bizon, N., Serban, G., Hoarcă, I.C.: Environmental protection - blockchain solutions for intelligent passenger transportation of persons. In: Proceedings of the 2021 13th International Conference on Electronics, Computers and Artificial Intelligence (ECAI), pp. 1–6 (2021). https://doi.org/10.1109/ECAI52376.2021.9515026
21. Jabbar, Y., et al.: Blockchain technology for intelligent transportation systems: a systematic literature review. IEEE Access **10**, 20995–21031 (2022). https://doi.org/10.1109/ACCESS.2022.3149958
22. Ganzha, M., Maciaszek, L., Paprzycki, M., Ślęzak, D. (eds.): Proceedings of the 17th Conference on Computer Science and Intelligence Systems, ACSIS, vol. 30, pp. 685–694 (2022)
23. Karatas, R., Sertkaya, I.: Self sovereign identity based E-petition scheme. Int. J. Inf. Secur. Sci. **9** (2020)
24. Chen, Y., Gu, J., Chen, S., Huang, S., Wang, X.S.: A full-spectrum blockchain-as-a-service for business collaboration. In: Proceedings of the 2019 IEEE International Conference on Web Services (ICWS), pp. 219–223 (2019). https://doi.org/10.1109/ICWS.2019.00045
25. Hyperledger Foundation: Hyperledger Fabric Documentation. Hyperledger Wiki (2023). https://hyperledger-fabric.readthedocs.io/. Accessed 14 Dec 2024
26. Reddy, B., Aithal, P.S.: Blockchain based service: a case study on IBM blockchain services & hyperledger fabric. Int. J. Case Stud. Bus. IT Educ. (IJCSBE) **4**(1), 94–102 (2020). https://doi.org/10.2139/ssrn.3611876
27. Ongaro, D.: In search of an understandable consensus algorithm (extended version). Stanford University (2014). https://raft.github.io/raft.pdf. Accessed 14 Dec 2024
28. Awati, R.: Consensus algorithm. TechTarget. https://www.techtarget.com/whatis/definition/consensus-algorithm. Accessed 14 Dec 2024
29. W3C: Decentralized Identifiers (DIDs) v1.0. W3C Recommendation (2022). https://www.w3.org/TR/did-core/. Accessed 14 Dec 2024
30. W3C: Verifiable Credentials Data Model v2.0. World Wide Web Consortium. https://www.w3.org/TR/vc-data-model/. Accessed 14 Dec 2024
31. Hyperledger Foundation: Hyperledger AnonCreds: Anonymous Credentials with Zero-Knowledge Proofs. Hyperledger Wiki. https://wiki.hyperledger.org/display/anoncreds. Accessed 14 Dec 2024
32. Polygon ID: Zero Knowledge Identity for Web3: Polygon (2022). https://polygon.technology/blog/introducing-polygon-id-zero-knowledge-own-your-identity-for-web3. Accessed 14 Dec 2024
33. Haider, F.: Compact sparse merkle trees (2018). https://doi.org/10.31219/osf.io/8mcnh

34. Sherriff, A., Young, K., Shea, M.: Editorial: establishing self sovereign identity with blockchain. Front. Blockchain **5**, 955868 (2022). https://doi.org/10.3389/fbloc.2022.955868
35. Saritas, H.B., Kardas, G.: A model driven architecture for the development of smart card software. Comput. Lang. Syst. Struct. **40**(2), 53–72 (2014). https://doi.org/10.1016/j.cl.2014.02.001
36. Arslan, S., Kardas, G.: DSML4DT: a domain-specific modeling language for device tree software. Comput. Ind. **115**(103179), 1–13 (2020). https://doi.org/10.1016/j.compind.2019.103179

Enhancing User Experience in Artificial Intelligence Systems: A Practical Approach

Alexander Zender(✉)[ID], Bernhard G. Humm[ID], and Anna Holzheuser[ID]

Darmstadt University of Applied Sciences, Schöfferstr. 3, 64295 Darmstadt, Germany
{alexander.zender,bernhard.humm}@h-da.de, anna.holzheuser@gmail.com

Abstract. An important aspect of Artificial Intelligence (AI) systems is their User Experience (UX), which can impact the user's trust in the AI system. However, UX has not yet been in the focus of AI research. In previous research, we have evaluated the UX of the AI system OMA-ML, uncovering weak points and proposing several recommendations for ensuring a positive UX in AI systems in general. In this paper we show that implementing those recommendations leads to measurable UX improvements. We present the interaction workflow of OMA-ML, based on CRISP-DM. Based on this, we present UX-improving features implemented in a new version of OMA-ML and the results from a second UX evaluation. The UX of OMA-ML could successfully be improved in four interactive principles (suitability for the user's tasks, self-descriptiveness, user engagement and learnability). We argue that an iterative approach to UX potentially leads to more human-centered AI.

Keywords: AI systems · User Experience

1 Introduction

Artificial Intelligence (AI) systems, in particular ones using Machine Learning (ML), are present in our everyday use, e.g. facial recognition in smartphones [31] or translation tools using natural language processing (NLP) [29]. An important aspect of AI systems is their User Experience (UX). UX in the context of AI systems assesses a user's overall experience with the AI system [27]. Understanding the user's needs and behaviors is necessary, as a bad UX may contribute to an AI system's failure [21]. While the UX is an important aspect of an AI system, there is limited discussion about it in the AI community.

We discussed this in previous research [6] and aimed to raise awareness by using the case study for the AI system OMA-ML[1] (Ontology-based Meta AutoML) [13,39]. Based on the case study, 104 UX issues were found, categorized, and resolved. Additionally, we proposed 12 measures and 4 recommendations to ensure a positive UX for AI systems. Based on the same methodology

---
[1] https://github.com/hochschule-darmstadt/MetaAutoML

[6], the interaction of 29 participants using the enhanced version of OMA-ML was evaluated.

In this paper, we show that implementing such recommendations leads to measurable UX improvements. We present the results from the new case study and the UX improvements implemented in a new version of OMA-ML. Based on the ISO 9241-110[2] interaction principles, OMA-ML was improved in the following interaction principles: suitability for the user's tasks, self-descriptiveness and user engagement compared to the previous evaluations weak points and even exceed in the learnability interaction principle beyond the target state, defined by a UX expert in previous research [6].

This article is an extended version of our previous publication at FEDCIS 2024 [38]. It includes a previously unpublished interaction workflow of OMA-ML.

The remainder of this paper is structured as follows: Sect. 2 outlines related work. Section 3 presents the OMA-ML interaction workflow. In Sect. 4, the UX evaluation methodology is discussed. Section 5 lists the UX improvements made to OMA-ML. The results from the second UX evaluation are presented in Sect. 6. Finally, Sect. 7 concludes the paper and discusses future work.

2 Related Work

AI systems are gaining increasing importance, with new powerful AI applications being released regularly. Most recently, AI systems using generative AI have gained prominence with applications such as ChatGPT [30], offering *human-like interactions* but also enabling new ways of powering AI systems such as code completion tools [32]. While the underlying AI algorithm is an important aspect of an AI system's success, it also depends on how it interacts with the user [24]. This is why UX is important, as it represents a collection of strategies for understanding a user's needs and behaviours with the system to create useful, stable systems and services [28].

However, in the past, the AI, UX and Human Computer Interaction (HCI) communities applied AI and specifically ML on a more technical approach for the creation of new methods to support the UX process itself [35] or the creation of new interfaces to interact with systems (e.g. voice interfaces) [3,7]. The HCI research community also proposes guidelines for human-AI interactions [4]. In the AI community, a focus is emerging for a user-centered approach for AI systems. One prominent research area in AI that applies this is Explainable AI (XAI) [36]. XAI is a research field that emerged to focus on explaining the decision-making of AI models to the user [8] and providing insight into the data [9]. Understanding how a model came about a decision can increase usability and give the user confidence in the system, and usability is a critical part of the UX. Usability accesses how easy a user interface is to use and refers to methods for improving the ease of use during the system's design process [26]. Our

---

[2] https://www.iso.org/obp/ui/#iso:std:iso:9241:-110:ed-2:v1:en.

previous work proposed a list of recommended measures to ensure a good UX for AI systems [6]. These recommendations are based on the interaction principles formulated in ISO 9241-110:2020[3] and the results from the usability study of OMA-ML. The OMA-ML interaction workflow is introduced in the next section.

3 OMA-ML Interaction Workflow

OMA-ML is an AI system that automatically generates ML pipelines without requiring programming or AI expertise. OMA-ML aims to target business domain experts (experts in an application domain such as medicine) and AI experts. Both user groups have different backgrounds and requirements that an AI system such as OMA-ML must reflect in order to be adopted. Business domain experts have profound knowledge and insight into their domain data but potentially lack the necessary programming or AI expertise to access ML models. AI experts can program and have the AI expertise to analyze the domain data. Still, they must apply the sometimes repetitive and laborious data science workflow (e.g., CRISP-DM [19]) to create ML models.

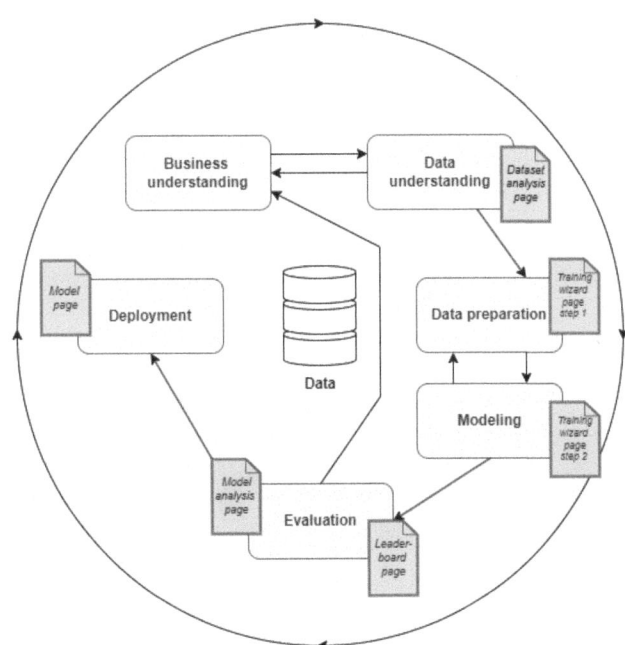

Fig. 1. OMA-ML interaction workflow based on CRISP-DM, adapted from [34]

---

[3] https://www.iso.org/obp/ui/#iso:std:iso:9241:-110:ed-2:v1:en.

Allowing the best usability for both user groups is not trivial. OMA-ML accomplishes this with a Graphical User Interface (GUI) based interaction workflow to reduce the required entry knowledge for its users. OMA-ML uses the CRISP-DM data science workflow as the schema for its interaction workflow. Figure 1 shows the CRISP-DM workflow [34] extended by the OMA-ML pages responsible for the respective workflow stages.

During the **business understanding** phase, users familiarize themselves with the business domain and understand its requirements. The goal is to gain insight and knowledge of the project objectives from a business perspective. The user must perform this step independently; OMA-ML does not provide any automation or support for this step.

In the next step, **data understanding**, the expert gathers, describes, explores, and accesses the quality of the domain data. At this step in the workflow, the OMA-ML interaction workflow begins. Users upload their domain data into the AI system, which then automatically analyzes the data and generates a data insight report. The report consists of visualizations to give insight into the data. The visualizations display the individual variable distributions, interactions, correlations, and missing values. In Fig. 2, a screenshot from the OMA-ML *dataset analysis* page is shown. It shows the dataset correlation matrix of the diabetes dataset[4].

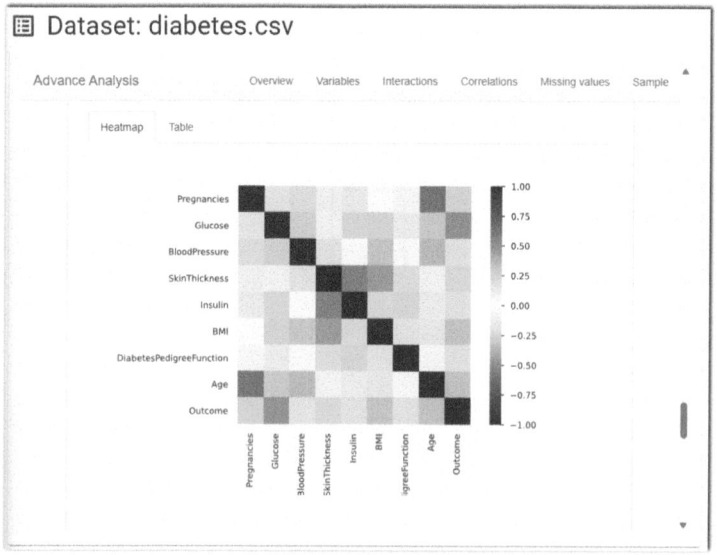

Fig. 2. OMA-ML Dataset analysis page

---

[4] https://www.kaggle.com/datasets/akshaydattatraykhare/diabetes\discretionary-dataset.

Both user groups benefit from the GUI-based report. AI experts improve their efficiency by focusing on understanding the data instead of manually analyzing it. Business domain experts gain access to insights into their data, which they were potentially unaware of.

Next, in the **data preparation** step, the data is augmented, aiming to transform the data into a format compatible with ML models; this process can include data cleaning, selection, modification, or generation. This is a laborious process, requiring significant data science expertise and insight into the data. OMA-ML automates this by using the dataset analysis results, automatically determining the best-matching and convertible data types. During the first training configuration step on the *training wizard* page, the user is presented with a dataset preview displaying the results from this analysis. The user can adjust each column's data types and ML roles individually, as seen in Fig. 3.

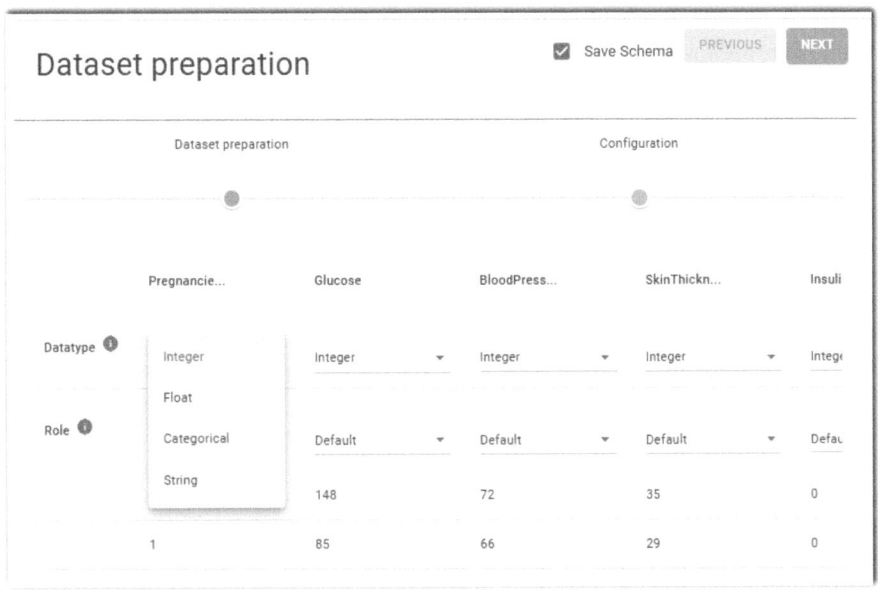

Fig. 3. OMA-ML Training configuration wizard page - step 1

OMA-ML also identifies compatible ML roles for each column during the dataset analysis; an ML role indicates ML-specific preprocessing that will be applied to this column. OMA-ML supports four ML roles: 1) Target: the column will be used as the prediction target for supervised learning ML tasks; 2) Index: columns which contain unique values for each row; 3) Ignore: the column will be dropped from the training process; 4) Default: no specific preprocessing is applied. OMA-ML automatically applies the user-defined data configuration before starting the training process.

Both user groups can adjust configuration options for a column, and OMA-ML performs the processing. OMA-ML also offers the option of applying *training strategies* [39], which can perform preemptive data preprocessing before the training begins during the next wizard step, e.g., Principle Component Analysis (PCA) [2]. OMA-ML employs Automated Machine Learning (AutoML) [11], an approach that automates the data preparation and modeling steps of the data science workflow. This is done by implementing several AutoML solutions and executing them in parallel (Meta AutoML, [14]) The underlying AutoML solutions may configure their unique data preprocessing for the data, making manual preprocessing redundant.

The next step is **modeling**, during which the ML approach (e.g., Random Forest) is selected, its hyperparameter adjusted, and the test framework defined. The test framework engulfs the division of data into training and test datasets. The configuration of the ML approach and its hyperparameters is only possible in a limited scope. OMA-ML focuses on the meta configuration of the process and hyperparameters made available by the AutoML solutions as shown in Fig. 4.

The figure shows the second step of the training configuration wizard. The UX design of this wizard is targeted at the different user groups of OMA-ML. Business domain experts only have to provide three required configuration parameters (Fig. 4a): a) the ML task, e.g., classification; b) the target for supervised ML tasks; c) the maximum training runtime. AI experts may configure numerous in-depth configuration parameters by opening the detail view (Fig. 4b), e.g., to change the active AutoML solutions, enable training strategies, and allow the configuration of individual AutoML hyperparameters.

After invoking the training process, OMA-ML automatically creates its test framework by dividing the data into 80% training dataset and 20% test dataset. The training dataset is passed to the AutoML solutions.

After the AutoML solutions have completed their trainings, OMA-ML performs the **evaluation** using various ML metrics computed with the test set. Figure 5 shows the leaderboard page, which allows users to compare the resulting ML models generated by the AutoML solutions according to various prediction performance metrics (e.g., accuracy for classification tasks), as well as other criteria like training runtime, prediction runtime, and environmental measures (CO_2-eq).

In addition, users may inspect ML models using the model analysis page, an *explainable AI (XAI)* module. This will be discussed in detail in Sect. 5.

In the final step, **deployment**, the AI application's installation, maintenance, and monitoring are planned. OMA-ML provides two different deployment options for its users accessible from the *model page* shown in Fig. 6. The first option is the *online prediction* functionality (Fig. 6a). Business domain experts may upload a new unlabeled sample set, and OMA-ML will automatically invoke the ML model and make new predictions using the new sample set. The resulting predictions are accessible using the GUI and downloadable as a CSV file.

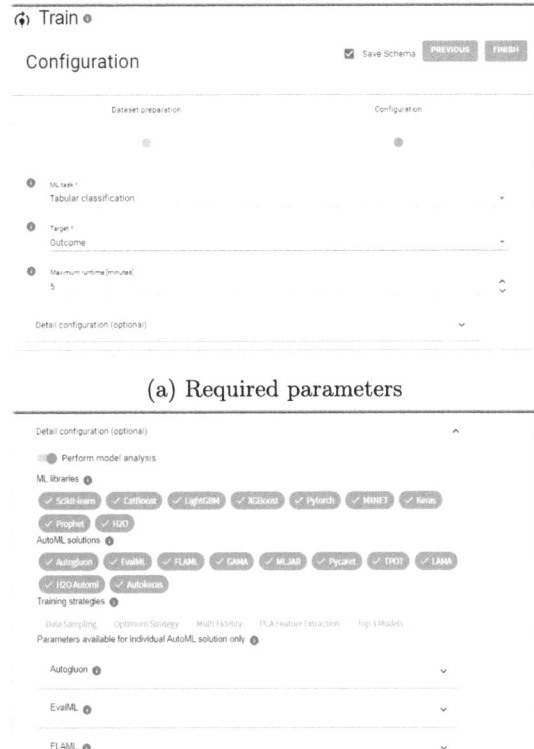

(a) Required parameters

(b) Optional parameters

Fig. 4. OMA-ML training configuration wizard page - step 2

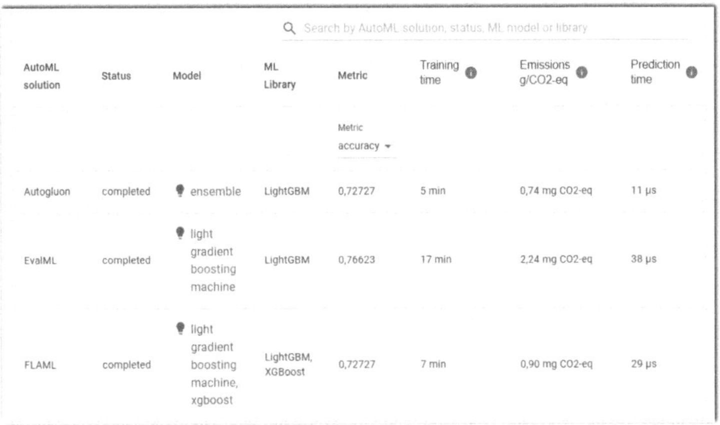

Fig. 5. OMA-ML leaderboard page

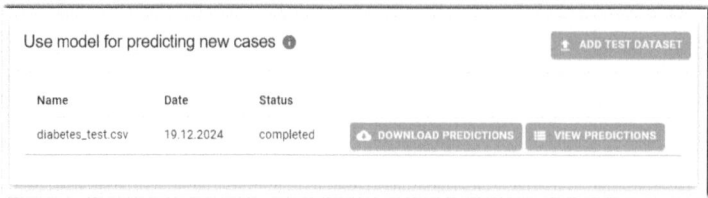

(a) Perform online prediction

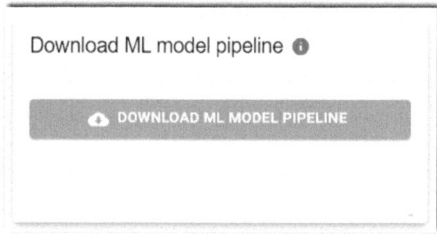

(b) Download ML model

Fig. 6. OMA-ML deployment options

The second option is the *Download* functionality (Fig. 6b). A ZIP file containing the generated ML model and executable Python code is downloadable. AI experts can use the Python code to perform local predictions using the ML model or integrate it into their AI application.

This concludes the OMA-ML interaction workflow. The following section introduces the UX evaluation methodology.

4 Methodology

Evaluating the usability of an AI system can be a three-stage process, see Fig. 7. First, a *use case model* [5] is developed to set the scope of the UX research. The use cases are defined following the interaction workflow.

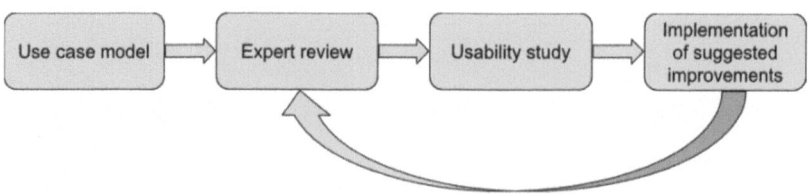

Fig. 7. UX evaluation methodology

Next, an *expert review* is conducted. During the expert review, a UX expert inspects the AI system, uncovering potential usability issues. Expert reviews assess the design by heuristics and guidelines or principles [12]. An important set of guidelines to evaluate usability is the ISO Standard 9241-110:2020[5], specifically the 7 outlined interaction principles: suitability for the user's tasks, self-descriptiveness, conformity with user expectations, learnability, controllability, use error robustness, and user engagement. These interaction principles are used to measure the AI system's usability. Based on the use case model, the UX expert determines the target state for each interaction principle. The interaction principles are measured on a scale of 1 to 5 [6]. The UX expert then evaluates the AI system to uncover usability issues and rate the AI system's actual state for each interaction principle. To rate the actual state, the German ISO 9241-110 [1] provides a checklist to determine whether the interaction principle requirements are met. Expert review is an effective method for catching issues. However, it may miss domain-specific issues or needs that would otherwise be found by the target audience [12].

This is revolved by performing a *usability study*. For this study, qualitative research techniques are chosen to comprehend what users value the most in their experiences [23]. One result of the usability study is a collection of UX issues together with suggested UX improvements. The suggested UX improvements can then be *implemented* in the AI system.

We have established a use case model for OMA-ML, conducted an expert interview, and performed a usability study. We published our results in [6]. Based on 104 UX issues detected, we then implemented the suggested UX improvements in OMA-ML (see following Sect. 5). We have then conducted a second expert interview and usability study with the improved version of OMA-ML in order to validate whether the implemented improvements, indeed, have a positive effect on the UX of OMA-ML. We provide details of the second expert interview and usability study in Sect. 6.

5 UX Improvements

In the first usability study of OMA-ML, a total of 104 UX issues were recorded. Some of the UX issues were minor, such as misunderstandings of button functionalities due to ambiguous icons or labels. For example, the dataset upload button depicted a cloud icon. This led to confusion with some participants, as they believed the dataset would be uploaded into a cloud service. In fact, most issues were major usability problems related to the participants having issues understanding what to do on a page or with elements on a page.

We identified three problem areas within OMA-ML which required a rework for better usability: (A) First-time user onboarding: when participants used the system for the first time, they were unsure how to proceed or what to do; (B) Self-descriptiveness: Participants from both user groups had difficulties understanding what some of the displayed information meant or what they were supposed to do; (C) Explainable AI: The information provided by the XAI modules

---

[5] https://www.iso.org/obp/ui/#iso:std:iso:9241:-110:ed-2:v1:en.

were too convoluted that even AI experts did not understand what they were looking at and quickly lost interest.

To address the first two problems, we followed the 10 usability heuristics by Nielsen [25], most importantly, heuristic number 10: *Help and Documentation* by implementing different types of help systems. Users can be supported by using two types of help systems: *Proactive Help*, and *Reactive Help* [15]. The goal of proactive help is to help the user familiarize with a user interface. This can be achieved by one of two revelations: (1) *Push Revelations*: The application provides help context without regard to the user's task, (2) *Pull Revelations*: the applications provide contextual information to the user's task. The second help system type is reactive help, which aims to answer questions and troubleshoot problems [15].

An AI system may provide a better UX if both help system types are present. Within OMA-ML, this is accomplished by providing an *interactive walkthrough* and contextual help using *tooltips* for proactive help, as well as a *documentation and search* pages for reactive help.

The XAI problem was addressed by reworking the modules. The existing modules were replaced by packages developed by the data science community. While these packages do not advertise with a focus on usability, they are popular based on their GitHub stars rating. Having an understandable XAI module is imperative for any AI system. It helps the user understand their data and ML models. Moreover, it may increase the trust in the AI system [10]. Making the AI system more transparent and providing an understandable explanation is important for adopting the AI system [22].

Next, the individual components used to improve the UX of OMA-ML are presented.

Interactive Walkthrough

An interactive walkthrough is a technique used for more complex applications to facilitate onboarding for new users. Onboarding is the process during which users get familiar with a new interface [16]. While it is recommended to let users experience the application independently and that tutorials such as a walkthrough may have no positive impact [17,20], they could be helpful in the context of complex AI systems. An interactive walkthrough may ease the onboarding, enabling them to learn by doing [16]. In Fig. 8, a screenshot from the OMA-ML home dashboard page with the enabled interactive walkthrough can be seen. The current walkthrough step explains the card *Recent datasets* and instructs the user to select a dataset to proceed.

The interactive walkthrough greets first-time users upon their first login and should be like a practice run of the AI system. At any point during the walkthrough, the user can prematurely exit and explore the system independently. However, the system offers the option on the documentation page to restart the walkthrough whenever the user wishes.

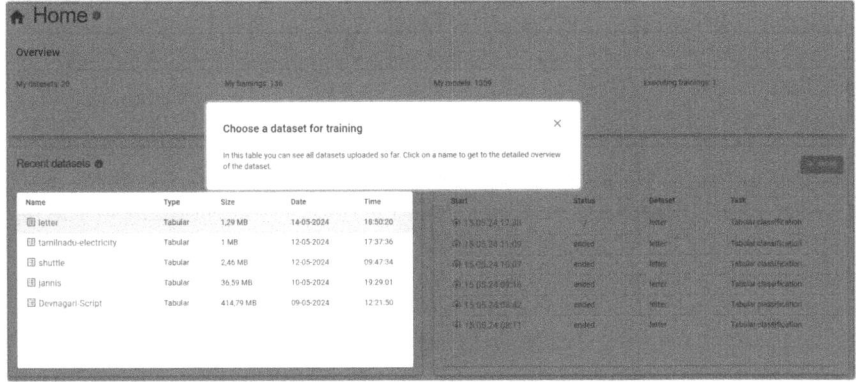

Fig. 8. OMA-ML home dashboard page with enabled interactive walkthrough

Documentation and Search

Documentation is an important part of UX. The main goal of documentation for reactive help is to help with user questions, troubleshoot their problems, and provide further detailed documentation for users aspiring to become expert users [15]. To achieve this, the documentation should follow some guidelines [15]: (A) It must be comprehensive and detailed; (B) it should be written following the rules of the web [33]; (C) it should make use of graphics and videos as secondary information source; (D) optimize for search; (E) group help topics into relevant categories; (F) highlight top content that is frequently viewed.

In Fig. 9, a screenshot of the OMA-ML documentation page can be seen.

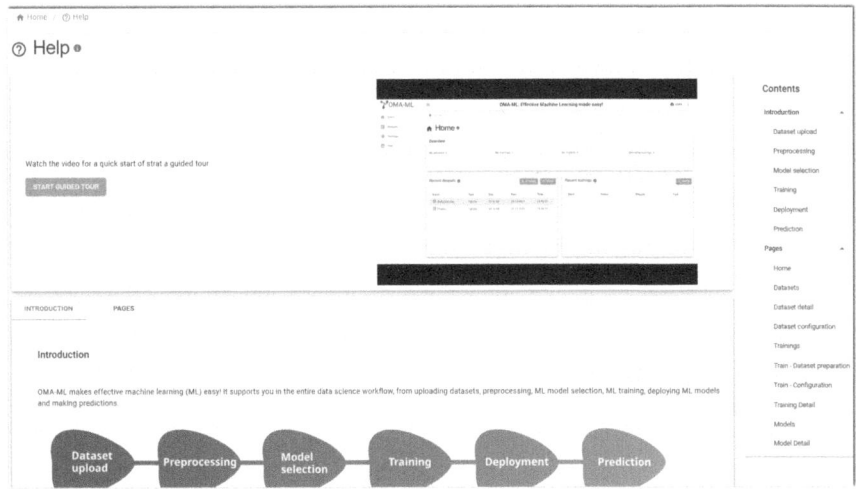

Fig. 9. OMA-ML documentation page

The documentation page consists of two sections. In the upper section, the user has a button to restart the interactive walkthrough and can view an explanatory video that follows the user interaction concept [6] and explains the process and individual pages.

The lower section provides graphical and brief written documentation for the individual steps of the user interaction concept [6] and each page within OMA-ML. Quick access links are available for the user on the right of the documentation page, listing the process steps and individual pages.

Furthermore, search functionality is available, as shown in Fig. 10. The search function aggregates all the knowledge from the underlying ontology (See [37] for more information) and the documentation page.

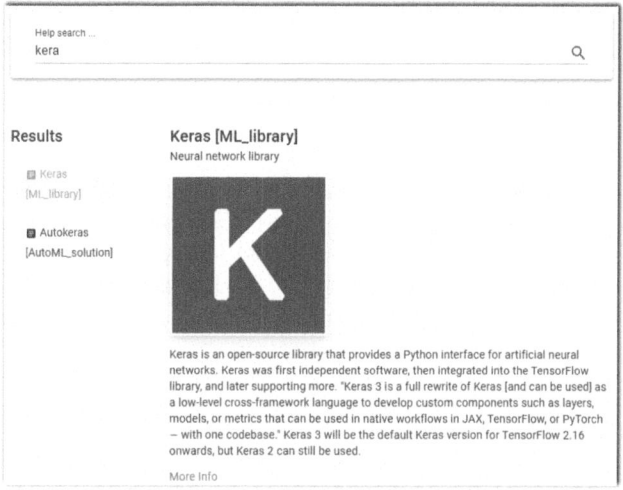

Fig. 10. OMA-ML search page

A user can search any keyword used within the system and is then presented with a search result page. Depending on the search result, a written explanation with a graphic is shown, or the corresponding help page section is displayed. In this example, the search term is *"Keras"* and the result are the ML library[6] Keras and the AutoML solution AutoKeras[7].

Tooltips

A tooltip is a brief, informative message that appears when a user interacts with an element in a GUI [18]. Tooltips are one method that can be used as a pull revelation for the user, providing information at the moment it is needed [20].

---

[6] https://keras.io/.
[7] https://autokeras.com/.

However, it is important to respect guidelines when incorporating them into an AI system [18,20]. Most importantly, they shall not be used to provide vital information for the user to complete their task and be used consistently. This was one of the major UX issues in the first OMA-ML study. Business domain experts and AI experts had difficulties understanding the meaning of the AI terminology in the context of the AI system because there was no explanation. While business domain experts would not have the general background expertise to understand the meanings, AI experts would also question their expectations. This was addressed by including tooltips for any AI-specific term displayed in the system. Depending on the nature of the element, one of two different approaches was used. First, buttons and selection options display a tooltip by hovering over them. For example, in Fig. 11, the tooltip briefly describes the selectable option of tabular classification.

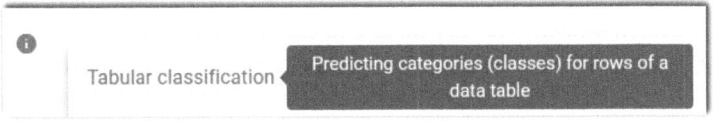

Fig. 11. OMA-ML tooltip help for tabular classification

Secondly, a popup tips element was used for any element displaying information or requesting input. A popup tip is the sister element of the tooltip normally used for touchscreen devices [18]. It is paired with an "i" icon instead of being paired with an element. The OMA-ML example can be seen in Fig. 12. In this screenshot, the mouse hovers over the information icon next to a domain-specific term within the system.

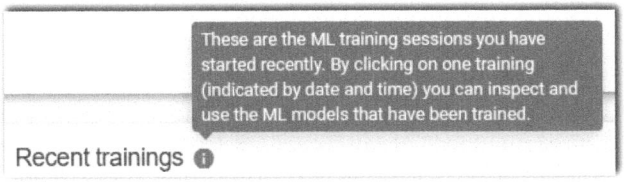

Fig. 12. OMA-ML tooltip help for recent trainings

In this example, the tooltip briefly explains what the card *recent training* displays and what happens when clicking on one element within that card. This is a *progressive disclosure* approach [20], as it makes the existence of the tooltip visible to the user. Teaching the user information is not only available with interaction elements but also labels or elements to provide AI knowledge as well as task explanations.

Explainable AI

XAI provides a suite of techniques that enable human users to understand, trust, and produce more explainable models [9]. It is an important aspect of an AI system, almost as important as the main AI functionality, as the trust a user has towards an AI system influences the adoption decision of the AI system [22]. AI explainability can be accomplished by incorporating techniques from the four XAI categories [9]. (A) *Data Explainability*: provides visualisation of the data giving insight into the dataset; (B) *Model Explanation*: provides techniques to understand the decision-making within black and white box models; (C) *Feature-Based Techniques*: methods to describe how input features contribute to the model output; (D) *Example-Based Techniques*: Techniques to provide explainability using dataset specific examples.

XAI research provides a toolkit of techniques to make the data and models explainable [9]. However, there are also ready-to-use modules available covering one or multiple XAI categories.

Two third-party XAI ready-to-use modules were incorporated in the XAI module of OMA-ML. The first is *ydata-profiling*[8] for data explainability. Ydata-profiling provides an Exploratory Data Analysis (EDA) by automatically performing univariate, multivariate, text, file analysis and discovering dataset challenges. In Fig. 2, a screenshot of the EDA dashboard generated by data-profiling within OMA-ML can be seen. In the screenshot, only a section of the dashboard can be seen; this section displays the correlation matrix between dataset features.

The second XAI module is *explainer dashboard*[9]. This XAI module generates an interactive dashboard by analyzing an ML model with a corresponding dataset. It supports techniques from the remaining XAI categories (model explanations, feature-based techniques, and example-based techniques). In Fig. 13, a screenshot of the explainer dashboard can be seen within OMA-ML.

Depending on the ML model, different information is displayed. In this case, the dashboard contains information about the importance of features, classification statistics, individual predictions, what-if analyses, and feature dependence. In the screenshot, the what-if tab is displayed. This tab provides functionality to experiment with the feature values and live evaluate how the model adjusts its prediction probability.

While neither module lists UX as a focus of their work, their popularity can be deducted from the number of GitHub stars they received (12.1k for ydata-profiling and 2.2k for explainer dashboard as of May 2024). The data science community is actively using and continuously improving these tools.

6   UX Evaluation of OMA-ML

The improved version of OMA-ML has undergone a second UX evaluation, consisting of an expert interview and a usability study following the same methodology as the first UX evaluation (see Sect. 4). Figure 14 shows the results of the

---
[8] https://github.com/ydataai/ydata-profiling.
[9] https://github.com/oegedijk/explainerdashboard.

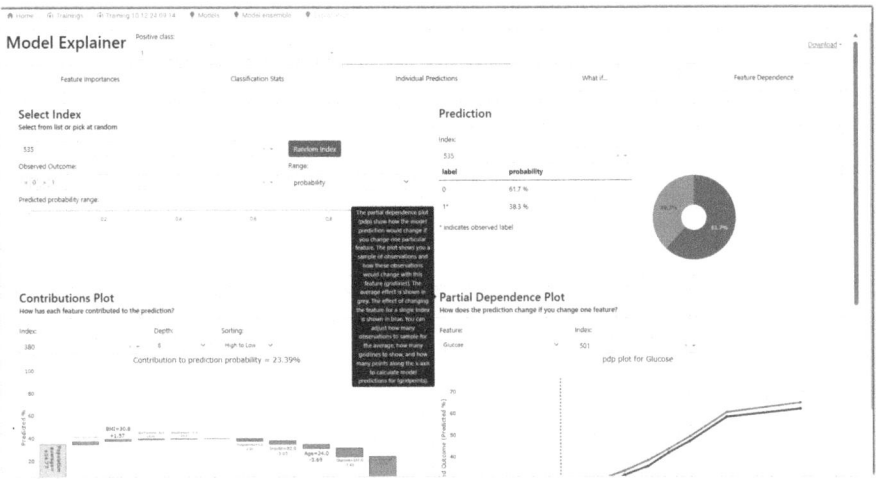

Fig. 13. OMA-ML ML Model analysis page

Fig. 14. Spider chart comparing the target state vs the results from the first and second usability study

first UX evaluation as published in [6]. The chart presents, for each of the 7 interaction principles, the states on a scale of 1 to 5. The blue data points represent the target state, defined by UX experts based on the use case model. The orange data points represent the state of OMA-ML after the first expert review. A total of four interaction principles with weak points were identified: suitability for the user's tasks, self-descriptiveness, conformity with user expectations and user engagement.

Results From the Second Expert Review. Figure 14 also shows the results of the second expert interview (green data points). Considerable improvements can be seen for the interaction principles suitability for the user's task and learnability. Learnability even outperforms the target state. Further improvement is in the interaction principles user engagement and self-descriptiveness. No considerable improvement could be noted for controllability (which already outperformed the target state in the first UX evaluation), use error robustness, and conformity with user expectations.

Results From the Second Usability Study. Each usability test lasted, on average, between 1,5-2 hours per participant. A total of 29 usability tests were performed; participants from both user groups were included: 9 AI experts and 20 business domain experts with backgrounds in medicine, manufacturing, and economics. The participants' ages were between 25 to 65 years. Only 3% of the participants had previous usage experience with the OMA-ML system, 66% of the participants did not know OMA-ML, and 31% had some knowledge about it.

The result of the usability studies is a collection of 120 usability issues. Each usability issue was assigned the interaction principle it infringes: suitability for the user's tasks (26), self-descriptiveness (27), conformity with user expectations (38), learnability (2), controllability (7), use error robustness (14), user engagement (6). Next, a severity rating was performed using the method described in [6], and potential resolution approaches were added to each usability issue. Compared to the first usability study, the majority (78) of the usability issues have a severity rating of 2 (minor usability problem) or lower.

In total, it can be stated that implementing the suggested UX improvements from the first UX evaluation considerably and measurably enhanced the UX of OMA-ML.

7 Conclusions and Future Work

UX focuses on creating a positive and meaningful experience for users and takes on a critical role during the design and development phase of any application. A bad UX can lead to rejection by the user. This is of particular importance when it comes to AI systems. As one part of UX, the usability gets determined by the trust of the underlying AI system. This is especially important to AI systems such as OMA-ML. As without trust, the user may not adopt the system. However, UX has not yet been a major focus in AI research. Nonetheless, the XAI research area is providing a suite of tools to support AI systems to provide explainability and trust in AI systems.

For the purpose of understanding and successfully improving the UX of an AI system, it is important to take an *iterative* qualitative and user-centric research approach, using expert review and usability tests based on the 7 interaction principles. The expert review uncovers UX issues, and the usability tests help to find usability problems from the target user group's perspective. Afterwards, the issues are resolved, and the updated version should be re-evaluated to uncover further UX issues and weak points. Using the case study of OMA-ML, we could show that the UX improvements to the interface and new XAI modules improved the system's UX in 3 of the 4 interaction principle weak points previously uncovered in the first UX evaluation.

While OMA-ML is not yet reaching its target state in all interaction principles, further UX improvements may be seen after the next UX evaluation iteration. The usability study found a total of 120 new UX issues. After resolving these issues, a new iteration of the UX evaluation can be performed, potentially uncovering new ways to improve OMA-ML.

We recommend performing UX evaluations iteratively and regularly. This can lead to successfully improving the UX of AI systems, potentially leading to more human-centered AI.

Acknowledgments. This work is funded by the German federal ministry of education and research (BMBF) in the program Zukunft der Wertschöpfung (funding code 02L19C157), and supported by Projektträger Karlsruhe (PTKA). The responsibility for the content of this publication lies with the authors.

Disclosure of Interests. The authors have no competing interests to declare that are relevant to the content of this article.

References

1. Din en iso 9241-110:2020-10, ergonomie der mensch-system-interaktion-teil 110: Interaktionsprinzipien (iso 9241-110:2020); deutsche fassung en iso 9241-110:2020
2. Abdi, H., Williams, L.J.: Principal component analysis. Wiley Interdisc. Rev. Comput. Stat. **2**(4), 433–459 (2010). https://doi.org/10.1002/wics.101
3. Abdul, A., Vermeulen, J., Wang, D., Lim, B.Y., Kankanhalli, M.: Trends and trajectories for explainable, accountable and intelligible systems. In: Mandryk, R. (ed.) Proceedings of the 2018 CHI Conference on Human Factors in Computing Systems, pp. 1–18. ACM Conferences, ACM, New York, NY (2018). https://doi.org/10.1145/3173574.3174156
4. Amershi, S., et al.: Guidelines for human-AI interaction. In: Brewster, S. (ed.) Proceedings of the 2019 CHI Conference on Human Factors in Computing Systems, pp. 1–13. ACM Digital Library, Association for Computing Machinery, New York, NY, United States (2019). https://doi.org/10.1145/3290605.3300233
5. Bittner, K., Spence, I.: Use case modeling. The Addison-Wesley object technology series, Addison-Wesley, Boston, Mass (2003)
6. Brand, L., Humm, B.G., Krajewski, A., Zender, A.: Towards improved user experience for artificial intelligence systems. In: Alonso, S., Iliadis, L., Jayne, C., Maglogiannis, I., Pimenidis, E. (eds.) EANN 2023. CCIS, vol. 1826, pp. 33–44. Springer, Cham (2023). https://doi.org/10.1007/978-3-031-34204-2_4

7. Chromik, M., Lachner, F., Butz, A.: Ml for ux? - an inventory and predictions on the use of machine learning techniques for UX research. In: Lamas, D., Sarapuu, H., Šmorgun, I., Berget, G. (eds.) Proceedings of the 11th Nordic Conference on Human-Computer Interaction: Shaping Experiences, Shaping Society, pp. 1–11. ACM Digital Library, Association for Computing Machinery, New York, NY, United States (2020). https://doi.org/10.1145/3419249.3420163
8. Colley, A., Kalving, M., Häkkilä, J., Väänänen, K.: Exploring tangible explainable AI (TangXai): a user study of two xai approaches. In: Bowen, Pantidi et al. (Hg.) 12.02.2023 – Proceedings of the 35th Australian, pp. 679–683. https://doi.org/10.1145/3638380.3638426
9. Dwivedi, R., et al.: Explainable AI (XAI): core ideas, techniques, and solutions. ACM Comput. Surv. **55**(9), 1–33 (2023). https://doi.org/10.1145/3561048
10. Ferreira, J.J., Monteiro, M.S.: What are people doing about XAI user experience? A survey on AI explainability research and practice. In: Marcus, A., Rosenzweig, E. (eds.) HCII 2020. LNCS, vol. 12201, pp. 56–73. Springer, Cham (2020). https://doi.org/10.1007/978-3-030-49760-6_4
11. Feurer, M., Klein, A., Eggensperger, K., Springenberg, J.T., Blum, M., Hutter, F.: Efficient and Robust Automated Machine Learning. MIT Press, Cambridge (2015). https://doi.org/10.5555/2969442.2969547
12. Harley, A.: UX expert reviews. https://www.nngroup.com/articles/ux-expert-reviews/
13. Humm, B.G., et al.: Machine intelligence today: applications, methodology, and technology. Informatik Spektrum, pp. 1–11 (2021). https://doi.org/10.1007/s00287-021-01343-1, https://link.springer.com/article/10.1007%2Fs00287-021-01343-1
14. Humm, B.G., Zender, A.: An Ontology-Based Concept for Meta AutoML. In: Maglogiannis, I., Macintyre, J., Iliadis, L. (eds.) AIAI 2021. IAICT, vol. 627, pp. 117–128. Springer, Cham (2021). https://doi.org/10.1007/978-3-030-79150-6_10
15. Joyce, A.: Help and documentation (usability heuristic #10). https://www.nngroup.com/articles/help-and-documentation/
16. Joyce, A.: Mobile-app onboarding: an analysis of components and techniques. https://www.nngroup.com/articles/mobile-app-onboarding/
17. Joyce, A.: Mobile tutorials: wasted effort or efficiency boost?. https://www.nngroup.com/articles/mobile-tutorials/
18. Joyce, A.: Tooltip guidelines. https://www.nngroup.com/articles/tooltip-guidelines/
19. KDnuggets: CRISP-DM, still the top methodology for analytics, data mining, or data science projects - kdnuggets (22102024). https://www.kdnuggets.com/2014/10/crisp-dm-top-methodology-analytics-data-mining-data-science-projects.html
20. Laubheimer, P.: Onboarding tutorials vs. contextual help. https://www.nngroup.com/articles/onboarding-tutorials/
21. Mahmoud, M., Badawi, U., Hassan, W., Alomari, Y., Alghamdi, F., Farag, T.: Evaluation of user experience in mobile applications **15**, 2021 (2021)
22. Meg Kurdziolek: explaining the unexplainable: explainable AI (XAI) for UX. https://uxpamagazine.org/explaining-the-unexplainable-explainable-ai-xai-for-ux/
23. Merriam, S.B.: Qualitative research and case study applications in education. A joint publication of the Jossey-Bass education series and the Jossey-Bass higher and adult education series, Jossey-Bass Publishers, San Francisco, Calif., rev. and expanded. edn. (1998)

24. Moustakis, V.S., Herrmann, J.: Where do machine learning and human-computer interaction meet? Appl. Artif. Intell. **11**(7–8), 595–609 (1997). https://doi.org/10.1080/088395197117948
25. Nielsen, J.: 10 usability heuristics for user interface design. https://www.nngroup.com/articles/ten-usability-heuristics/
26. Nielsen, J.: Usability 101: introduction to usability. https://www.nngroup.com/articles/usability-101-introduction-to-usability/
27. Norman, D.A.: The Design of Everyday Things. MIT Press, Cambridge (2013). revised and expandes editons
28. Pennington, B., Chapman, S., Fry, A., Deschenes, A., McDonald, C.G.: Strategies to improve the user experience. Ser. Rev. **42**(1), 47–58 (2016). https://doi.org/10.1080/00987913.2016.1140614
29. Polakova, P., Klimova, B.: Using DeepL translator in learning English as an applied foreign language - an empirical pilot study. Heliyon **9**(8), e18595 (2023). https://doi.org/10.1016/j.heliyon.2023.e18595
30. Ray, P.P.: ChatGPT: a comprehensive review on background, applications, key challenges, bias, ethics, limitations and future scope. Internet Things Cyber-Phys. Syst. **3**, 121–154 (2023). https://doi.org/10.1016/j.iotcps.2023.04.003
31. Ríos-Sánchez, B., Silva, D.C.D., Martín-Yuste, N., Sánchez-Ávila, C.: Deep learning for face recognition on mobile devices. IET Biometrics **9**(3), 109–117 (2020). https://doi.org/10.1049/iet-bmt.2019.0093
32. Sarkar, A.: Will code remain a relevant user interface for end-user programming with generative AI models? In: van der Storm, T., Hirschfeld, R. (eds.) Proceedings of the 2023 ACM SIGPLAN International Symposium on New Ideas, New Paradigms, and Reflections on Programming and Software, pp. 153–167. ACM, New York, NY, USA (2023). https://doi.org/10.1145/3622758.3622882
33. Schade, A.: Inverted pyramid: writing for comprehension. https://www.nngroup.com/articles/inverted-pyramid/
34. Shearer, C.: The crisp-DM model: the new blueprint for data mining. J. Data Warehous. **5**(4), 13–22 (2000)
35. Stige, Å., Zamani, E.D., Mikalef, P., Zhu, Y.: Artificial intelligence (AI) for user experience (UX) design: a systematic literature review and future research agenda. Inf. Technol. People (2023). https://doi.org/10.1108/ITP-07-2022-0519
36. Wang, D., Yang, Q., Abdul, A., Lim, B.Y.: Designing theory-driven user-centric explainable AI. In: Brewster, S. (ed.) Proceedings of the 2019 CHI Conference on Human Factors in Computing Systems, pp. 1–15. ACM Digital Library, Association for Computing Machinery, New York, NY, United States (2019). https://doi.org/10.1145/3290605.3300831
37. Zender, A., Humm, B.G.: Ontology-based meta AutoML. Integr. Comput. Aided Eng. **29**(4), 351–366 (2022). https://doi.org/10.3233/ICA-220684
38. Zender, A., Humm, B.G., Holzheuser, A.: Successfully improving the user experience of an artificial intelligence system. In: Proceedings of the 19th Conference on Computer Science and Intelligence Systems (FedCSIS), pp. 253–258. Annals of Computer Science and Information Systems, IEEE (2024). https://doi.org/10.15439/2024F2707
39. Zender, A., Humm, B.G., Pachmann, T.: Improving the efficiency of meta AutoML via rule-based training strategies. In: 2023 18th Conference on Computer Science and Intelligence Systems (FedCSIS), pp. 235–246 (2023). https://doi.org/10.15439/2023F708

S3E'24 – Thematic Session on Advances in Programming Languages (APL)

Programming Cocktail Analysis Based on the Cognitive Load Theory, a First Approach

Alvaro Costa Neto[1,2,3]([✉]) [iD], Maria João Varanda Pereira[2] [iD], and Pedro Rangel Henriques[3] [iD]

[1] Instituto Federal de Educação, Ciência e Tecnologia de São Paulo, Barretos, Brazil
`alvaro@ifsp.edu.br`
[2] Research Centre in Digitalization and Intelligent Robotics (CeDRI), Polytechnic Institute of Bragança, Bragança, Portugal
`mjoao@ipb.pt`
[3] ALGORITMI Research Centre/LASI - DI, University of Minho, Braga, Portugal
`prh@di.uminho.pt`

Abstract. The daily activities of those involved in software development are inherently related to the technologies they use. Languages, libraries, frameworks, and tools tend to accumulate as projects evolve and change, effectively forming Programming Cocktails. Unfortunately, the burden of learning, using, and managing these technologies also tends to closely follow this growth, spawning a myriad of concepts that need to be handled concurrently. This complexity usually requires several factors to be analysed, in order to limit its negative effects. These factors range from security risks to costs and cognitive load, just to mention a few. This paper presents an ontology-based modelling framework that can be used to create an overview of Programming Cocktails. The instantiation of this ontology results in Cocktail Identity Cards, which can then be augmented with one or more of the previously mentioned factors. Finally, the paper also presents a first approach to the cognitive load analysis of Programming Cocktails, based on John Sweller's Cognitive Load Theory.

Keywords: Programming Cocktails · Cognitive Load Theory · Tech Stack · Programming Technologies · Development Complexity

1 Introduction

The development process of an application invariably requires the use of certain technologies, such as languages (for programming, specification, *etc.*), libraries, frameworks and tools. This process may be either monoglot, requiring no more than a base language and, occasionally, a handful of libraries, or it may be polyglot, with several languages, frameworks, libraries, and tools.

Whenever a project demands—or is propelled by—the presence of multiple technologies, the actors involved in the construction of the application must learn, use and manage them. The epistemological challenges that arise in these contexts resemble the ones that have been researched in Computer Programming Education for decades [18]. These studies range from tools to aid students and teachers [21,37,51,54], educational methodologies [1,39,41], analysis of success and failure factors [22,57] to more psychological endeavours [2,11,13,49]. New languages, frameworks and libraries that are unfamiliar to programmers must be learnt and understood [19,22] during the entire life cycle of an application. In the presence of such a myriad of technologies, a new caveat appears: beyond understanding, programmers must also manage a surge in cognitive load as their minds are required to cope with so many options and requirements for implementation.

Research into dealing with these challenges usually present themselves as comparative surveys [20,34,56] that list different programming technologies and their main characteristics. They usually aim to establish a clear landscape and support decisions on which technologies are best suited to specific contexts based solely on individual properties of each technology. Inherently, these studies fail to take into account any possible combination thereof, focusing their efforts in relating and comparing pre-determined aspects. It then becomes clear that a comparative study is not enough to understand how these programming technologies relate to each other in real-life scenarios. The concepts that relate to these technologies, and their interconnections must be formally and structurally mapped. Knowledge must be constructed to cover not only each Ingredient (technology), but the Cocktail (combination) itself. A possible answer to this challenge relies in the use of ontologies [23,44], a formal method to structure knowledge, to conceptualize and instantiate information from Cocktails, establishing reasonable inferences on its landscape of programming technologies.

This paper is an *extended version* of [14]. It provides further insights and developments on Programming Cocktails through the augmentation of their Identity Cards. It also provides a first approach to evaluate the cognitive load inherent to a Cocktail based on the Cognitive Load Theory by John Sweller [45].

This article is divided into six more sections. Section 2 presents the definitions for Programming Cocktails, their Ingredients and other related concepts. Section 3 details a survey of real-life Cocktails conducted with several software development companies. Section 4 presents the ontology that was created to formally model Programming Cocktails, and the instantiated concept of Cocktail Identity Cards. Section 5 provides the overview of how Identity Cards can be augmented with several types of analysis to improve its usefulness. Section 6 presents the Cognitive Load Theory and a first approach to adapt it for use with Programming Cocktails and their Identity Cards. Finally, Sect. 7 concludes the paper with a summary of lessons learned, and presents the next steps in the research of Programming Cocktails.

2 Programming Cocktails

Before delving into the intricacies of application development and the complex relations between the components that are used to build them, it is of good measure to define what *Programming Cocktails* and *Ingredients* actually mean.

It is comprehensible that the use of such relaxed terms to describe logical and structured concepts might seem as a stretch (or even sarcastic) at first sight. Maybe just an analogy, that is furiously gripping itself on the edge of an undeniably sharp, sleek and mathematically sound cliff. Nevertheless, it is in fact very meaningful to this article's context and objectives. Anyone who has ever tried to concoct actual cocktails should be able to described them by more than a list of components. The results are sometimes clean and homogeneous, with strong and decisive tastes. In other cases, the components barely mix together, presenting fuzzy (even chunky) separations that stubbornly remain. In the worst scenarios, when the list of ingredients, their measures, and combinations are poorly chosen, the final result may become undrinkable.

Analogously, the term *Programming Cocktail* defines a combination of computer programming technologies—such as programming languages, libraries and frameworks—that is used to develop specific software applications. *Ingredients* are the components of a *Cocktail*. It is important to note that a Cocktail is associated with a specific application or service, and its Ingredients may also appear in the Cocktail for other application under the same development context[1]. Suppose a company develops three applications:

- **Application A:** HTML, CSS, JavaScript, and ReactJS;
- **Application B:** HTML, CSS, JavaScript, MySQL, and PHP;
- **Application C:** C++, and Unity.

It might seem that, as a whole, there is one Cocktail for the company: the union of the sets formed by each application's Cocktail. Nonetheless, for the purposes of this study, each Cocktail is taken independently, even if it means to consider Ingredients more than once in the same development context. In short, there are three Programming Cocktails in the previous example, one for each application (A, B, and C).

As is expected, a few decisions had to be made while defining these terms. The first and foremost was: which development technologies should be considered Ingredients? At first sight, there are countless technologies that are involved in the development of an application. From standard and well-known programming languages, through Domain-Specific Languages (DSL) for diverse specifications, configuration and communication; to niche libraries, full-stack frameworks, editors and debuggers, the list of candidates to be identified as Ingredients is varied and long. A qualitative threshold was defined to separate what would be considered part of a Cocktail. A programming technology was identified as an Ingredient only if it is *directly applied to the development*[2] *process of an application.*

On the other hand, several technologies are commonly used during deployment or execution of an application, such as Database Management Systems (DBMS), queue coordinators, *etc.*. Despite their influence on the design

---

[1] *Development context* represents the set of factors that influence the actual construction of an application, including, but not limited to, its team, technologies, tools, organization, and requirements.
[2] *Development* here indicates a generalised concept which includes, but is not limited to, programming tasks.

and implementation of an application, these technologies are not considered Ingredients, they are *Resources*. Examples include: Apache Web Server [4], ActiveMQ [3], MySQL [35], and memcached [16].

The second decision concerned the definition of categories for the Ingredients. For the purposes of this study, an Ingredient may be categorized as one of four possibilities:

- **Language:** encompasses any kind of text or graphics-based language. May be used for programming, specification, description, communication, scripting, so on and so forth. Examples: C [25], Python [40], HTML [33], CSS [32], SQL [12], *etc.*.
- **Library:** a portion of code (either in source form or pre-compiled) that augments programming languages and their standard libraries with extra functionality. Examples: LibSSH [28], RayLib [42], *etc.*.
- **Framework:** scaffolding augmentations to programming languages. Albeit similar to libraries, frameworks add functionality while imposing some form of structure to the source code (syntactic, semantic, or paradigmatic) or the use of pre-defined components[3]. Examples: SwiftUI [5], React Native [30], *etc.*.
- **Tool:** specifies any tool that is directly used for development, such as editors, Integrated Development Environments (IDE), debuggers *etc.*.

There might be cases in which the borders between these categories become tenuous. In these situations, an Ingredient that has multiple roles in the development process might need to be either sliced into its constituent parts, or included in more than one category. As an example, testing frameworks, such as JUnit [52], usually include both libraries and servers to allow for concurrent testing. These Ingredients could possibly be separated into their individual roles (*JUnitLibrary* and *JUnitServer*, per example) or included in both categories (Library and Tool).

The reasoning behind these decisions became clear through the construction of the ontology (explained in Sect. 4), with its foundational rationale extracted from real-world Cocktails, surveyed from several multi-national companies in Portugal.

3 Cocktails Assemblage

As previously stated, obtaining the current uses of Programming Cocktails was paramount to establishing an overall picture of computer programming technologies. To this intent, several companies were contacted in a survey for information about which Programming Cocktails they have used. Their feedback allowed for the construction of the ontology's main concepts (presented in Sect. 4) and the consequent structuring of the knowledge surrounding Programming Cocktails.

---

[3] Given that there is no standard for distinguishing between libraries and frameworks, this definition may collide with others'.

3.1 Survey

Starting in October 2023, several companies that have offices in Portugal were contacted via email for a survey of Programming Cocktails. The email (shown in the Appendix) described the context of the study and asked for the programming technologies each company has used, divided by applications in which each Cocktail was used. Companies were specifically asked to answer informally via email, in order to stimulate participation and consequently obtain faster and more numerous responses. Given previous experiences, online survey questionnaires, such as those created via platforms akin to Google Forms[4] tend to be postponed, resulting in fewer answers. While the amount of companies that responded was far from ideal, this number would possibly be even lower if a formal system was used.

Up to the time of this paper's submission[5], 213 companies were contacted and of those, 15 responded with several Cocktails they have used in the past, or still use in the present.

A few important considerations:

– Given the informal nature of the survey, some answers had to be either supplemented (in the case of obvious missing elements, such as Cocktails with React that missed JavaScript) or followed up with further communication;
– Some answers pointed to the fact that the *borders between some systems are a bit fuzzy*, and their Cocktails represent overall divisions that are shared between groups of applications. Such is the case with systems that are heavily structured around micro-services, as example;
– Despite the fact that only Portuguese offices of the surveyed companies were contacted, the majority of them have international endeavours or are multinational themselves, which reduces the locality bias of the answers;
– Exhaustiveness was never the goal for the survey. Given that the programming technologies landscape is ever changing in a fast pace, the survey was designed to support the construction of knowledge about Programming Cocktails, which in turn, may eventually be applied to future works and studies.

Currently, 49 Programming Cocktails have been obtained, spanning a total of 124 different Ingredients and Resources, that range from programming languages and frameworks, to database management systems and resource cache management applications.

3.2 Data Overview

As previously mentioned, statistical data analysis is not the main goal of this study. Nonetheless, a few statistical facts can be extracted from the Programming Cocktails that were gathered in the survey.

---

[4] Available at: https://www.google.com/forms/.
[5] All data discussed in this paper should be considered from the same time period, unless stated otherwise.

Table 1. Summarised example of the Cocktails spreadsheet.

Ingredient	Type	Lang.	Task	App1	App2	...	AppN
.NET	Framework	C#	Full-stack development			...	X
C#	Language	C#	Server implementation		X	...	
C#	Language	C#	Full-stack development	X		...	
⋮							
YAML	Language	YAML	Communication		X	...	

In order to better organize the survey results, an online spreadsheet[6] was created, listing Ingredients on the lines and Cocktails on the columns (Table 1 represents a summarised example of the actual spreadsheet). Column A contains the names of the Ingredients. The columns from B to D categorize each Ingredient into, respectively, its type[7] (*Language, Library, Framework* or *Tool*), the Language with which it was used, and the Task it was applied to (Tasks will be further explained in Subsect. 4.2). In the eventual case of an Ingredient either being used with more than one Language, or applied to more than one Task, its line would be duplicated and its categories adapted as needed. A hypothetical example would be the .NET Framework, which can be used with several different programming languages, and would require such treatment. Finally, from E onwards, each Cocktail was listed in its own column, with their Ingredients' rows marked to represent their inclusion. As an example, in Table 1, the column *App2* represents the second Cocktail that was gathered and includes both C# and YAML.

In total, 63 different Ingredients have been collected:

- 23 Languages;
- 14 Libraries;
- 22 Frameworks;
- 4 Tools.

As per Resources, 61 have been gathered. Overall, each Cocktail has an average of 8 Ingredients and Resources, which a 4.6 standard deviation. Some other observations include:

- 2 Cocktails are based either on *Low Code* or *No Code* Ingredients;
- Most of the Cocktails belong to Web Development (32 in total);
- The most frequent Ingredients are (from most to least used):
    - **Language:** HTML, CSS, JavaScript, SQL, C#;
    - **Library:** OData, Bootstrap, (all the other tied in one use);

---

[6] A read-only version is available at: https://bit.ly/4aFjSjj.
[7] Resources have also been included in the spreadsheet and are categorized as such, despite not being Ingredients *per se*.

- **Framework:** React, Node.js, .NET, Angular, ASP.NET;
- **Tool:** Visual Studio, Visual Studio Code, PowerPages, Liferay;
– The most frequent combination of a programming language and a framework is JavaScript with React, followed by JavaScript with Node.js, C# with .NET, and JavaScript with Angular;
– 7 Cocktails use only one language;
– At the time of writing, no Cocktails have been collected that directly apply any Artificial Intelligence (AI) support or technology.

As previously mentioned, micro-services architectures presented a challenge in defining borders between systems—and consequently, their Cocktails. In these cases (5 in total), their Cocktails were defined taking into account a group of micro-services that implement logical parts of the whole system. The logic behind this definition was dependent on the system itself, and as such, stipulated by the company that provided the Cocktails.

4 Ontology for Programming Cocktails

The data collected through the survey has a purpose: to allow for better understanding of Programming Cocktails, which entails the construction and structuring of knowledge. Our research group has had several interactions with and has made several contributions to the study of ontologies [6–9, 27, 29, 50], both in their construction and definition. Consequently, from several approaches that could be applied to achieve the construction of knowledge about Programming Cocktails, an ontology seemed a straightforward and appropriate choice. It allowed for the formal definition of Programming Cocktails' main concepts, the generation of *Identity Cards*, an ontology-based characterisation mechanism for Cocktails, and the organization of their Ingredients.

Moreover, the ontology will be paramount for future use in coming studies, that will deal with the evaluation of Cocktails in cognitive load metrics. The construction of the ontology was then, in practice, a two-fold endeavour, as it aided in structuring and understanding the data that was collected through the survey (its initial goal), while also providing a foundation on which several studies might surge.

4.1 OntoDL

The initial version of the ontology was created using a spreadsheet to organize and list its concepts, relations, instances, and connections. While suitable for the beginning phases, when the number of elements was small, as the ontology grew it became evident that other solutions would offer better scaling and future-proofing. A visual representation would be ideal to quickly present the connections between the ontology's elements. Given previous experiences and its simple yet capable syntax, OntoDL [15] was chosen as the main source for the definition and instantiation of the ontology. OntoDL is a Domain-Specific

Language (DSL) that was created for modelling ontologies, as an alternative to more verbose options such as the Web Ontology Language (OWL) [55]. It has been used in several projects, including the WebOntoDL application[8], which can interpret ontologies written in OntoDL and translate them to several other formats, such as DOT[9] and OWL. It contains a syntax that is reminiscent of the mathematical formal definition of ontologies. It also allows the use of keywords in Portuguese or in English, which could be a beneficial factor for exchange and contribution from third parties.

The basis for OntoDL's syntax relies on five main structures: the name of the ontology, the list of concepts, the list of individuals, the list of relation types and the triples that actually declare relations. Listing 1.1 shows the basic declaration for each structure. A few basic rules:

- The language follows basic principles of ignoring whitespaces and line-breaks, as well as the use of curly brackets as group delimiters;
- The order of the declarations matters;
- Concepts, relationships and triples are mandatory;
- Comments are line based, beginning with the percent sign (%) and ending with a line-break;
- There are pre-defined relation types for specialization (`isa`), composition (`pof`), and instantiation (`iof`);
- Triples are directional, and may be formed using any combination of concepts and individuals.

There are more rules for defining properties, axioms and other elements, that have not been used in this paper. With the foundation firmly established on OntoDL, the first step to create a valid ontology that would allow for reasoning on the surveyed Programming Cocktails was to model its main concepts.

4.2 Open Conceptual Model

Before delving into the actual ontology and its concepts, it is important to establish a graphical notation that will be used and referenced in figures that represent them. Figure 1 shows the basic elements and how they are graphically styled, more specifically for OntoDL's pre-defined relations. Other relationships use a simple arrow. This notation is emblematic because it allows for quick identification of element types (concepts or individuals), and pre-defined relation types that carry specific semantics (instantiation, specialization and composition).

---

[8] Available at: https://webontodl.epl.di.uminho.pt.
[9] DOT is a graphics format written in plain text that is used to define visual elements in a diagrammatic form. It is part of the Graphviz project, available at https://graphviz.org.

Listing 1.1. Basic syntax for OntoDL.

```
% Identifiers must follow the C standard.
Ontology OntologyName

% The order of declarations matters.
concepts { Concept1, Concept2, ... }

individuals { Individual1, Individual2, ... }

% Whitespace and line-breaks are ignored.
relationships {
    RelationType1,
    RelationType2,
    ...
}

triples {
    % Triples may relate both concepts and individuals,
    % in any combination.
    Concept1      =RelationType1=> Concept2;
    Individual4   =RelationType2=> Individual5;
    % Specialization.
    ConceptChild  =isa=> ConceptFather;
    % Composition.
    ConceptPart   =pof=> ConceptWhole;
    % Instantiation.
    IndividualA   =iof=> ConceptA;
}
% The period indicates the end of the ontology.
.
```

The main concepts of the ontology were incrementally created. The first concepts meant to establish a foundation, based on the fact that each *Cocktail* is directly associated to a *System* that either is or has been under *Development*. Listing 1.2 and Fig. 2 present them.

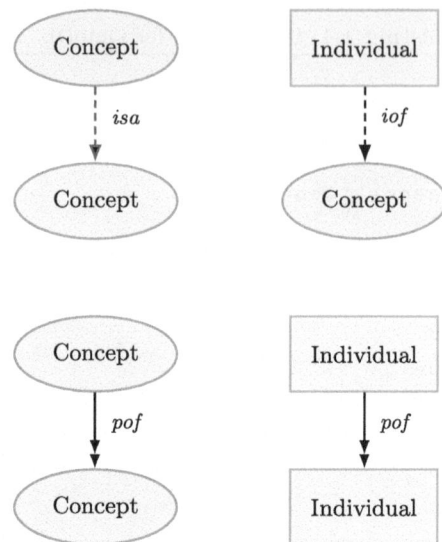

Fig. 1. Graphical notation for the ontology.

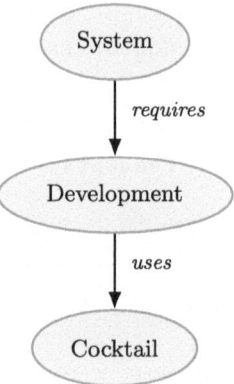

Fig. 2. Initial concepts for the ontology.

The next step in the development of the conceptual model was the addition of the Ingredients and their types. The results of the survey reaffirmed the initial proposal for their types (Language, Library, Framework and Tool), but also highlighted a basic problem: some tools that were listed by the companies did not participate directly in the development process. In some cases, such as the main Operating System that programmers chose or a note taking application, it was evident that their inclusion as Ingredients would be a stretch that could backfire in later developments. Other elements were not so easy to distinguish, such as Database Management Systems, and Queue Managers.

Listing 1.2. Initial concepts for the ontology.

```
Ontology Cocktails

concepts {
    System,
    Development,
    Cocktail
}

relationships {
    uses,
    requires
}

triples {
    % Foundation.
    System        =requires=> Development;
    Development   =uses=>     Cocktail;
}
.
```

At that moment, a decision had to be made: would these tools be included as Ingredients? Which category would they belong to? At first, the intention was to include all of them as Tools, but as more Cocktails were obtained, it became clear that this choice could easily distort the category's meaning. In the end, in order to avoid this negative effect, the concept of a *Resource* was created to implement this solution. A Resource represents an external system (or service) that is used at runtime by the application, but that does not participate directly during the development process. For obvious cases, such as Operating Systems, the separation between a Tool and a Resource was clear. Alas, that was not always the case. Some Resources required some kind of implementation in the development phases, such as a communication library, or a configuration language. In these cases, the runtime of the system (or service) was considered a Resource, while any mandatory Application Programming Interface (API), library, framework or language that was used to interact with it was considered an Ingredient (of the correct type). As an example, in order to communicate with MySQL, an external library or framework (such as *libmysqlclient*) is usually included as part of the project. Given that the runtime of the MySQL server provides support for the *execution* of the application, it would be considered a *Resource*. On the other hand, *libmysqlclient* would be considered a *Library*, as it participates directly in the development phase to program the interaction to the server. In order to highlight this difference in purpose (supporting the application execution *versus* the development process), the concept of the Resource was moved from its initial relationship (a specialization of Ingredient) to a supporting role to the System itself. Listing 1.3 and Fig. 3 show the inclusion of these concepts to the ontology. It can be seen that while the concepts of Language, Library, Framework and Tool are specializations of the more general concept of an Ingredient, Resource is directly connected to the System concept.

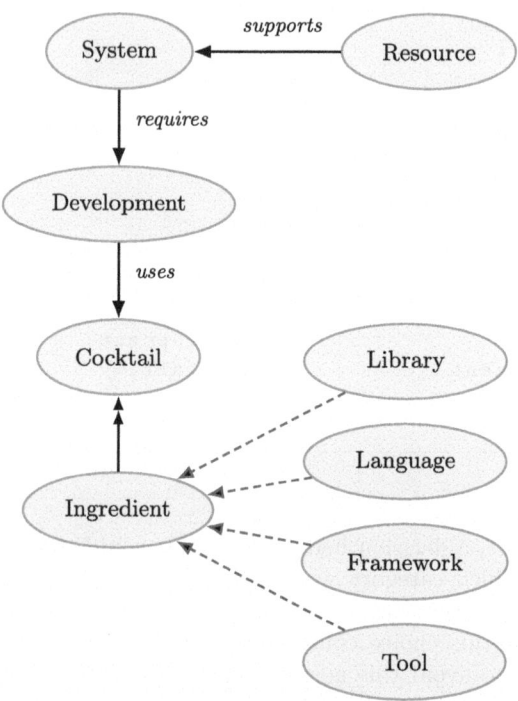

Fig. 3. The inclusion of Ingredients and Resources to the ontology.

The last two additions to the conceptual model consisted in a series of relationships that highlighted the central role of Languages in the Cocktail, and the definition of Tasks. Languages are usually the central element in the development of almost any kind of System. In fact, it is very unusual that a Language choice will depend on other types of Ingredients, such as Frameworks, or Libraries. The reverse, although, is commonplace: the choice of a Language usually dictates which other Ingredients will be part of the Cocktail.

Listing 1.3. The inclusion of Ingredients and Resources to the ontology.

```
Ontology Cocktails

concepts {
    System,
    Development,
    Cocktail,
    Resource,
    Ingredient,
    Language,
    Library,
    Framework,
    Tool
}

relationships {
    uses,
    requires,
    supports
}

triples {
    % Foundation.
    System        =requires=> Development;
    Development   =uses=>     Cocktail;

    % Runtime resources (OS, DBMS, etc.)
    Resource      =supports=> System;

    % Ingredients and their types.
    Ingredient    =pof=> Cocktail;
    Language      =isa=> Ingredient;
    Library       =isa=> Ingredient;
    Framework     =isa=> Ingredient;
    Tool          =isa=> Ingredient;
}
.
```

In order to illustrate and define Language's central role, three relationships were added, each connecting one of the other Ingredient types to it (see the *extends*, *encloses* and *supports* relationships that terminate in *Language* in Listing 1.4 and Fig. 4).

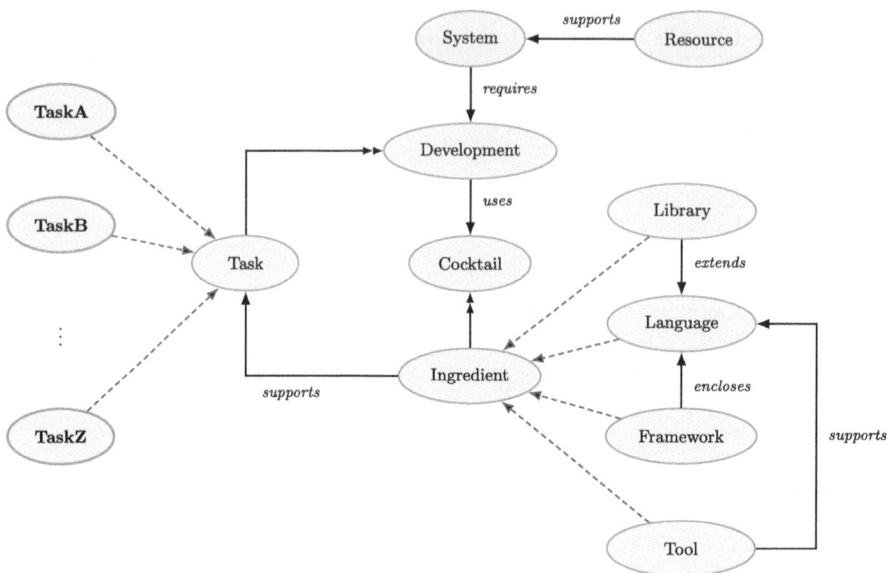

Fig. 4. The conceptual model for the ontology.

The definition of Tasks and how they were modelled was the last step in the construction of the conceptual model for the ontology. As with any specification for concepts that rely heavily on a particular context, there is no optimal solution. A few strategies were considered:

- A general concept is created in order to future-proof the definition, such as *ProgrammingTask*, or equivalent. It does not conceive any particular information about real Tasks that are effectively conducted in the development context. By doing so, the model will not require further updates, while remaining valid for any future Programming Cocktails. The drawback relies on the lack of effective representation, given its generalist nature;
- Given a survey of Programming Cocktails, a set of pre-defined Tasks is established in order to achieve more practical representation than one general concept. These Tasks are fixed and any future use of the ontology will require "fitting" of the actual development context into the set of pre-defined Tasks. This option has the evident risk of rapidly becoming outdated, specially in dynamic domains, such as Web Development. It may also require distortions on the division of Tasks in order to fit the pre-defined concepts, potentially losing its representativeness;
- The conceptual model becomes open and adaptable to specific development contexts. This was the chosen strategy for the ontology. Given that the main intention is to construct knowledge on Programming Cocktails and that each project, team, company, or organization has specific demands and requirements, keeping the ontology adaptable was a better solution to the definition of Tasks.

Listing 1.4. The conceptual model for the ontology.

```
Ontology Cocktails

concepts {
    System,
    Development,
    Cocktail,
    Resource,
    Ingredient,
    Language,
    Library,
    Framework,
    Tool,
    Task,
    TaskA, TaskB, ..., TaskZ
}

relationships {uses, requires, supports, extends,
    ↪ encloses}

triples {
    % Foundation.
    System        =requires=> Development;
    Development   =uses=>     Cocktail;
    % Runtime resources (OS, DBMS, etc.)
    Resource      =supports=> System;
    % Ingredients and their types.
    Ingredient    =pof=> Cocktail;
    Language      =isa=> Ingredient;
    Library       =isa=> Ingredient;
    Framework     =isa=> Ingredient;
    Tool          =isa=> Ingredient;

    % Language's central role.
    Library       =extends=>  Language;
    Framework     =encloses=> Language;
    Tool          =supports=> Language;
    % General Task concept.
    Task          =pof=>      Development;
    Ingredient    =supports=> Task;
    % Context-specific Tasks. These tasks depend on the
    % development context and its structure.
    TaskA         =isa=> Task;
    TaskB         =isa=> Task;
    ...
    TaskZ         =isa=> Task;
}
.
```

The final solution for the ontology and how it must deal with Tasks relies on adapting the Task concept (via specialization) to include in the model a logical division of Programming Tasks, fit for the context in case.

As an example, a company with different projects might establish different conceptual models for their ontologies. Suppose that the first project is a simple Web Application, with just a few Ingredients. In this case, the team behind it might simplify the conceptual model and only specialize general Tasks, such as *FrontEndProgramming* and *BackEndProgramming*. In another project, with multiple Ingredients and a much larger problem to solve, the team might find it appropriate to specialize *Task* into a more granular level, such as *LandingPageStructuring*, *ClientInterfaceStyling*, *DatabaseCommunication*, so on, and so forth. This is what the term *open* in *open conceptual model* means.

This strategy future-proofs the conceptual model by making it adaptable, while providing both flexibility and a solid foundation for Programming Cocktails analysis.

4.3 Cocktail Identity Cards

The conceptual model of an ontology is crucial to define its structure, how the modelled concepts are related, and what level of detail is expected for the overall organization of knowledge. Nonetheless, the concepts, besides being fundamental, are usually materialized into *individuals*, on their occurrences in the context being modelled.

The conceptual model of the ontology was applied to the Cocktails in order to test its validity and aid in structuring the information from the survey. Initially, all individuals and concepts were pictured, which resulted in a convoluted image and many overlapping connections. In order to establish a clearer picture of each Cocktail, the focus shifted to showing the individuals, their relations and, when necessary, some concepts to avoid misidentification of the individuals. The concepts that were kept in the diagram were:

- *Resource* to explicitly show which supporting systems and services each application used;
- *Language*, *Library*, *Framework*, and *Tool*, to categorise each *Ingredient*;
- *Task* specializations to identify the parts of the application that each *Ingredient* tackles.

In all of these cases, a concept is only added to the diagram if a relation to or from it is also present. As an example, if there are no libraries in the Cocktail, the *Library* concept will not be shown.

The instantiation of an application from the survey is presented in Fig. 5[10]. It is a Question & Answer (Q&A) Web Application used for internal communication (and documentation) in the company. It requires three different

---

[10] The names of the applications have been changed to a generic *App#* format for privacy concerns. Nonetheless, they have all been gathered in the survey and represent real software.

supporting systems for its execution[11]: Elasticsearch [17], MongoDB [31], and RabbitMQ [10]. The three basic *Ingredients* for almost any Web Application are present (HTML, CSS, and JavaScript), as are two well known *Frameworks* (Node.js and React.js).

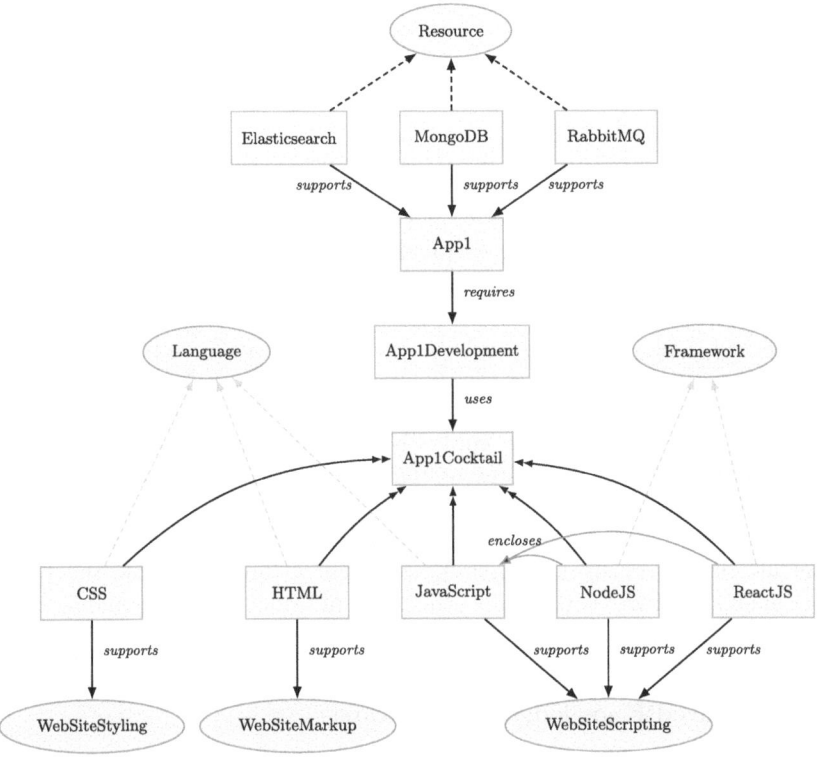

Fig. 5. An example of a Cocktail Identity Card modelled for a Q&A Web Application.

The three *Task* concepts (*WebSiteStyling*, *WebSiteMarkup*, and *WebSiteScripting*) have been determined based on the main areas of the development context. They do not represent specific tasks, as these have not been provided by the company. Their role is to exemplify how *Ingredients* relate to their supported *Tasks*.

As a first proof of concept, the instantiation in Fig. 5 is able to visually represent each development component and how they relate to the application. It does so in a compact form, with enough elements to quickly provide interesting insights into the Cocktail:

– Dependency on external services and systems is directly represented by the number of *Resources* that support the *System*;

---
[11] Instantiated from the *Resource* concept.

- Dependency on *Ingredients* is represented by the number of the equivalent instances;
- Possible redundancies (too many *Ingredients* of the same type supporting the same *Task*) are quickly identified;
- *Tasks* that are too reliant on many *Ingredients*—a possible weakness point—can be directly identified by their number of *support* relations.

The instantiation provides enough information about the application and its development (specially its Cocktail) that it is effectively an *Identity Card* (CIC). It has been successfully applied to the other Cocktails obtained from the survey, providing CICs to all of them. Figure 6 shows two more CICs for comparison.

The Identity Card shown in Fig. 6a represents a mobile educational game. In this case, the tasks have been chosen in a more granular manner, in order to better represent specific parts of development context. Figure 6b also represents a mobile application, but not a game. It is a Covid-pass related front-end application. Differently from Fig. 6a, which applied a multi-platform engine (Unity [53]) to create and deploy the game to both mobile application stores (Apple's App Store and Google's Play Store), Fig. 6b shows how one application may require more than one development context, since it used mutually exclusive technologies for each platform (Swift for Apple's ecosystem, and Kotlin for Google's). In both cases, the CICs quickly present the previously listed properties for their Programming Cocktails.

The Identity Cards are valuable for quick identification of several Cocktail properties, as previously shown, but also form a foundation for the further, deeper analysis. Risks, costs, or any other form of valuation that would be layered on top of their relations could become valid augmentations to the CICs.

4.4 Structured Knowledge on Cocktails

The instantiations are valuable in their own merit, by organising the relations between the technologies that application development depends on. Nonetheless, its construction, by itself, relayed valuable information about the survey.

The definition of the category columns in the spreadsheet (mentioned in Subsect. 3.2) is a direct and practical result in this case. The initial version of these columns had several problems, from the lack of domain definitions, to redundancy in values. Since the categorization of the Ingredients will be paramount in future studies, columns B to D are of great importance. After the definition of the ontology and its application to the several Cocktails that have been gathered, the final version of the category columns was finally obtained.

The first category column (*Type*, column B) was a direct implementation of the *Ingredient* specializations (*Language*, *Library*, *Framework* and *Tool*). It is a direct definition of the ingredient's nature. The next column (*Language*, column C) represents what language is used for each other type of ingredient. It was derived directly from the relationships that the different types of ingredients establish to *Language* in the conceptual model (see the bottom-right relations in

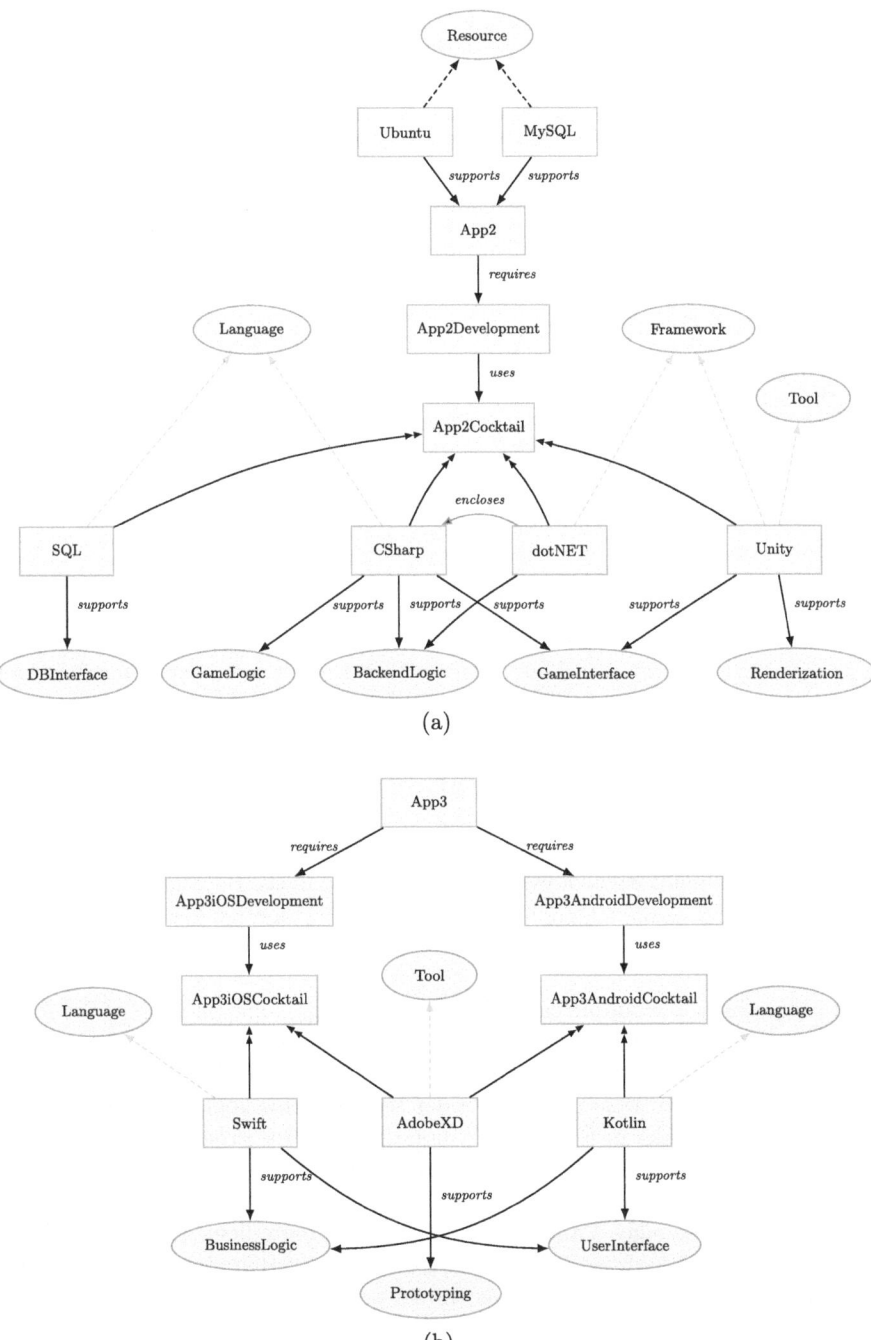

Fig. 6. Identity Cards for two different applications: a mobile educational game (a) and a Covid-pass management front-end (b).

Fig. 4). Finally, column D (*Task*) represents the *Task* specializations, as previously explained. In the case that an ingredient is applied to more than one task, or used with more than one language, its line would be duplicated and changed to reflect these variations.

Another direct result from the construction of the ontology was the possibility to determine which languages are more auto-sufficient (have fewer libraries and frameworks connected to them) or more dependant of complements.

A third point-of-view for knowledge construction based on the ontology relates to project management. A few possibilities include:

- By superimposing the Identity Cards, teams and companies can quickly identify which ingredients they are more dependent on, or have more experience with;
- The definition of the *Task* specializations render an opportunity to identify common threads between projects, in order to standardize or evaluate how teams are structured, personnel is allocated, *etc.*
- The Identity Cards provide quick documentation about a project's technological evolution. Given that it can also be encoded in OntoDL, it can be easily registered in Version Control Systems (VCS), such as Git [43].

As with any kind of structural representation, this ontology may be applied to analyse and support decisions on many facets of project developments, from simple documentation to critical factors such as risk and dependency.

5 Identity Cards Augmentation

The Cocktail Identity Cards form a foundational result that can be augmented to support several qualitative, or even quantitative, analysis. Beyond the immediate applications previously stated in Subsect. 4.4, the Identity Cards can also be directly superimposed with values that correspond to specific metrics—akin to a weighted graph.

An hypothetical example can better illustrate the augmentation of the Identity Cards. Consider a development team that needs to evaluate and report security risk in its working context, for a specific project. Among the several analysis that need to take course in order to reach this goal, the evaluation of inherent security risks in each of the Ingredients of its Programming Cocktail would be essential for success. By taking into account both internal metrics, and published results, such as technical reports from the ISO's Working Group in Programming Languages Vulnerabilities [24], each Ingredient's inherent vulnerabilities and security risks can be qualified. Not only that, but the integration between certain Ingredients, such as frameworks and programming languages, can also be evaluated and taken into account for the analysis.

The drawing in Fig. 7 presents how the Identity Card (bottom part of Fig. 5) of a Programming Cocktail would be augmented with the security risk analysis. The composition relations between each Ingredient (CSS, HTML, JavaScript, NodeJS and ReactJS) and the Cocktail represent inherent security risks that each one of them contributes to the project. These labels (*HIGH* or *LOW*) easily indicate that some Ingredients are naturally more prone to vulnerabilities than others and that would require more attention of developers to avoid security mistakes. Beyond that, the relations between both frameworks (NodeJS and ReactJS) and their languages would also influence the risk level. Finally, this piecewise analysis could also be recursively applied to the upper instantiations in the Identity Card in order to reach an overall picture of security risk for this project.

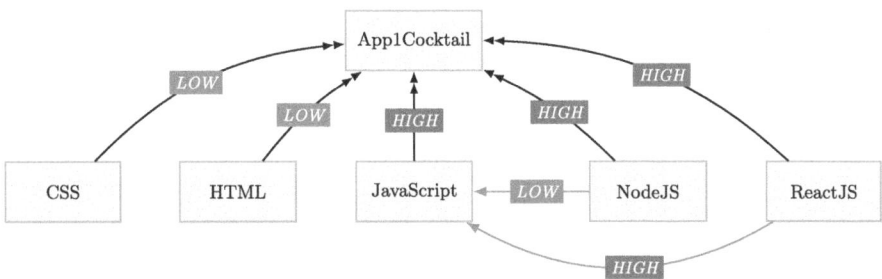

Fig. 7. A possible augmentation of a Cocktail Identity Card with security risk analysis.

Another benefit of this augmentation technique is that it is flexible by its own design and construction. Given that the origin of the Identity Cards is the conceptual model, which is itself an ontological model, any other concepts or properties that are needed to complement the analysis can easily be added to cope for specific needs of the team. The instantiation of a new Conceptual Model will reflect automatically these changes in the project's Identity Cards.

Continuing the example of the security risk analysis, if the interpreters for the programming languages and the client-side rendering engines could contribute to security risks, both concepts could be added to the Conceptual Model, as shown in Fig. 8. The instantiation into Identity Cards would then take these new concepts into account and the same type of augmentation that was applied to each Ingredient and their relations would also be used in the connection between languages and their processing programs.

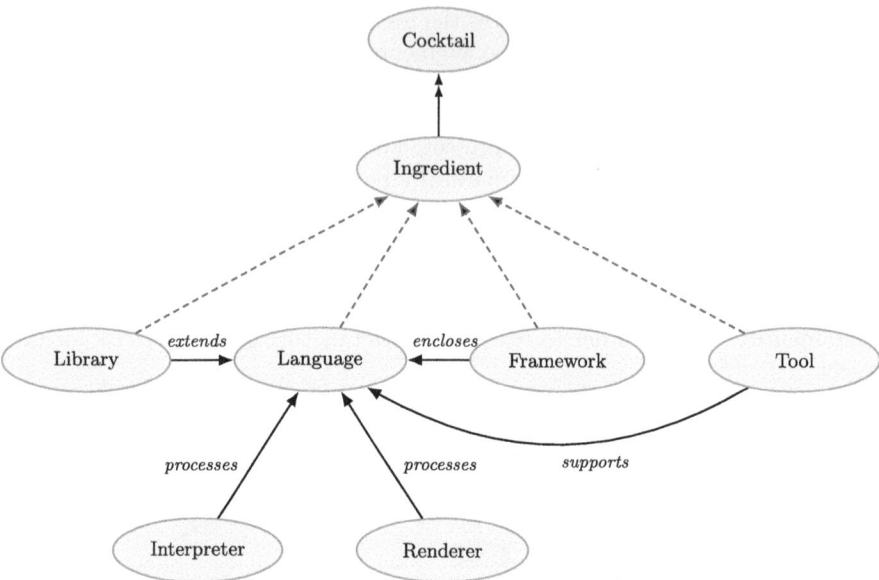

Fig. 8. A possible adaptation of the conceptual model to better fit a security risk analysis scenario.

6 Cognitive Analysis, a First Approach

Cognitive Load Theory was introduced by John Sweller in 1988 through his seminal paper [45]. Despite the constant development of the theory since then [26, 36, 46–48], the main ideas behind Sweller's original article still hold true.

Sweller proposed a Production System model to represent problem-solving mental facilities. Following the ideas that come from Piaget's Constructivism [38], a person only learns when new mental schemes[12] are created. Whenever a problem needs to be solved, those previously assimilated schemata are then used to construct a solution to the problem. This construction method also uses information that is obtained directly from the context (e.g. data given by an exercise's statement), or that can be derived from it. In doing so, the individual tackles both long-term memory (where the schemata reside) and *working memory*. The latter is of utmost importance to this theory, given that it is a very limited and volatile resource, while also being the essential mental scratch pad in which all problem-solving happens. In fact, it is very similar to the *permanent* versus *volatile memory* conundrum that computers face, in which permanent storage is abundant and slow, while volatile memory is reduced in size, but much faster. Any processes that need to be executed, have to load its necessary operations and data from permanent to volatile memory, and, so do humans

---

[12] The collective term for scheme is also known as *schemata*.

whenever a problem needs to be solved. The occupation level of working memory is Sweller's definition of *cognitive load*.

Just as computers may run out of volatile memory and freeze if not properly managed, humans tend to leave important (or even essential) information behind whenever working memory is stressed. This, according to Sweller, not only diminishes the possibility of solving the problem, but also leaves no space for actual learning to happen. The only way to allow individuals to learn during problem-solving is then to avoid increasing cognitive load beyond one's capacity.

6.1 Production System Model

In order to simulate, measure and analyse cognitive load during problem-solving situations, Sweller proposed a *Production System Model* that simulates how problems are mentally solved. In this model, any solution to a problem is composed of states, from the beginning—when only knowns, unknowns, constraints and operations are available—to the very end, when a final result is found.

The functioning of the model is based on inference rules that represent the logical steps that can be taken to solve a problem. Through the author's own words [45, p. 264]:

> A production system is a set of *inference rules* that have *conditions* for applications and *actions* to be taken if the conditions are satisfied[13].

The conditions, actions and strengths[14] are grouped into *productions*. In order for a production to activate (meaning, its actions to take place), the contents of working memory is compared against the set of conditions of all productions currently available, and the strongest in the set is chosen to be activated.

It is important to note that beyond the problem's data and context, productions are also kept in working memory while a solution takes place. In fact, the main objective of Sweller's paper was show that means-ends exercises are more taxing to an individual's cognitive load than those with non-specific goals. One of the strongest arguments for that conclusion was the necessity of keeping productions in working memory while solving a problem. Given that means-ends exercises have more productions available at any state of the solution than those with non-specific goals, the main argument behind Sweller's article was proven to be true. In summary [45, p. 265]:

> It seems plausible to suggest that the more productions that need to be considered at each step in the problem and the more statements[15] that need to be matched in order to decide between productions, the greater is the "cognitive load."

---

[13] Emphasis added by the authors of this article.
[14] A production's strength is akin to an operator's precedence, dictating which one should activate in case of a conditional tie.
[15] *Statement* is a general term that corresponds to any fact currently available about the problem and the solution, such as unknowns, conditions, *etc.*

6.2 Problem-Solving Example

In order to trace a parallel to how Sweller's theory could be applied to computer programming, it is useful to review and understand the *productions* in one of his examples. In his seminal paper, Sweller proposed a simple kinematics problem to demonstrate how cognitive load could be approximated in its resolution using different strategies. The problem involved a car that accelerates from rest, and presents a pre-calculated average velocity. Despite simple, it is illustrative on how a problem can be solved and what the productions really mean.

The specifics of the example—which are beyond the scope of this article—can be found in Sweller's paper [45, p. 269]. In fact, for the purposes of computer programming, it is more important to highlight what the productions represented and their characteristics.

As can be seen in Table 2 (adapted from [45, p. 267]), the productions represent the logical steps that need to be taken in order to solve a simple problem, such as the one the example proposed. In fact, these productions are atomic and effective enough to solve any kind of problem in which a set of unknowns, equations and initial values are given, and that, by simple substitution, a final answer can be found.

Table 2. Productions in Sweller's original paper.

Prod.	Conditions	Actions	Strength
1	A problem has a specified goal and an equation is known in which the goal is the only unknown	The goal becomes known	1.2
2	A problem has a specified goal and an equation is known which contains the goal and one or more unknowns not previously set as subgoals	The unknowns not previously set as subgoals and other that the goal become subgoals	1.0
3	An equation is known which contains subgoals and one or more unknowns not previously set as subgoals	The unknowns not previously set as subgoals become subgoals	1.0
4	An equation is known in which a subgoal is the only unknown	The subgoal becomes a known	1.1
5	A problem does no have a specified goal and an equation can be found with only one unknown	The unknown becomes a known	1.0

The cognitive load for solving the problem was calculated by taking into account not only the problem's statements, but also the total number of productions for the that type of solution in each step. In fact, it became the main supporting argument that problems without specific goals require a lower cognitive load than their means-ends equivalents.

6.3 Cognitive Load Theory and Programming Cocktails

The results of Sweller's original paper established a new branch of pedagogical and psychological research, focusing on the general theory behind cognitive load measurements. Given that computer programming problems are very similar to (or even derived from) general mathematical problems, it seems logical to establish equivalences to measure cognitive load, and support application development.

Problem solving in computer programming tends to follow recurrent patterns that could be mapped into productions, just as Sweller did to solve simple equation problems. Table 3 shows an example of this mapping for the use of repetition structures (loops). While it does not take into account every single detail of the implementation of repetitive portions of the source code, it provides an idea of what the cognitive productions would be.

Similar productions can be created for the several sub-problems that frequently occur when programming computers—conditioning, modularization, organization, *etc*. The analysis can also be segmented in levels (lexical, syntactic, semantic and logical) to contemplate different aspects of development, ranging from concrete and direct (e.g. rules for writing valid identifiers) to more abstract tasks (e.g. how to organize the several constituent parts of a source code).

This strategy is fit for the augmentation of Identity Cards. While the real cognitive load would only be calculable when realising a programming task, the linguistic and structural characteristics of the Ingredients in a Programming Cocktail can provide a cognitive overview of the project. As an example, each language in use may contribute with more ways to solve a repetition problem, by providing not only different syntactic constructs (such as loop structures: `while`, `for`, `foreach`, an so on), but also paradigmatic implementations and restrictions[16]. This would inevitably raise the number of cognitive productions and, by consequence, the cognitive load during development. This rationale not only agrees with intuitive perception—many languages bring more "confusion" or "entropy" to the development—but also is founded on a solidly researched, developed and proven theory.

---

[16] That is not to say that only syntactic features should be taken into consideration for cognitive load analysis. The example in this statement only simplifies the explanation of how more than one ingredient in a Programming Cocktail can affect the overall cognitive load under Sweller's theory.

Table 3. Productions that map the general use of repetition structures in computer programming. This is not meant to be exhaustive, neither in scope, nor in abstraction coverage.

Prod.	Conditions	Actions	Strength
1	A sequence of instructions need to be executed repeatedly until a condition is met	The sequence becomes a *repetition block* and the condition becomes its *repetition factor*	1.0
2	A *repetition block* exists and its *repetition factor* is a known integer quantity	The *repetition block* is enclosed in a *counting loop* that starts at zero and runs up to the quantity of repetitions is reached	1.1
3	A *repetition block* exists and its *repetition factor* is a known integer quantity	The *repetition block* is enclosed in a *pre-conditional loop* with a counter variable that starts at zero and runs up to the quantity of repetitions is reached	1.0
4	A *repetition block* exists and its *repetition factor* is a collection of items	The *repetition block* is enclosed in a *collection loop* that starts at the first item and runs up to the last one	1.1
5	A *repetition block* exists and its *repetition factor* is a collection of items	The *repetition block* is enclosed in a *pre-conditional loop* with a reference variable that starts at the first item and runs up to the last one	1.0
⋮	⋮	⋮	

7 Conclusion

This extended paper presented a modelling framework for Programming Cocktails based on an ontology that was created to structure knowledge around their uses. The instantiation of this ontology resulted in Cocktail Identity Cards, that allow for further analysis of a project's programming technologies and their interrelations. Furthermore, a first approach for augmenting such Identity Cards with cognitive load features has also been shown to be possible.

The very act of constructing the ontology has already structured knowledge for the surveyed Cocktails. Nonetheless, the ontology itself and the Identity Cards present more interesting opportunities, allowing for quick visualization, identification and extraction of knowledge for Programming Cocktails. The flexibility of the modelling mechanisms also allow for different augmentations and adaptations to easily occur, even to cope with specific needs in a development context.

Future developments of this project will extend the methodology that gathered and identified Cocktails, and finalise the cognitive load augmentation of the Identity Cards with a comprehensive mapping of cognitive productions for typical programming tasks in different levels of abstraction.

Acknowledgments. This work has been supported by FCT - Fundação para a Ciência e Tecnologia within the R&D Units Project Scope: UIDB/00319/2020.

The work of Maria João and Alvaro was supported by national funds through FCT/MCTES (PIDDAC): CeDRI, UIDB/05757/2020 (DOI: 10.54499/UIDB/05757/2020) and UIDP/05757/2020 (DOI: 10.54499/UIDP/05757/2020); SusTEC, LA/P/0007/2020 (DOI: 10.54499/LA/P/0007/2020).

Disclosure of Interests. The authors have no competing interests to declare that are relevant to the content of this article.

References

1. Almeida, M.V.P., Alves, L.M., Pereira, M.J.V., Barbosa, G.A.R.: Easycoding: methodology to support programming learning, vol. 81, pp. 1–8. Open Access Series in Informatics (OASIcs), Schloss Dagstuhl-Leibniz-Zentrum für Informatik (2020). https://doi.org/10.4230/OASIcs.ICPEC.2020.1. https://drops.dagstuhl.de/opus/volltexte/2020/12288
2. Alves, J., Costa Neto, A., Pereira, M.J.V., Henriques, P.R.: Characterization and identification of programming languages, vol. 104, pp. 1–15. Open Access Series in Informatics (OASIcs), Schloss Dagstuhl - Leibniz-Zentrum für Informatik (2023). https://doi.org/10.4230/OASIcs.SLATE.2022.14. https://drops.dagstuhl.de/opus/volltexte/2022/16760
3. Apache Software Foundation: Apache activemq. https://activemq.apache.org
4. Apache Software Foundation: Apache http server project. https://httpd.apache.org
5. Apple: Swiftui. https://developer.apple.com/xcode/swiftui/
6. Araújo, C., Lima, L., Henriques, P.R.: An ontology based approach to teach computational thinking. In: Marques, C.G., Pereira, I., Pérez, D. (eds.) 21st International Symposium on Computers in Education (SIIE), pp. 1–6. IEEE Xplore (2019). https://doi.org/10.1109/SIIE48397.2019.8970131
7. Araújo, C., Henriques, P.R., Cerqueira, J.J.: Creating Learning Resources based on Programming concepts. In: Bollin, A., Futschek, G. (eds.) Local Proceedings of the 15th International Conference on Informatics in Schools – ISSEP 2022, pp. 35–46. The Austrian Library Association, open-access net-library, Klagenfurt; Wien, Auatria (2022). https://doi.org/10.48415/2022/issep.2022
8. Araújo, C., Henriques, P.R., Cerqueira, J.J.: Ontocne, characterizing learning resources for training computational thinking. In: 2023 International Symposium on Computers in Education (SIIE), pp. 1–6 (2023). https://doi.org/10.1109/SIIE59826.2023.10423710
9. Barbosa, D.R.: CnE-Ar: teaching of computational thinking to adults in reconversion. Master's thesis, Minho University, Braga, Portugal (2021). MSc dissertation
10. Broadcom: Rabbitmq. https://www.rabbitmq.com
11. Casalnuovo, C., Barr, E.T., Dash, S.K., Devanbu, P., Morgan, E.: A theory of dual channel constraints. In: Proceedings of the ACM/IEEE 42nd International Conference on Software Engineering: New Ideas and Emerging Results, ICSE-NIER 2020, pp. 25–28. Association for Computing Machinery, New York (2020). https://doi.org/10.1145/3377816.3381720

12. Chamberlin, D.D.: Early history of SQL. IEEE Ann. Hist. Comput. **34**, 78–82 (2012). https://doi.org/10.1109/MAHC.2012.61. https://ieeexplore.ieee.org/document/6359709
13. Costa Neto, A., Araújo, C., Pereira, M.J.V., Henriques, P.R.: Programmers' affinity to languages, vol. 91, pp. 1–7. Open Access Series in Informatics (OASIcs), Schloss Dagstuhl - Leibniz-Zentrum für Informatik (2021). https://doi.org/10.4230/OASIcs.ICPEC.2021.3. https://drops.dagstuhl.de/opus/volltexte/2021/14219
14. Costa Neto, A., Pereira, M.J.V., Henriques, P.R.: An ontology to understand programming cocktails. In: Bolanowski, M., Ganzha, M., Maciaszek, L., Paprzycki, M., Ślęzak, D. (eds.) Proceedings of the 19th Conference on Computer Science and Intelligence Systems (FedCSIS). Annals of Computer Science and Information Systems, vol. 39, p. 453–464. IEEE (2024). https://doi.org/10.15439/2024F7885
15. Dias, A.M.C.: ONTODL+, an ontology description language and its compiler. Master's thesis, Minho University, Braga, Portugal (2021). MSc dissertation
16. Dormando: Memcached. https://www.memcached.org
17. Elastic: Elastisearch. https://www.elastic.co/elasticsearch
18. Fenichel, R.R., Weizenbaum, J., Yochelson, J.C.: A program to teach programming. Commun. ACM **13**, 141–146 (1970). https://doi.org/10.1145/362052.362053. https://dl.acm.org/doi/10.1145/362052.362053
19. Figueiredo, J., García-Peñalvo, F.J.: Building skills in introductory programming. In: Proceedings of the Sixth International Conference on Technological Ecosystems for Enhancing Multiculturality, pp. 46–50. ACM, New York (2018). https://doi.org/10.1145/3284179. https://dl.acm.org/doi/10.1145/3284179.3284190
20. Fourment, M., Gillings, M.R.: A comparison of common programming languages used in bioinformatics. BMC Bioinform. **82**(9) (2008). https://doi.org/10.1186/1471-2105-9-82. https://bmcbioinformatics.biomedcentral.com/articles/10.1186/1471-2105-9-82
21. Freitas, T.C., Costa Neto, A., Pereira, M.J.V., Henriques, P.R.: NLP/AI based techniques for programming exercises generation, vol. 104, pp. 1–15. Open Access Series in Informatics (OASIcs), Schloss Dagstuhl - Leibniz-Zentrum für Informatik (2023). https://doi.org/10.4230/OASIcs.SLATE.2022.14. https://drops.dagstuhl.de/opus/volltexte/2022/16760
22. Gomes, A., Mendes, A.J.: Learning to program: difficulties and solutions. In: Proceedings of the 2007 International Conference on Engineering and Education (ICEE), International Network on Engineering Education and Research, pp. 283–287 (2007). http://icee2007.dei.uc.pt/proceedings/papers/411.pdf
23. Gruber, T.R.: A translation approach to portable ontology specifications. Knowl. Acquis. **5**(2), 199–220 (1993)
24. International Organization for Standardization: ISO/IEC/JTC 1/SC 22/WG 23 document register. https://www.open-std.org/JTC1/SC22/WG23/docs/documents
25. Kernighan, B.W., Ritchie, D.M.: C Programming Language, 2 edn. Pearson (1988)
26. Krell, M., Xu, K.M., Rey, G.D., Paas, F.: Editorial: recent approaches for assessing cognitive load from a validity perspective. Front. Educ. **6** (2022). https://doi.org/10.3389/feduc.2021.838422. https://www.frontiersin.org/journals/education/articles/10.3389/feduc.2021.838422
27. de La Salete Teixeira, M.: Adequa, a platform for choosing Games suitable to Students' Profile. Master's thesis, Minho University, Braga, Portugal (2021). MSc dissertation
28. LibSSH: Libssh. https://www.libssh.org

29. Martins, L., Araújo, C., Henriques, P.R.: Digital collection creator, visualizer and explorer. In: Rodrigues, R., Janoušek, J., Ferreira, L., Coheur, L., Batista, F., Oliveira, H.G. (eds.) 8th Symposium on Languages, Applications and Technologies (SLATE 2019). OpenAccess Series in Informatics (OASIcs), vol. 74, p. 15:1–15:8. Schloss Dagstuhl–Leibniz-Zentrum fuer Informatik, Dagstuhl, Germany (2019). https://www.dagstuhl.de/dagpub/978-3-95977-114-6
30. Meta Platforms: React native. https://reactnative.dev
31. MongoDB: Mongodb. https://www.mongodb.com
32. Mozilla Foundation: CSS: Cascading style sheets. https://developer.mozilla.org/en-US/docs/Web/CSS
33. Mozilla Foundation: HTML: Hypertext markup language. https://developer.mozilla.org/en-US/docs/Web/HTML
34. Odeh, A.H.: Analytical and comparison study of main web programming languages: ASP and PHP. TEM J. **8**, 1517–1522 (2019). https://doi.org/10.18421/TEM84-58. http://www.temjournal.com/content/84/TEMJournalNovember2019_1517_1522.pdf
35. Oracle: Mysql. https://www.mysql.com
36. Paas, F., van Merriënboer, J.J.G.: Cognitive-load theory: methods to manage working memory load in the learning of complex tasks. Curr. Dir. Psychol. Sci. **29**(4), 394–398 (2020)
37. Pereira, M.J.V., Henriques, P.R.: Visualization/animation of programs in alma: obtaining different results. In: Proceedings of the IEEE Symposium on Human Centric Computing Languages and Environments, pp. 260–262 (2003). https://doi.org/10.1109/HCC.2003.1260242. https://ieeexplore.ieee.org/document/1260242
38. Piaget, J.: The Psychology of Intelligence, 1 edn, vol. 92. Routledge (2001)
39. Plass, J.L., Homer, B.D., Kinzer, C.K.: Foundations of game-based learning. Educ. Psychol. **50**(4), 258–283 (2015). https://doi.org/10.1080/00461520.2015.1122533
40. Python Foundation: Welcome to python.org (2019). https://www.python.org
41. Robertson, S.A., Lee, M.P.: The application of second natural language acquisition pedagogy to the teaching of programming languages: a research agenda. ACM SIGCSE Bull. **27**(4), 9–12 (1995). https://doi.org/10.1145/216511. https://dl.acm.org/doi/10.1145/216511.216517
42. Santamaria, R.: raylib. https://www.raylib.com
43. Software Freedom Conservancy: Git. https://git-scm.com
44. Studer, R., Benjamins, V.R., Fensel, D.: Knowledge engineering: Principles and methods. Data Knowl. Eng. **25**(1), 161–197 (1998)
45. Sweller, J.: Cognitive load during problem solving: effects on learning. Cogn. Sci. **12**(2), 257–285 (1988)
46. Sweller, J.: Evolution of human cognitive architecture. Psychol. Learn. Motiv. **43**, 215–266 (2003). https://doi.org/10.1016/S0079-7421(03)01015-6. https://www.sciencedirect.com/science/article/pii/S0079742103010156
47. Sweller, J.: Cognitive load theory. Psychol. Learn. Motiv. **55**, 37–76 (2011). https://doi.org/10.1016/B978-0-12-387691-1.00002-8. https://www.sciencedirect.com/science/article/pii/B9780123876911000028
48. Sweller, J., van Merriënboer, J.J.G., Paas, F.: Cognitive architecture and instructional design: 20 years later. Educ. Psychol. Rev. **31**, 261–292 (2019)
49. Tavares, P.C., Gomes, E.M.F., Henriques, P.R.: O Impacto da Animação e da Avaliação Automática na Motivação para o Ensino da Programação. Ph.D. thesis, Minho University, Braga, Portugal (2017)

50. Teixeira, S., Boas, R.V., Oliveira, F., Araújo, C., Henriques, P.R.: Ontojogo: an ontology for game classification. In: 2020 IEEE 8th International Conference on Serious Games and Applications for Health (SeGAH), pp. 1–8. IEEE Xplore, Vancouver, BC, Canada (2020). https://doi.org/10.1109/SeGAH49190.2020.9201876
51. Teixeira, S.A.: Automatic grading of programming exercises. Master's thesis, Minho University, Braga, Portugal (2023, to be published)
52. The JUnit Team: Junit. https://junit.org
53. Unity Technologies: Unity real-time development platform. https://unity.com
54. Vasconcelos, P.: Haskelite: a step-by-step interpreter for teaching functional programming, vol. 104, pp. 1–15. Open Access Series in Informatics (OASIcs), Schloss Dagstuhl - Leibniz-Zentrum für Informatik (2023). https://doi.org/10.4230/OASIcs.SLATE.2022.14. https://drops.dagstuhl.de/opus/volltexte/2022/16760
55. W3C: Web ontology language (OWL). https://www.w3.org/OWL/
56. Walia, N., Kalia, A.: Programming languages for data mining: a review. Int. J. Comput. Trends Technol. **68**, 38–41 (2020). https://doi.org/10.14445/22312803/IJCTT-V68I1P109. https://ijcttjournal.org/archives/ijctt-v68i1p109
57. Wilson, B.C., Shrock, S.: Contributing to success in an introductory computer science course: a study of twelve factors. In: Proceedings of the 32nd SIGCSE Technical Symposium on Computer Science Education, pp. 184–188. Association for Computing Machinery (2001). https://doi.org/10.1145/364447.364581. https://dl.acm.org/doi/10.1145/364447.364581

S3E'24 – Thematic Session on Model Driven Approaches in System Development (MDASD)

Improve the Design Workflow of Hardware Engineers Using a Textual DSL With Immediate Graphical Feedback

Twan Bolwerk[1,2](✉), Marco Alonso[2], and Mathijs Schuts[1,2]

[1] Philips, Best, The Netherlands
{twan.bolwerk,mathijs.schuts}@philips.com
[2] Radboud University, Nijmegen, The Netherlands
marco.alonso@philips.com

Abstract. Cyber-Physical Systems are designed and developed using multi-disciplinary teams that require handovers from one discipline to another. These handovers often involve text documents written in natural language, which can be imprecise, ambiguous, and lead to errors. To address this issue, we created a textual Domain Specific Language with immediate graphical feedback. This language allows mechanical and mechatronic engineers to communicate more effectively during handovers by providing a formalized system description that can be easily visualized in real-time. Our approach also incorporates multiple industry standards, which enables bi-directional navigation between languages, making it easier for teams to collaborate across different disciplines and prevent errors from being made. We applied and evaluated our approach in relation to medical robots at Philips IGT.

Keywords: Domain Specific Language · DSL · Industry Case · Multi-disciplinary · Graphical Feedback · Medical Robots

1 Introduction

A Cyber-Physical System (CPS) [4] is a complex system composed of both hardware and software components. These systems are designed and developed with multi-disciplinary teams. Often, a CPS consists of moving parts such as in the case of robots, cars, airplanes, etc. For the hardware component development, mechanical and mechatronics engineers are involved. The mechanical engineer creates 3D models of the physical components using a Computer Aided Design (CAD) tool [38] and performs measurements, i.e., on weight and tolerances. The mechatronics engineer makes these physical systems move by creating control solutions using tools such as Matlab and Simulink [26]. Both disciplines use their own specialized software tools. Currently, the workflow involves manually written documents that are used to handover designs and measurement information from the mechanical engineer to the mechatronics engineer. Due to the informal nature of these documents, they can be imprecise, ambiguous, and prone to errors. Additionally, changes between document versions may go unnoticed.

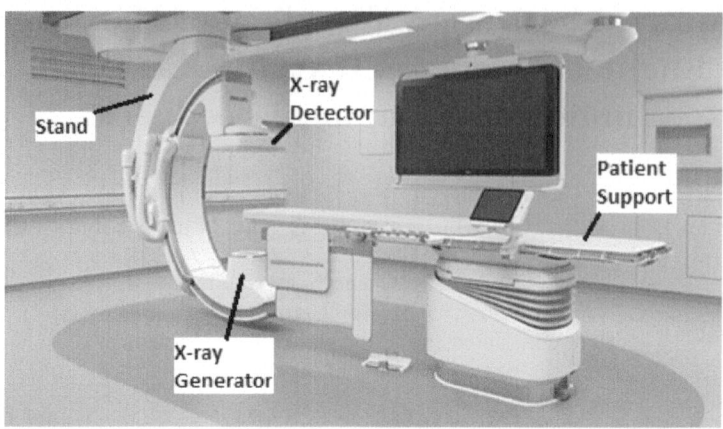

Fig. 1. Interventional X-ray system

At Philips IGT, we create interventional X-ray systems such as the Azurion system in Fig. 1, which are used for minimally invasive procedures. These large medical robots feature motorized moving parts that can be operated using joysticks [35].

In this paper, we present an improved workflow for the development of these CPSs. After a mechanical component has been modelled using a CAD tool, the mechanical engineer can export the 3D model in the Unified Robot Description Format (URDF) [21], which is based on eXtensible Markup Language (XML) [8]. However, one downside of URDF is that weights and tolerances are not included, and cannot be added. Additionally, it lacks an import mechanism for reusing components across similar robots. These limitations can be addressed using the XML macro language (Xacro) [2], which requires manual editing to add weights and tolerances. Both formats are in XML, which is not a user-friendly way of editing. Furthermore, we place these files in a version controlled system, but merging XML-based files is challenging.

This paper introduces an improved workflow and tool enhancements aimed at overcoming these challenges. We created a textual Domain Specific Language (DSL) [12] called Geometry Specific Language (GSL) or GeometrySL. The language extends Xacro but is not based on XML. Instances of this language are placed in a version controlled system and handed over from mechanical engineers to mechatronics engineers. By using formal GSL files instead of informal documents, we reduce the likelihood of errors due to handovers. The GSL provides immediate live graphical feedback when editing the textual instance, showing which part is being edited within the robot's 3D model. It also has facilities for graphically comparing two versions of a robot, highlighting parts that are different in a 3D model. Additionally, it supports bi-directional navigation from a graphical part to the corresponding DSL fragments and vice versa. This allows seamless navigation between graphical views, URDF instances, Xacro instances, GSL instances, and back again using shortcuts.

To the best of our knowledge, the novelty of this research lies in the creation of the GSL, a DSL that defines how differences between robot representations are visualized. By leveraging multiple languages, including industry standards like Xacro and URDF, this approach enables bi-directional navigation and offers a unique method for visualizing differences in robot descriptions. This paper is an extended version of a conference paper [7]. Compared to the conference version, we present new capabilities in the tool, including a graphical side-by-side view of robot models.

In addition, a detailed evaluation of the new workflow has been conducted with mechatronic engineers at Philips IGT. This evaluation provides insights into how the tool performs in real-world applications and its impact on productivity and collaboration.

This version of the paper discusses the research conducted to establish an effective evaluation framework. By reviewing related work on tool and workflow assessment, we used a combination of existing methodologies for evaluating the new tool.

Also comprehensive comparison of the old and new workflows is presented. This discussion highlights the advantages of the new approach, including reduced reliance on XML editing, improved usability, and better support for version control systems.

By addressing these aspects, this paper provides an overview of the new workflow and its impact on CPS development. The proposed improvements aim to reduce engineering bottlenecks, enhance collaboration, and enable a more intuitive design process for large medical robots.

The paper is organized as follows. In Sect. 2, we provide an overview of related work on technology. We describe the current and proposed workflows in more detail in Sect. 3. The GSL, Xacro and URDF languages are presented in Sect. 4. Section 5 describes the design of the tool. The resulting tool is shown in Sect. 6. In Sect. 7, we describe our evaluation approach and in Sect. 8, we evaluate our tool. Discussion is in Sect. 9. In this section, we also discuss how our work is related to the work of others. And we conclude our paper in Sect. 10.

2 Related Work

Shen et al. [37] categorized recent studies on DSL based on three concerns: concrete syntax, abstract syntax and semantics. They analyzed the parsing and mapping strategies of these studies to classify them into categories such as external/internal, textual/graphical, modeling/visualizing/embedding. This study aims to address research gaps in DSL categorization. The vertical axis of Fig. 2 lists literature references while horizontal axis list the following categories:

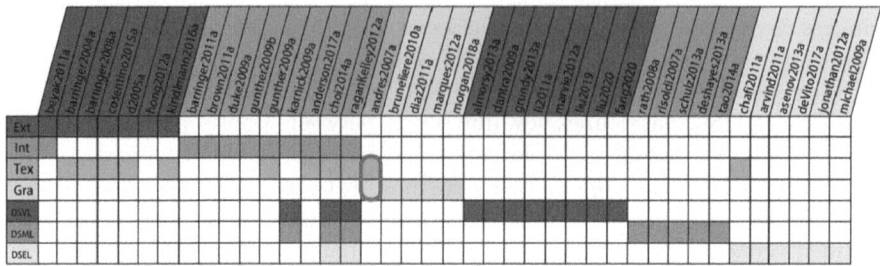

Fig. 2. DSL categories from [37].

- **External (Ext):** Standalone languages with their own syntax and grammar, distinct from any host language, providing specific solutions within a particular domain.
- **Internal (Int):** Embedded within an existing general-purpose programming language, leveraging the host language's syntax and features to implement domain specific constructs.
- **Textual (Tex):** Use text-based syntax, similar to traditional programming languages, designed for domain experts familiar with coding or scripting.
- **Graphical (Gra):** Employ visual representations such as diagrams and flowcharts to define domain specific constructs, useful for users preferring visual over textual representation.
- **Domain Specific Visual Language (DSVL):** A subset of graphical DSLs using specialized visual notations to represent domain concepts, facilitating understanding and communication among stakeholders.
- **Domain Specific Modeling Language (DSML):** Focus on creating models specific to a domain using specialized syntax and semantics, providing tools for simulation, validation, and code generation.
- **Domain Specific Embedded Language (DSEL):** A type of internal DSL embedding domain specific constructs within a host language, integrating domain specific functionality directly into general-purpose language code.

The figure features a red box highlighting the scarcity of research focused on Gra and Tex DSL combinations. While enabling live graphical feedback reduces cognitive load, improves collaboration and communication in engineering projects. This study bridges computing science and behavioral research domains to improve DSL design with live graphical feedback for better communication and collaboration in complex engineering projects.

To visualize property changes in language instances, we need to consider their visibility. Munzner's book [24] recommends automatic highlighting with varied colors, shapes, or positions can emphasize distinctions between properties. The "pop-out" effect in Munzner's book helps users spot differences quickly without focused attention.

In [16], Joshua Horowitz et al. define programming qualities. The focus is on immediate feedback (liveness), domain specific editing (richness) and composability. Composability enables the inclusion of external libraries or components, separating responsibilities over multiple sources. Programming tasks often require using multiple composed tools, so effects should be visible with minimal distraction and effort. Liveness and richness often fail to retain their composability according to Horowitz et al. conclusion. They identified a trend where interfaces lacking composability are standalone applications that offer limited utility in practice. This research explores the intersection of liveness, richness and composability by adhering to these qualities using familiarity with 3D graphical tools for hardware-engineers' workflow improvement and tool intuitiveness enhancement.

Van Rozen et al. [33] recognized the need for program execution observation in traditional programming, which requires re-execution of updated source code from the beginning. This process is time-consuming and distracting when valuable states are lost or difficult to reproduce. To address these challenges, they propose a more fluid and live experience in programming using Textual Model Diff (TMDiff) [30]. Tmdiff uses two key techniques: origin tracking (tracing semantic model elements back to their defining source code) and text differencing (identifying corresponding model elements when aligned names have the same origin). The deltas found by TMDiff are converted into run-time edit operations, which can be applied atomically using rmpatch. Custom state migrations extend rmpatch to avoid information loss or invalid run-time states. Events like user interactions and changes in source code are recorded for undo functionality, persistent application state and back-in-time debugging. They evaluated existing methods (Xtext and EMFCompare) using Eclipse Modeling Framework (EMF) and found TMDiff's scope-handling ability more flexible. Their goal is to minimize distractions and preserve intermediate visual state for a smoother programming experience.

In [11], Cooper et al. present requirements and challenges to integrate graphical editors using Sirius within EMF. They note that while Sirius allows creation of custom modeling editors, it has a steep learning curve. To address this limitation, they propose five requirements for a hybrid textual-graphical workbench: syntax-aware editing, scoping and referencing, rename refactoring, error/warning marker display and accessibility to the textual model. These requirements aim to improve productivity, reduce errors and facilitate collaboration by providing seamless integration between graphical and textual models. Their proposed solution aligns with a case study on hybrid modelling workbenches.

A DSML for UML profiles was created by combining Papyrus and Xtext using EMF. One unique feature is shared storage base for both textual and graphical views, reducing synchronization efforts. The tool is tested their by four scenarios (Create1, Modify1, Create2, Modify2) with experienced developers in the UML language. Results showed that creating elements and setting properties were faster in textual notation while constructing state machines was quicker in the graphical view. Renaming operations were faster in textual mode due to regex search and replace efficiency. The hybrid solution was superior in efficiency, doubling the speed in mentioned scenarios. This demonstrates potential of combined graphical-textual approach for DSMLs [1].

In game development, rapid adjustments of rules are made using tools like Machinations[1]. Van Rozen et al. created a DSL called Micro-Machinations (MM) using the tool Rascal [29] to balance games. MM allows for direct visualization model editing, shortening feedback loops and reducing design iteration times by improving flexibility and adaptability. The Rascal Language WorkBench (LWB) with SPIN model checker [5] is used for analyzing MM, providing an IDE that reads textual MM and displays a visual model interactively. The MM Lib is embedded in the game itself to tackle interoperability, traceability and debugging challenges [41]. An immediate feedback loop greatly improves multi-disciplinary team collaboration in gaming domain similar to engineering domains.

Perez et al. [27] created DSVL using both textual and graphical views with AToM tool[2]. They followed meta-model centric approach where EBNF grammar was generated based on the meta-model, allowing decision to be made later whether to use graphical or textual syntax. Another issue is that produced Abstract Syntax Tree (AST) from parsing is not formally defined causing problems in integration with multi-view DSL proposed by them. They noticed that it is more natural to describe equations in a textual notation.

A more extensive version of this work can be found in [6].

3 Workflow

In this section, we describe the current workflow of hardware engineers at Philips IGT and we propose a new improved workflow. The workflow involves two actors: mechanical engineers and mechatronics engineers.

3.1 Current Workflow

The workflow process follows a waterfall approach, where mechanical engineers measure the system in the factory. These measurements are then communicated via various Office tools to mechatronics engineers. The tools used by these actors are depicted in Fig. 3 and illustrate their interactions. The interactions between the tools can occur either automatically, with data being stored or transferred automatically between tools, or manually inputted by the user.

We describe the actions per actor:

- Mechanical engineer. The mechanical engineer creates the hardware design of the system using the CREO[3] tool for opening and editing 3D CAD files. They also measure the real-world properties of the system, perform calculations in Excel and document any changes compared to the original CAD model using Word. These updates are presented via PowerPoint [36].
- Mechatronic engineer. The mechatronic engineer manually compares previous measurements saved as Matlab instances with the changed properties

---

[1] https://machinations.io/.
[2] http://atom3.cs.mcgill.ca/.
[3] https://www.ptc.com/en/products/creo/.

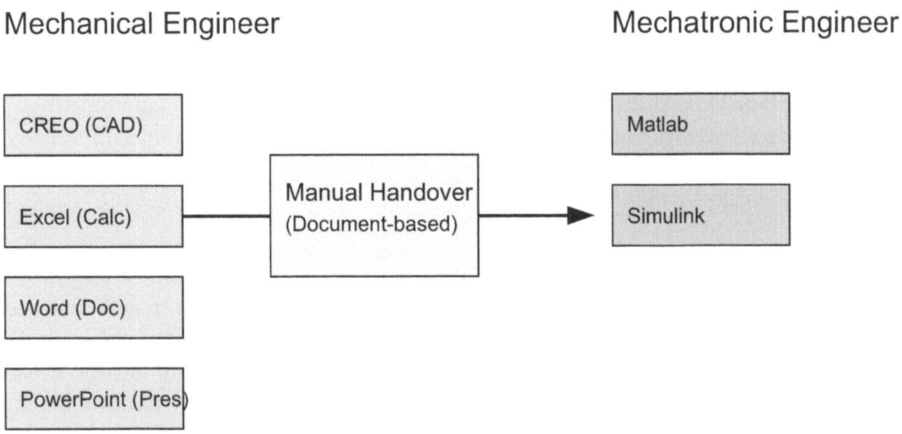

Mechanical Engineer Mechatronic Engineer

Fig. 3. Tools and actors

recorded in CAD and Excel to determine if the system still meets the specifications. For example, they ensure that the system adheres to the predefined tolerances for each link[4]. These assessments are crucial for maintaining the system's performance and reliability, and are calculated using complex calculations and simulations in Matlab and Simulink [45].

In sum, the handover from the mechanical engineer to the mechatronics engineer currently relies on informal document-based communication. This can result in misunderstandings and potential errors due to missed changes or ambiguities.

3.2 Proposed Workflow

In the proposed workflow, all Microsoft Office tools are replaced by Domain Specific Modelling (DSM) [13] using a single Geometry Specification Language (GSL) with live graphical feedback. It replaces the Microsoft Office tools by a unified language capable of presenting changes, serving as documentation and evaluating mathematical expressions that can be used to describe and calculate properties.

By eliminating the reliance on Microsoft Office tools and therefore multiple sources of truth, the complexity associated with using these tools is reduced. This can be observed in Fig. 4 compared to Fig. 3.

A CAD file can be converted into URDF which we are able to translate to our own DSL. The mechanical engineer can input measurements manually in an expressive manner similar to an Excel spreadsheet but now in the GSL. Meanwhile, the mechatronic engineer can compare previous measurements stored in the single source of truth DSL which is stored within Philips' version control system. Using a textual DSL makes, i.e., merging branches easy.

---

[4] A link in robotics refers to a rigid component that forms part of a robot's structure, connecting to other links through joints.

3.3 Use Cases

In this section, we describe two main use cases. One involves presenting the textual DSL in a graphical manner and another focuses on visualizing differences between two versions of the DSL in a graphical representation. Differences between robot models can be visualized either by highlighting specific changes or through a side-by-side comparison.

Present. The first use case demonstrates effective communication of measurement changes between mechanical and mechatronic engineers. It serves as a visual representation tool, enabling the presentation of changes through visualization. By hovering over the textual representation using the cursor as a pointer, the view automatically focuses on the specific physical link of the robot being hovered over. This visualization feature enhances communication by clearly highlighting and displaying the changes made to each physical link of the robot. It provides a seamless and intuitive way for stakeholders to understand and interpret updated measurements for every physical link in the robot.

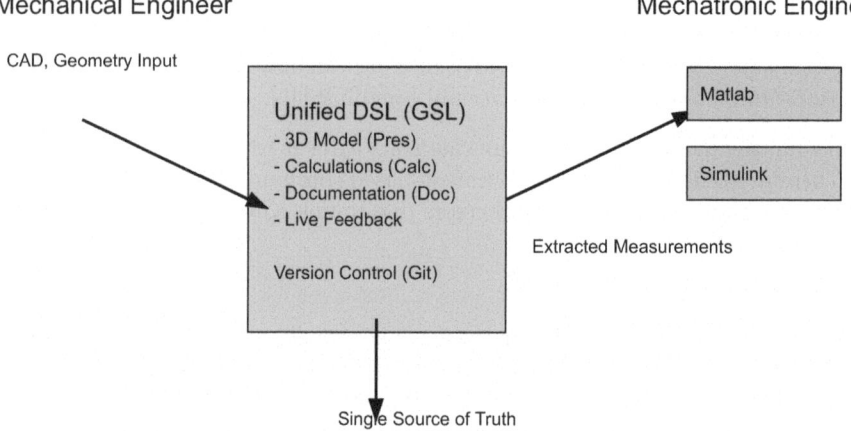

Fig. 4. Actors and tools workflow with DSL.

The mechanical engineer can efficiently navigate, inspect, and present the robot's hardware properties using the tool's textual and graphical representations. This use case showcases how engineers can leverage the tool's features to communicate and demonstrate the robot's hardware-properties.

Highlight. The highlight use case offers an efficient solution for mechatronic engineers to automatically identify and highlight changed physical links between robot or component versions. This internal scenario eliminates the need for manual input of values into Matlab, as it leverages automatic highlighting and live graphical feedback. Engineers can quickly and accurately pinpoint variations between link versions using this feature, reducing reliance on manual comparisons and potential errors.

Side-by-Side. The side-by-side view provides users with greater control by allowing them to visually detect changes such as variations in the color and size of links. This approach makes differences graphically more apparent compared to highlighting, which merely indicates where a change has occurred without offering a clear visual representation.

4 Languages

In this section, we introduce the Language WorkBench (LWB) used to implement our tool as needed in order to understand this paper. We describe the URDF, Xacro and GSL languages. Finally, we provide example instances of these three languages.

4.1 Language Workbench

A LWB provide concepts and mechanisms to define language syntax, semantics, and code generation for a language. They facilitate model-driven engineering by allowing developers and domain experts to work with high-level abstractions that closely resemble the specific problem domain. This can lead to more efficient development processes, maintainable code, and closer collaboration between different stakeholders. LWBs bridge the gap between generalized programming languages and the unique requirements of specialized domains [9].

There are many language workbenches (LWBs) available. Both Eclipse Modeling Framework (EMF) and Rascal[5] are used at Philips; however, Rascal provides support for Visual Studio Code (VS Code). Given that VS Code[6] is the preferred tool at Philips and aligns with our previous experience using Rascal, we decided to use it for our tool.

Rascal [19] is a type-safe programming language featuring immutable data, built-in pattern matching, search, and relational calculus. It is a functional and procedural programming language with Java-like syntax. We introduce the language in this section as needed to understand the code fragments presented in this paper. The code snippets in Listing 1.1 are reused from [34].

```
1 loc l =
2   |file:///Users/kees/.bashrc|(100,20,<2,0>,<2,20>)
3
4 data Boolean = true() | false() | and(Boolean lhs,
5   Boolean rhs);
6 //extending Boolean with another constructor
7 data Boolean = or(Boolean lhs, Boolean rhs);
```

---

[5] https://www.rascal-mpl.org.
[6] https://code.visualstudio.com.

```
 8 data Statement = \if(Expression c, Statement tt,
 9   Statement ff);
10
11 for (int i <- [1 .. 5]) println(i);
12
13 str w = "world"
14 println("Hello, <w>!");          //prints "Hello, world!"
```
Listing 1.1. Rascal code fragments

Rascal has numerical types such as int and booleans, represented by bool. It supports polymorphic lists, maps for collections and loc for location constants. Rascal also provides the following built-in functions for working with maps:

1. Map := A list that uses any kind of data as index (called keys), to store a value.
2. rangeR := Expects a map and returns a map of key, value pairs that match the values.
3. range := Returns a list of values.
4. domain := Returns a list of keys.

On Line 2 there is a constant loc that points to a file with the file scheme and selects the part on line 2 between the left margin and the 20th column. Locations are used to refer to files, store information extracted from files and help in referring back to source locations.

In Rascal, Algebraic Data Types (ADTs) can be user-defined with their constructor functions. The fragment on Lines 4–9 shows a declaration of an ADT for the representation of Boolean expressions using three constructors. The next line extends the same ADT by adding an alternative to the existing declaration. Reserved keywords are not permitted as names of algebraic constructors; hence, if is escaped with \if when used as the name of an algebraic constructor.

Control structures such as for can be used to iterate over a value, while str literals in Rascal are not delimited by line endings.

We utilized the following two Rascal libraries: Salix and TypePal. Salix is a library that facilitates the development of web-based GUI programs; it runs user code on the server side instead of client-side execution. The library employs the Model View Controller (MVC) pattern by sending HTML patches to the browser and interpreting messages from the browser on the server to update the view accordingly. TypePal is a typechecking and validator library for Rascal, designed to analyze and enforce type constraints, ensuring correct usage of types and detecting potential type-related errors in DSL instances. TypePal provides static type checking capabilities and can be used to improve the reliability and correctness of language instances [40].

4.2 URDF

Utilizing URDF offers numerous advantages, notably its capability to express a wide range of hardware properties, with the exception of tolerances. Moreover,

URDF facilitates seamless conversion from formats like CAD files, streamlining the integration of engineering disciplines for our use case. Furthermore, the compatibility of URDF with visualization tools such as RViz[7] underscores its ability in conveying essential information using a 3D graphical representation.

The downside of URDF is its inability to scale and its cumbersome XML format, which is difficult to maintain and causes issues in the archiving system when merging changes. As the model becomes more complex, the lack of reusable components results in larger file sizes.

4.3 Xacro

To address the issue of large URDF files, especially for complex 3D robot models like interventional X-ray systems, a solution based on modularization and composition using the Xacro language can be employed. Xacro provides a way to create modular and reusable components, making robot descriptions more manageable and organized.

Although Xacro simplifies URDF composition and introduces expression evaluation, it still relies on an XML format that is neither user-friendly nor intuitive, making it difficult to version control and prone to merging issues.

4.4 GeometrySL

To overcome the previously described limitations, we introduce GeometrySL (GSL), which extends XacroSL. GeometrySL encapsulates Xacro and converts it to a more user-friendly syntax, making it easier to archive and merge changes. It enabled the creation of a more intuitive syntax that supports custom property definitions (including tolerances) and provides enhanced visualization options. The aim is to offer a more intuitive, flexible language for 3D robot modeling, addressing the drawbacks associated with traditional XML-based URDF descriptions.

Creating GeometrySL adds flexibility in defining and designing custom syntax, making it more intuitive to use and easier to extend with new semantics and introduce custom properties, enhancing its expressiveness and adaptability for different use cases.

One of these new use cases is the integration of visual semantics. This allows mechanical engineers to describe desired appearances of views using a language that engineers can understand. This approach enables better collaboration by providing live graphical feedback.

4.5 Example Instances

Next, we will describe three features using language instances–custom features, modular includes, and highlighting differences between two robot versions. Due

---
[7] http://wiki.ros.org/rviz.

to confidentiality concerns, we use Franka's Panda robot[8] as an example instead of our interventional X-ray system.

```
1  robot {
2    link {
3      name="lbr_iiwa_link_0"
4      inertial {
5        origin := {
6          rpy="0 0 0"
7          xyz="-0.1 0 0.07"
8        }
9        mass := { value="0.2" }
10       tolerance := { value="200" }
11       inertia := {
12         ixx="0.05"
13         ixy="1"
14         ixz="0"
15         iyy="0.06"
16         iyz="0"
17         izz="0.03"
18       }
19     }
20     visual {
21       origin := {
22         rpy="0 0 0"
23         xyz="0.2 0.1 0"
24       }
25       geometry {
26         mesh := { filename="meshes/link_0.stl" }
27       }
28     }
29     collision {
30       origin := {
31         rpy="0 0 0"
32         xyz="0 0 0"
33       }
34       geometry {
35         mesh := { filename="meshes/link_0.stl" }
36       }
37     }
38   }
39 }
```

Listing 1.2. GeometrySL instance example

Listing 1.2 shows an example of GeometrySL for the Panda robot, demonstrating how to define a link. A link has a name and various features such as inertial, visual, and collision properties. Inside the inertial feature, we added a custom property called "tolerance". This property can be exported to Xacro

---
[8] https://support.franka.de/docs/franka_ros.html.

but not to URDF. The instance also references STereo Lithography (STL) files, which is a format used to describe 3D objects using triangles.

```
robot {
  name="lbr_iiwa"
  xmlns:xacro="http://www.ros.org/wiki/xacro"
  include "lbr_iiwa_link_0.gsl"
  ...
  include "lbr_iiwa_link_7.gsl"

  include "lbr_iiwa_joint_1.gsl"
  ...
  include "lbr_iiwa_joint_7.gsl"
}
```

Listing 1.3. GeometrySL instance example for modular includes

In Listing 1.3, an instance of GeometrySL is shown that describes the Panda robot. It includes other instances of GeometrySL to describe links and joints of the Panda robot. A link is represented as a mesh, while a joint defines the relation between exactly two joints.

```
<?xml version="1.0"?>
<robot name ="lbr_iiwa"
  xmlns:xacro="http://www.ros.org/wiki/xacro" >
<xacro:property name ="color" value ="Green"/>
<xacro:property name ="half" value ="0.1"/>
<xacro:include filename
  ="lbr_iiwa_link_0.gsl.xacro"/>
...
<xacro:include filename
  ="lbr_iiwa_link_7.gsl.xacro"/>

<xacro:include filename
  ="lbr_iiwa_joint_1.gsl.xacro"/>
...
<xacro:include filename
  ="lbr_iiwa_joint_7.gsl.xacro"/>
</robot>
```

Listing 1.4. Xacro instance example for modular includes

Listing 1.4 shows an example of how to represent the same information from Listing 1.3 in the Xacro language. It uses XML syntax instead.

```
<?xml version="1.0" ?>
<robot name="lbr_iiwa">
  <link name="lbr_iiwa_link_0">
    <inertial>
      <origin rpy="0 0 0" xyz="-0.1 0 0.07"/>
      <mass value="0.2"/>
      <inertia ixx="0.05" ixy="1" ixz="0"
```

```
8          iyy="0.06" iyz="0" izz="0.03"/>
9        </inertial>
10       <visual>
11         <origin rpy="0 0 0" xyz="0.2 0.1 0"/>
12         <geometry>
13           <mesh filename="meshes/link_0.stl"/>
14         </geometry>
15         <material name="Grey"/>
16       </visual>
17       <collision>
18         <origin rpy="0 0 0" xyz="0 0 0"/>
19         <geometry>
20           <mesh filename="meshes/link_0.stl"/>
21         </geometry>
22       </collision>
23     </link>
24     ...
25     <link name="lbr_iiwa_link_7">
26       ...
27     </link>
28     <joint name="lbr_iiwa_joint_1" type="revolute">
29       <parent link="lbr_iiwa_link_0"/>
30       <child link="lbr_iiwa_link_1"/>
31       <origin rpy="0 0 0" xyz="0 0 0.1575"/>
32       <axis xyz="1 0 1"/>
33       <limit effort="300" lower="-2.96705972839"
34         upper="2.96705972839" velocity="10"/>
35       <dynamics damping="0.5"/>
36     </joint>
37     ...
38     <joint name="lbr_iiwa_joint_7" type="revolute">
39       ...
40     </joint>
41 </robot>
```

Listing 1.5. URDF instance example for expanded Xacro instance

Listing 1.5 shows an example of how to represent the same information as Listing 1.4 using URDF syntax instead. It includes expanded information from Listing 1.2, but does not include the "tolerance" property that was present in GeometrySL and Xacro.

```
1 highlight
2   robot "robot_v1.gsl"
3 difference
4   robot "robot_v2.gsl"
```

Listing 1.6. GeometrySL instance example for highlighting differences for two versions of a robot

Listing 1.6 demonstrates a language instance of GeometrySL that visually shows the differences between two versions of the robot.

```
1  compare
2    robot "robot_v1.gsl"
3  with
4    robot "robot_v2.gsl"
```

Listing 1.7. GeometrySL instance example for compare with for two versions of a robot

Listing 1.7 shows a language instance of GeometrySL that will show both robot instances side-by-side.

5 Design

In this section, we describe how we realized the use cases presented in Sect. 3.

5.1 Conversion Tool

One of the benefits of using URDF, a widely adopted and standardized format is that other tools often have conversion features. For instance, the Blender tool[9] can be utilized as an intermediary that enables conversion from CAD export files into URDF. Blender is open-source, has free licensing, and it has widespread community support. This not only makes Blender cost-effective but also ensures that the tool is consistently updated and improved by a global community of developers.

5.2 VS Code URDF Viewer

The VS Code URDF viewer[10] was utilized as the starting point, which incorporates BabylonJS[11], a JavaScript 3D graphics library. This library can load STL files and assemble them using URDF. However, it lacks certain features such as comparing changed properties, highlighting differences, bi-directional navigation and side-by-side views, and maintaining state after changes. Additionally, it requires the use of URDF, which has a non-user-friendly syntax and leads to large file sizes when designing systems like interventional X-ray systems. Nonetheless, despite these limitations, the VS Code URDF viewer serves as a beneficial starting point.

The visualization is extended with a context menu. The view's context menu enhances user experience by enabling the identification of links through right-click actions, revealing a menu that displays the link's name, depicted in Fig. 6. This visual representation establishes a direct connection between the textual and visual physical links of the robot, improving cohesiveness and comprehension of both representations.

The sliders facilitate joint movement, enhancing the view by providing an interactive experience. While primarily focused on static properties, this feature

---

[9] https://www.blender.org/.
[10] https://github.com/javahacks/vscode-urdf-viewer.
[11] https://www.babylonjs.com/.

can greatly improve the visualization of specific links. Furthermore, the "reload" and "auto" buttons play a vital role in updating the view with the latest changes made in the GSL textual editor, whether through manual input or automatic updates.

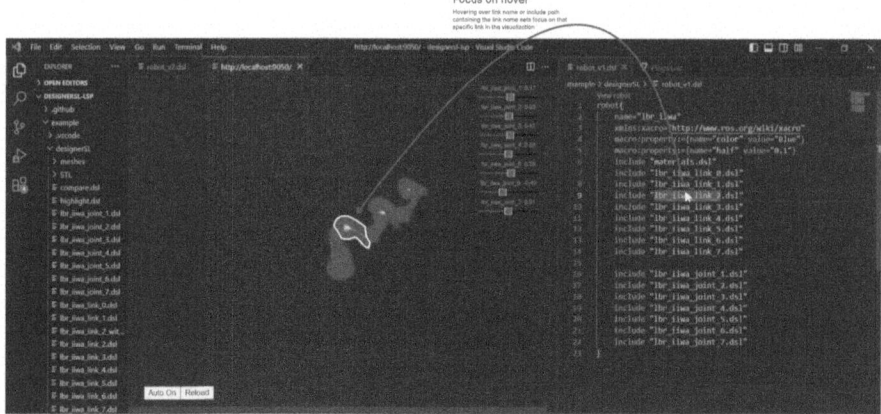

Fig. 5. Focus on hover link

5.3 Show Differences Between Robot Versions

The next use case is showing differences between two robot versions. When the GSL instances are defined as the corresponding physical links of the robot are displayed as solid while the remaining links become transparent, offering a visual distinction.

Listing 1.6 provides a GSL instance to compare two robot versions. In Fig. 6, we show the same GSL instance on the right and on the link we have the graphical view with differences.

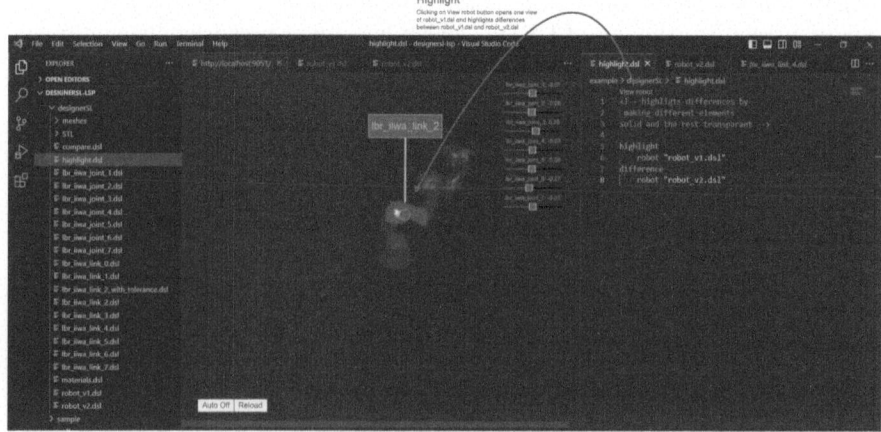

Fig. 6. Highlight robot

5.4 Present Robot

The first use case we are going to describe is how we present the robot. The conversion tool has been executed and the VS Code URDF viewer is running. Salix is utilized to present the robot by a polling feature that performs an action over a specified interval as short as one second. Although this feature may impose certain performance overhead, it helps our language to fulfill the "liveness" quality criteria by consistently checking for differences and updating the view accordingly. A toggle button labeled "auto" is provided, as shown in Fig. 5, which allows users to enable or disable the polling feature. This functionality offers a option to conserve system resources. With polling enabled the automatic updates are enabled, thus allowing for immediate feedback.

Upon detection of any discrepancy, a message with the updated model is send to our viewer which runs on a separate webserver thread. Rather than refreshing the complete web-view, the web-server can update the visualization gradually. This ensures that the robot is always maintained in the view during these gradual updates, reducing distractions from changing visual context. This feature enhances the user experience by providing a seamless transition during updates and maintaining continuity in the visualization.

Each time the user changes the source code and then saves the source code, a Rascal "summarize" event is triggered. In this event we set a flag to true, the polling mechanism that runs on a separate web-server thread then sends a HTTP message to our viewer. The viewer is equipped with a so-called listener (hooks) which update the visualization while preserving state. This significantly reduces distraction of reloading graphics and therefore improving usability.

The "polling" mechanism is used to focus on an element that is hovered over by the mouse. This improves the user's understanding of where the user is in source code. The focus mechanism sets the camera focus on that specific element and marks the element with a specific outline color as shown in Fig. 5.

In this approach, a custom Xacro parser has been developed to convert Xacro code into GeometrySL. The shell "exec" function from Rascal is leveraged to call the Xacro compiler.

5.5 Tool's Components Diagram

The component diagram in Fig. 7 illustrates the software components and their relationships.

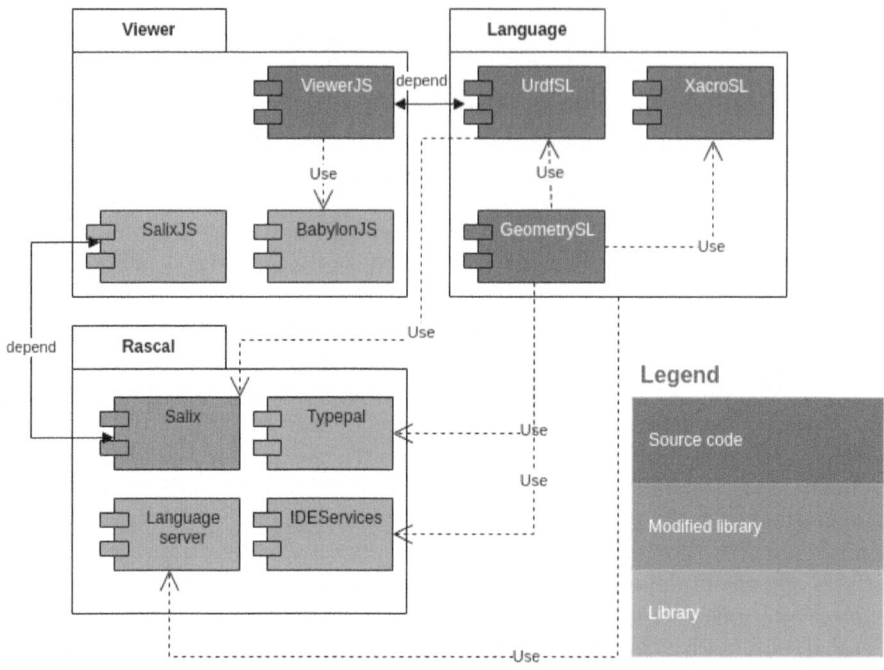

Fig. 7. Components.

Each component shown in Fig. 7 is mapped to its respective responsibility in Table 1.

Table 1. Responsibility per component

Component	Responsibility
ViewerJS and UrdfSL	Visualization of robots and changes
Babylon JS	3D visualization
SalixJS and Salix	Bi-directional navigation
TypePal	Checking path existence and navigation
LanguageServer	Integration with the IDE, using events (summarize, document, lenses)
IDEServices	Opening files in the IDE or opening interactive content
XacroSL	Expression evaluation and resolving include path, using Xacro
GeometrySL	Providing visual semantics and URDF conversion

5.6 Link Origin Tracing

In our work, we trace link origin throughout the transformation process from GeometrySL to Xacro and finally to URDF, and vice versa. This approach draws inspiration from Inostroza et al. [17], where they track string origins during transformations. However, our adaptation involves storing origin locations from physical links of the robot instead of strings and preserving this information across three transformations instead of one. This feature enables seamless navigation between the URDF source, GSL instance, and graphical representation of the robot model. As demonstrated previously, hovering over textual elements triggers the graphical element to be highlighted with a white outline. When holding down the Ctrl-key and clicking on a visual element, the user is directed to the corresponding section in the URDF source code. Conversely, clicking on a visual element without holding down Ctrl-key directs the user to the corresponding section in the GSL instance. With this approach bi-directional navigation is created. Upon hovering over text, the camera dynamically adjusts to center the active link, enhancing visual focus. When clicking on the link, a text editor is triggered, displaying the corresponding element's description for detailed examination. The tracing of robot link elements is chosen because links contain the visually represented graphical mesh, allowing for bi-directional navigation with the graphical representation.

By re-using the shared abstract data structure of Xacro, the compatibility with Xacro is maintained and the development time of GeometrySL is reduced. The shared data structure, illustrated in Listing 1.8, encapsulates both Xacro and GeometrySL and is located in the Shared folder of the class diagram.

```
data Id_ = id(str id);

data XACRO_Attribute = attribute(Id_ \type, str val)
  | xacro_attribute(Id_ \type1, Id_ \type2, str val);

data XACRO_Object = ... // irrelevant alternatives omitted
  | link(Id_ name,
      list [XACRO_Attribute] attributes,
      list [XACRO_Object] elements,
      loc origin=|unknown:///|); // link origin tracing

data XACRO = robot__(list[XACRO_Attribute] attributes,
    list [XACRO_Object] elements,
    loc origin=|unknown:///|); // link origin tracing
```

Listing 1.8. Shared XACRO datastructure

An important point to highlight in Listing 1.8 is that all objects and attributes are generic, allowing for easy extension of new robot property semantics such as tolerances. However, in order to support bi-directional navigation a more concrete data structure is needed. The link is specifically specified to incorporate storing origin locations.

```
tuple[XACRO_Object,
  map[str,XACRO]] translate(Object obj,
    map[str,XACRO] includes){
  <xacro_obj,includes> = translate(obj.\type, obj, includes);
  if (xacro_obj.\type.id == "link") {
    name = get(l.attributes, "name");
    return <link(id(name),
      xacro_obj.attributes,
      xacro_obj.elements,
      origin=obj@\loc), // keep track of link location
      includes>;
  }
  return <xacro_obj, includes>;
}
```

Listing 1.9. GeometrySL::Semantics

By opting for this generic data structure, it accommodates all valid XML formats, enabling the parsing and semantic translation of custom properties. However, a trade-off of this approach is that specific tasks like determining link origins requires iterating through all, as illustrated in Listing 1.11. Furthermore, the semantics of the generic data structure do not verify the validity of elements, accepting all inputs, whereas the UrdfSL semantics, as depicted in the Appendix' Listing 1.14, are more specific and restrictive.

```
map[str,loc] linkLocationMap = ();

map[str, loc] gatherLinkLocation(map[str,XACRO] xacros)
{
  map[str, loc] result = ();
  for (key <- xacros){
    result += gatherLinkLocation(xacros[key]);
  }
  return result;
}

map[str,loc] gatherLinkLocation(XACRO xacro){
  map[str, loc] result = ();
  for (obj <- xacro.elements){
    // pattern match on link elements
    if (link(_, _, _) := obj) {
      // map link name and location
      result += (obj.name.id:obj.origin);
    }
  }
  return result;
}
```

Listing 1.10. Gather link location algorithm

In Listing 1.10 the link location map is a relation that can be used in both directions. We can search on the link name but also look for its location to get the name of the link, a functionality that proves notably convenient.

5.7 Focus on Hover

Different Integrated Development Environment (IDE) events are utilized, specifically employing the documenter event. This event has information about where the cursor of the user is located. This active cursor information is used to determine what link is being inspected. In our implementation we even were able to look up the active link through include statements.

```
bool isCursorLocationInLocation(loc cursor, loc linkLocation){
  return cursor.begin >= linkLocation.begin &&
    cursor.end <= linkLocation.end;
}
```

Listing 1.11. Cursor location algorithm

In the link translation from GeometrySL to URDF we keep track of the identifier, the name of the link and its location see Listing 1.11. This goes in two directions, hence bi-directional. The identifier is used to find the corresponding location in the link location mapping and in the other direction to find the identifier based on its location. This location lookup checks if a certain location is in the same file and in between the row and column. If this is the case, it will return its identifier.

5.8 Bi-directional Navigation

With link-origin-tracing it possible to also use the 3D visualization to navigate through source code. When clicking on a visualized link it opens the corresponding section of code. This can be seen in Fig. 8.

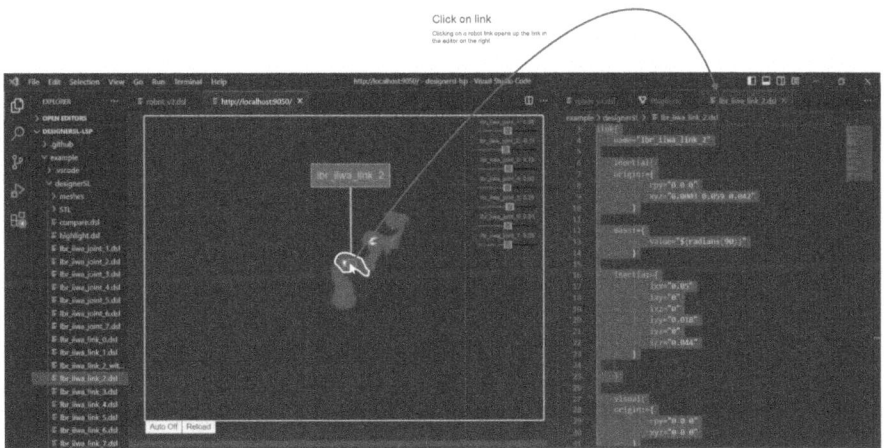

Fig. 8. Click on visual link.

5.9 Highlight Differences

The functionality of highlighting differences compared to previous version(s). Link origin tracing must be ignored, in order to strictly check for value equality, this is different opposed to [30] where origin is actually added and used to ensure file equality. The links are hashed such that they can be compared and stored more efficiently, see *removeOriginFromLink* function Listing 1.12.

```
map[str,str] removeOriginFromLink(list[URDF] links){
  map[str,str] result = ();
  for (link <- links){
    str uniqueHash = md5Hash(link.attributes + link.elements);
    result += (getName(link).val: uniqueHash);
  }
  return result;
}
```

Listing 1.12. Remove origin from link implementation

The URDF data structure consists of concrete data types for each URDF property. Each property has elements and attributes, parsed from the URDF robots. In order to compare robot1 (r1) and robot2 (r2), we extract from the elements mapping the "link" and store these in l1 and l2 respectively, such that we compare links only. Recall the explanation of the build-in map functions in Sect. 4.1. With rangeR we exclude the links in robot1 (r1) that do not exists in the robot2 (r2). Next the domain function is applied to the result, such that only the link identifiers are returned, since the keys are the link names, see Listing 1.12.

```
list [str] compare(URDF r1, URDF r2){
    l1 = getAll(r1, "link");
    l2 = getAll(r2, "link");
    return toList(domain(rangeR(
            removeOriginFromLink(l1),
              range(removeOriginFromLink(l2))))));
}
```

Listing 1.13. Compare algorithm

Note that we chose to apply the algorithm to the URDF data structure instead of GeometrySL or XacroSL due to the URDF's single-file nature, simplifying the process. We check for changes with the algorithm in Listing 1.13.

5.10 Compare Side-by-Side Differences

Alternatively to the approach of highlighting differences, we opted for a side-by-side comparison of two different versions of robot description files, as illustrated in Fig. 9. This approach allows mechatronic engineers to simultaneously view and compare the models in a split view, with one version displayed on the left and the other on the right. Differences in properties, structure, or elements can be visually identified, offering an intuitive and straightforward analysis. Interactive features, such as highlighting elements when hovering over them, further streamline the comparison process. This method leverages live graphical feedback, enabling engineers to efficiently analyze and validate the variations between two robot versions.

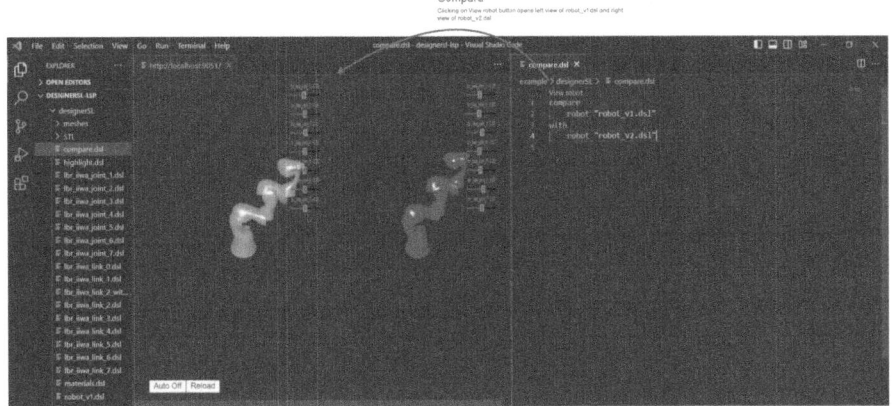

Fig. 9. Compare side-by-side.

6 Results

To view the final product in action, we recommend watching the demonstration videos. For confidentiality reasons, we use the Panda robot model instead of the Philips IGT interventional X-ray system.

The first video[12] illustrates two scenarios: presenting the robot and highlighting differences between two versions. The following steps are demonstrated:

1. The user clicks the left mouse button on a physical link of the robot in the graphical view.
2. The tool opens the corresponding GeometrySL instance and highlights the relevant text fragment.
3. The user switches to the textual view and opens the top-level GSL instance.
4. The user returns to the graphical view, presses the Ctrl key, and left-clicks on a link simultaneously.
5. The tool opens the corresponding URDF instance and highlights the associated text fragment.

---

[12] https://www.youtube.com/watch?v=n71kg1OKVus&ab_channel=fedcsis3391.

6. The user navigates back to the textual view and opens the top-level GSL instance again.
7. The user Ctrl-clicks on an included GSL file.
8. The tool opens the selected file.
9. The user navigates to the textual view and reopens the top-level GSL instance.
10. The user returns to the graphical view and presses the right mouse button.
11. The tool displays the name of the physical link.
12. The user left-clicks again on a physical link of the robot in the graphical view.
13. The tool opens the corresponding GeometrySL instance and highlights the relevant text fragment.

These steps demonstrate how the tool seamlessly integrates graphical and textual views, enabling users to navigate between robot elements and their underlying descriptions. This integration supports efficient analysis and modification workflows.

The second video[13] showcases the hover feature. The following sequence is presented:

1. The user changes the robot description file from version 1 to version 2.
2. The tool automatically updates the graphical view to reflect robot version 2.
3. The user types the keywords **highlight** robot version 1 **difference** robot version 2.
4. The tool graphically highlights the differences between the two robot versions by increasing their opacity.
5. The user navigates to the textual view and opens the top-level GSL instance.
6. Using Ctrl-click, the user selects an included GSL file.
7. The tool opens the selected file.
8. The user hovers over the included robot links.
9. While hovering, the tool highlights the corresponding links in the graphical view with a bold white outline.
10. The user identifies link 6, an **orange** component, in the graphical view and Ctrl-clicks on its associated GSL file.
11. The user navigates to the property color and changes it from **orange** to **black**.
12. The tool automatically updates the graphical view, changing the bold white outline and the color of link 6 from orange to black.

This sequence demonstrates how the tool integrates hover functionality, graphical feedback, and real-time updates, enhancing user interaction and streamlining the process of analyzing and modifying robot descriptions.

---

[13] https://www.youtube.com/watch?v=o_bJ8NsEODQ&t=9s&ab_channel=fedcsis3391.

The third video[14] provides a comprehensive overview of all the tool's features in action. It highlights the tool's ability to adjust the rotation of individual robot links using sliders and employs two distinct robot description files, `robot_v1.dsl` and `robot_v2.dsl`, for clarity.

In addition to the scenarios described above, the video demonstrates the side-by-side comparison feature, allowing users to easily observe differences between robot versions. The tool provides full control over how the graphical viewer represents robot descriptions. Users can choose between automatically highlighting differences, displaying the versions side-by-side, or focusing on a single version.

Moreover, the "compare with" and "highlight differences" keywords illustrate how the tool's functionality can be extended with additional keywords, enabling support for a variety of graphical representations. This flexibility and adaptability further enhance the tool's potential for future development and functionality expansion.

7 Evaluation Approach

Various articles on DSL evaluation, such as [20,39], and [18], rely on **questionnaires** to measure DSL usability. Despite the existence of alternative approaches like recording user interactions or analyzing user reactions [23], privacy concerns discourage their use. A **task-based evaluation** approach was chosen by Hoffman et al. [15] to assess the efficiency of the DSL.

Prior to the tasks, the test group received learning materials providing instructions on using the language. After performing the tasks, a questionnaire was used to gather initial impressions and obtain feedback on the learning materials. Participants' programming experience was considered in the result section with regard to the performance measure.

The task-based approach used questions and time as an indicator of efficiency. Answers to validate the accuracy of the users and time to measure the efficiency of each user. By keeping track of these two factors, the authors were able to mathematically measure efficiency; the researchers employed the Rate Correct Score (RCS) formula [44], defined as;

$$\text{RCS} = \frac{c}{\sum \text{RT}} \quad (1)$$

where c represents the number of correct responses and $\sum \text{RT}$ is the total reaction time for a trial [42]. This formula originates from the behavioral science field, and many adaptations of it exist, such as RCS.

Points Per Minute (PPM) introduced by Hoffmann et al. [15], similar to another measure called throughput [28], reflects correct responses per qualified time unit. In the case of PPM, the time unit is minute. Higher RCS, PPM, and throughput values suggest faster, more efficient task completion. However, a high

---

[14] https://www.youtube.com/watch?v=XiwrbvOOKiA&ab_channel=graphicaldesigner.

score in less time might not always surpass a higher overall score achieved over longer periods.

The balance between speed and accuracy should be carefully considered, keeping in mind the task or domain requirements. As noted by Kahraman & Bilgen [18], in addition to questionnaires, which may be highly subjective, the construct validity framework incorporates assessment evidence.

In this evaluation, the evidence could include log files collected during the participant's use of the tool, providing a more objective measure. The RCS and PPM serve as benchmarks for evaluating user efficiency. These benchmarks are utilized to assess future enhancements and determine whether they have effectively improved user efficiency.

8 Evaluation

For the evaluation of DesignerSL at Philips IGT, a preperation deployment is conducted followed by the evaluation of two phases: an alpha test phase and a beta test phase.

8.1 Deployment

In the preliminary evaluation, it was found that the installation process of the language(s) posed challenges for hardware engineers, as it involved installation of multiple programs. The Xacro functionality has been incorporated, and now only Python and the Rascal extension for Visual Studio Code (VS Code) are required.

8.2 Alpha

During the alpha testing phase, it was observed that the execution of import and command-line instructions was not intuitive for mechanical engineers with limited programming background.

To address this challenge, the decision was made to deploy the language as a VS Code extension. This approach involves creating a .vsx executable, simplifying the setup process. By relying on the installation of VS Code, the barriers to tool usage are reduced. As an interim solution, a script has been implemented to execute the command-line instructions with a single click, providing a more user-friendly experience.

Furthermore, the alpha testing revealed that not only links but also joints were being edited.

To enhance clarity, the aim is to visualize joints by highlighting both the parent and child links affected by the changes. This visual representation will provide users with a clearer understanding of the impact of their modifications.

In addition, the current tool converts a URDF to DesignerSL with a single click, but the links and joints are not separated into individual files.

As a future improvement, the workflow will be enhanced by automatically separating the links and joints into separate files. This modification will simplify maintenance and further streamline the transition from URDF to DesignerSL.

8.3 Beta

The beta test group conducted tasks derived from the use cases. To calculate the Points per Minute (PPM) metric, each task was accompanied by a question. The time taken for each task was recorded through the logs of the tool.

Upon completion of the tasks, the participants were asked to fill out a questionnaire about the usability of the language. The participant group comprised 5 mechatronic engineers and 4 software engineers, with the latter excluded from the test results due to their non-inclusion as intended users. The results revealed variations among mechatronic engineers in task completion within the 20-minute timeframe, as seen in Evalutation Results Table 2, which displays each task's completion time in minutes, RCS, and PPM results. The evaluation form and comments were also taken into account.

The following key points provide an in-depth analysis of these outcomes, emphasizing tasks completed consistently and mechatronic users' perceptions of the tool. It's worth emphasizing that mechatronic engineers didn't use the office stack that this new tool now supersedes. As a result, they do not utilize the document, presentation, and calculation use cases, and they do not make comparisons with these specific tasks (1, 2, 3, 4, 5). Their workflow involves notion of changes in measurements. Instead of manually comparing textual variations, they now benefit from visual feedback, which enables them to effortlessly observe changes, make comparisons, and identify and highlight differences, which are then used in Matlab to calculate and verify the performance of the system.

In Table 2, we have listed the mechatronic engineers who took part in the beta evaluation. Each column corresponds to tasks 1 through 6. A task was awarded full points when the result was correct. If a task was only partially correct, it received 0.5 points. Tasks that were not completed or received no response are denoted by a '-' symbol.

Table 2. Evaluation Results

Role	1	2	3	4	5	6	Minutes	RT in seconds	RCS	PPM
Mechatronic 1	1	1	1	1	1	1	15	900	0.006666667	0.4
Mechatronic 2	1	-	-	-	-	-	20	1200	0.000833333	0.05
Mechatronic 3	1	1	-	-	-	-	20	1200	0.001666667	0.1
Mechatronic 4	1	1	1	1	1	0.5	17	1020	0.005882353	0.352941176
Mechatronic 5	1	1	1	1	1	1	20	1200	0.005	0.3
Average PPM: 0.240588235										

1. **Points per Minute (PPM) metric**: To assess the efficiency of the users during task performance, the PPM metric was employed [42]. This calculation depends on the RCS [44]. The evaluation session had a total duration of 40 min, excluding the introduction and feedback round. The evaluation began

with a set of six initial steps designed to familiarize participants with the tool. Subsequently, participants engaged in a task-based approach, which lasted for 20 min and encompassed six tasks.
2. **Environment Impact**: The beta test group conducted the tasks in a conference room using their laptops. However, the lack of additional monitors made it difficult for them to use the tool with split-screen view, especially on smaller screens.
3. **User Interface Observations**: The group also made some observations about the user interface of the software:
    - "It looks really cool and visuals are responsive"
    - "The software does not allow changing the robot position after focusing on hover."
    - "Users prefer automatic updates."
    - "Opening the text editor replaces the view in Visual Studio Code, but this issue was resolved by using a web browser."
    - "It is really cramped up to work with on a single screen."
4. **Language Consensus**: The users liked the ability to use mathematical expressions like π and radians in the tool and the inclusion of files. The language was understandable especially when having a background with using URDF.
5. **Recommendations for Future Evaluations**: It would be more beneficial to conduct the next evaluation at each participant's workplace, as they would be more comfortable with their environment, would likely have access to dual monitors, and could use the web browser to view the robot instead of the integrated view in Visual Studio Code. This would prevent some of the issues participants encountered that hindered their ease of use.

The respondents had positive initial impressions and found various features of the language useful. They provided suggestions for improvements in live graphical feedback, such as highlighting, GUI controls and use of a secondary monitor. The language itself was commonly perceived as intuitive, although each participant held their unique perspective on what constitutes intuitiveness especially with regard to the visualization.

One of the participants expressed a dislike for the transparency of unchanged properties as it hinders comprehensibility, while another participant preferred a more detailed visualization of the changed attributes. This highlights the complexity of designing graphical representations that strike a delicate balance between providing detailed enough information while avoiding clutter that can impede comprehensibility.

The multiple choice response ratings are depicted in the boxplot Fig. 10, which illustrates the variability in the responses. To enhance readability, each question is correspondingly mapped in Table 3.

Table 3. Survey Multiple Choice Questions

Number	Question Text
6	The live graphical feedback helps me to understand what robot properties have changed
7	The live graphical feedback helps me to understand on what robot properties I am working
8	The graphical language helps me to communicate changed robot properties to my colleagues
9	How intuitive did you find the graphical language?
10	How intuitive did you find the live graphical feedback?
11	live graphical feedback would improve my ability to understand and work with robot properties?
12	Does the new workflow improve the communication between colleagues?

The boxplot in Fig. 10 illustrates the distribution of ratings for the multiple-choice questions listed in Table 3. The vertical axis represents the ratings, ranging from positive (5) to negative (1), with neutral responses at (3). The horizontal axis corresponds to the indices of the multiple-choice questions, reflecting the participants' responses.

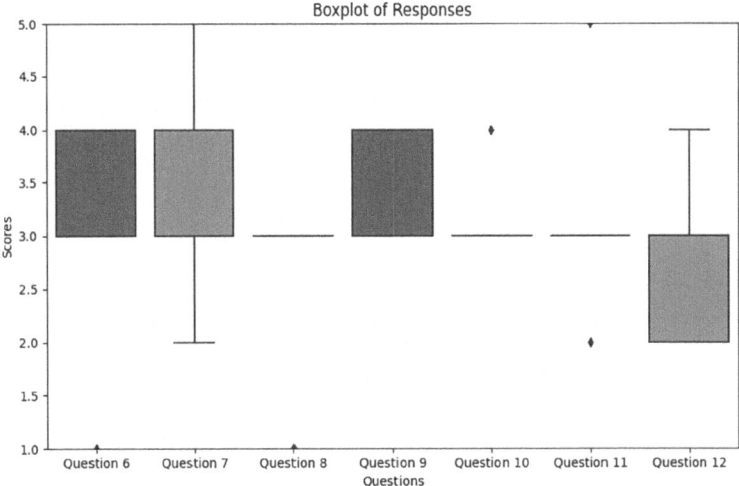

Fig. 10. Boxplot: Questionnaire responses.

Based on the given ratings, we can analyze the reception of the DesignerSL with live graphical feedback among mechatronic engineers for each question:

Question 6: The live graphical feedback helps me to understand what robot properties have changed.

- Mean rating: 3.0
- Standard deviation: 1.22

The engineers' ratings for this question vary, with a mean rating of 3.0.

The standard deviation of 1.22 suggests some level of disagreement or inconsistency among the engineers.

Some engineers may find the live graphical feedback helpful in understanding changes to robot properties, while others may not.

Question 7: The live graphical feedback helps me to understand on what robot properties I am working.

- Mean rating: 3.4
- Standard deviation: 1.14

The engineers, on average, rated the live graphical feedback slightly higher for this question, with a mean rating of 3.4. However, the standard deviation of 1.14 indicates that there is still some variability in their opinions. Some engineers find the live graphical feedback helpful in understanding the robot properties they are working on, while others may not perceive it as useful.

Question 8: The graphical language helps me to communicate changed robot properties to my colleagues.

- Mean rating: 2.6
- Standard deviation: 0.89

The engineers' ratings for this question are relatively low, with a mean rating of 2.6. The low mean rating suggests that the graphical language may not be perceived as effective in communicating changed robot properties to colleagues. The lower standard deviation of 0.89 indicates that the engineers' opinions are more consistent for this question compared to the previous ones.

Question 9: How intuitive did you find the graphical language?

- Mean rating: 3.4
- Standard deviation: 0.55

The engineers, on average, found the graphical language relatively intuitive, with a mean rating of 3.4. The low standard deviation of 0.55 suggests that there is a higher level of agreement among the engineers regarding the intuitiveness of the graphical language.

Question 10: How intuitive did you find the live graphical feedback?

- Mean rating: 3.2
- Standard deviation: 0.45

The engineers rated the live graphical feedback as moderately intuitive, with a mean rating of 3.2. The low standard deviation of 0.45 indicates that there is a relatively high level of agreement among the engineers regarding the intuitiveness of the live graphical feedback.

Question 11: live graphical feedback would improve my ability to understand and work with robot properties?

- Mean rating: 3.2
- Standard deviation: 1.10

The engineers' opinions are divided for this question, with a mean rating of 3.2 and a higher standard deviation of 1.10. Some engineers believe that live graphical feedback would improve their ability to understand and work with robot properties, while others may not share the same perception.

Question 12: Does the new workflow improve the communication between colleagues?

- Mean rating: 2.8
- Standard deviation: 0.84

The engineers' ratings indicate that the new workflow does not significantly improve communication between colleagues, with a mean rating of 2.8. The standard deviation of 0.84 suggests a moderate level of agreement among the engineers regarding the lack of improvement in communication.

Overall, based on the given ratings, it appears that the mechatronic engineers have mixed opinions about the DesignerSL with live graphical feedback. While they generally find the live graphical feedback and graphical language to be intuitive, their perception of the effectiveness in communicating changed robot properties and improving communication between colleagues is relatively low. There is also some variability in their opinions, as indicated by the standard deviations in the ratings.

The lower scores we observed in colleagues' visual communication of changes (questions 3 and 7) could be attributed to the task sequence. Specifically, task 6, which involves comparing and highlighting robot models, this was only completed by three participants. As not all participants reached this task, as evident in Evaluation Results Table 2 where column six and row participant '-' indicate task 6 was not completed, their feedback on this aspect was based on tasks that did not specifically cover this use case. Consequently, these responses may not offer a complete understanding of how the use cases compare and highlight were received by the mechatronic engineers. The limited exposure to these use cases is also reflected in the open questions of the questionnaire.

9 Discussion

In contrast to the existing literature reviewed in Sect. 2, which predominantly concentrates on visually representing properties of robots which can be visually represented such as positions of components and movements, our research places a strong emphasis on highlighting changes that cannot be visually represented, such as inertia and mass.

Leveraging the widely adopted URDF standard tapped into the existing knowledge base of end-users, simplifying their adoption and adaptation to the DSL. This underscores the notion that harnessing established standards can expedite the learning curve for new DSLs. Furthermore, through the incorporation of Xacro, we achieved composability within the language. Moreover, the development of GeometrySL expanded its capabilities with a visual language that empowers hardware engineers to precisely define how the robot is visually represented. This extension encompasses all known keywords and components while eliminating the cumbersome XML syntax, enhancing the user experience.

9.1 Bi-directional Navigation

The benefits of bi-directional interaction, as outlined by Witte et al. [43], is that it reduces cognitive load and improves the overall user experience. By integrating the view and text editor through a bi-directional approach, our tool aims to alleviate cognitive load and further enhance the user experience. It allow users to interact with visual links by clicking on them, instantly directing them to the specific location in the text editor where that element is specified.

Salix has been used in game development to improve collaboration among multiple disciplines [32], resulting in improved collaboration. By leveraging the Salix library, a successful prototype of bi-directional input visualization was achieved. This feature enables users to effortlessly click on visual elements, which then redirects them to the corresponding location within the text editor.

Building upon the insights from [16], our approach embraces the concept of richness by not only providing visual feedback but also integrating the textual and graphical representations. Although persistent changes are not supported via the visualization interface, this integration fosters a cohesive and intuitive user experience by establishing a strong connection between the two interfaces.

9.2 Workflow Comparison

To better understand the benefits of adopting a unified tool, we compare the workflows of hardware engineers without and with the tool. The "Without Tool" workflow represents the current state, where multiple standalone tools and manual processes are used. The "With Tool" workflow demonstrates the envisioned approach using an integrated domain-specific language to streamline tasks. The comparison highlights key differences in efficiency, integration, and user experience, as shown in Table 4.

Table 4. Workflow Comparison: Without Tool vs. With Tool

Aspect	Without Tool	With Tool
Tools and Formats	Relies on various tools, including CAD, Excel, Word, and PowerPoint	Utilizes a unified domain-specific language with integrated functionality
Integration Between Tools	Minimal integration; data is manually transferred between tools	Seamless integration, with CAD files converted via Blender into URDF format for use in the tool
Documentation and Presentation	Separate tools (Word and PowerPoint) are used for documentation and presentations	Unified within the tool, featuring live graphical feedback and customizable views
Change Management	Changes to CAD models are manually documented in Word and presented using PowerPoint	Changes are directly visualized and tracked in the tool, highlighting differences between versions with customized views
User Interaction	Requires manual interaction with multiple tools; data must be consolidated manually	Bi-directional navigation between textual and graphical representations enhances clarity and user experience
Integration with Archives	Separate archiving solutions are required for storage and retrieval	Fully integrated with Philips' existing archiving system for seamless file management
Communication	Disconnected tools and formats may hinder effective interdisciplinary collaboration	A unified domain-specific language and graphical feedback promote better interdisciplinary communication
Efficiency	Workflow is fragmented and complex, leading to inefficiencies	Streamlined and integrated, reducing complexity, enhancing productivity, and improving decision-making

9.3 Immediate Feedback

Earlier research [10] and [14] have indicated that immediate feedback significantly improves debugging. More recent studies also successfully applied immediate feedback in their DSL [3,22,25,31]. Additionally, incorporating immediate feedback ensures that the DSL adheres to the liveness quality, improving the programming experience.

In VS Code, the "summarize event" of the Rascal Language server library is triggered each time the file is saved. We take advantage of this event to re-render the visualization using the latest valid state of the DSL, ensuring an up-to-date representation of the data.

This approach of fully refreshing the visualization, causes a brief moment of disappearance and reappearance of the robot, upon saving the file. This can be improved in terms of user experience. A more gradual change that maintains the robot in the exact same state and keeps it constantly in view would provide a smoother and more user-friendly way of communicating the modifications, minimizing context-switches and enhancing overall usability. By avoiding the robot's disappearance, users can maintain continuous visual feedback and better understand the impact of their changes.

It makes sense to make this part of the summarize behavior the visualization serves a similar purpose as source code errors and warnings, and most languages perform these checks upon saving to achieve it. Additionally, this approach helps minimize the performance impact of running resource-intensive processes with each change.

Our language exhibits key qualities such as liveness, richness, and composability, as discussed in Horowitz et al.'s work on live programming [16].

Like mentioned in Munzner's book [24], we aim to create a solution that addresses the invisibility of property changes and enhances user experience by implementing these highlighting strategies while considering potential conflicts with user-defined materials, overlapping color use, or making components transparent for highlighting. We opted against animations due to their potential to cause change blindness, distracting users from subtle property changes. Instead, we focus on highlighting the changed links to clearly differentiate changes, enhancing user experience by ensuring modifications are easily perceived and understood within the graphical representation. The highlighting differences aim to make changes more distinguishable and improve the user experience.

TMDiff [30] utilizes an algorithm that relies on source location to detect changes, similar to existing tools like Linux's built-in diff and git diff. These tools typically compare lines of code, analyze differences on a line-by-line basis, and categorize changes as modified, deleted, or added.

In contrast, our solution specifically addresses the unique characteristics of URDF and GLS files, which represent robotic systems with distinct links and joints identified by their names. We introduce a novel approach by hashing the links and joints including their unique identifiers while excluding their source location into a hashmap. This allows us to efficiently determine whether links or joints already exist in the system, enabling effective management of modifications and comparisons.

Moreover, our visualization tool offers enhanced capabilities compared to TMDiff. While both systems can highlight changes per link and between linked entities (in the case of joints), our solution goes further by seamlessly accommodating rearrangements of links and joints. This means that even if the structure of the system is altered, our tool can accurately compare the old and modified versions, providing a more robust and flexible comparison mechanism for this use case.

In conclusion, our study has demonstrated that integrating liveness, richness, and composability into a DSL tailored for hardware engineers at Philips IGT, featuring enhancements like bi-directional navigation, live graphical feedback, and the inclusion of robot components, can significantly enhance usability and effectiveness. Furthermore, it has underscored the challenge of visualizing invisible hardware properties, which often hinges on personal preferences and perceptions. These findings make meaningful contributions to the ongoing development of DSLs within this domain, emphasizing the critical role of user feedback in designing intuitive graphical feedback languages.

10 Concluding Remarks

We improved the hardware development workflow at Philips IGT by creating a textual Domain Specific Language (DSL) called GeometrySL or GSL. This DSL was used to formalize handovers from mechanical engineers to mechatronic engineers, preventing mistakes during the exchange process.

The novel approach of leveraging industry-standards URDF and Xacro, alongside techniques such as origin tracing and the LWB Rascal has resulted in a live graphical feedback on differences between Cyber-Physical System (CPS) versions. It enables bi-directional navigation among the graphical representation, URDF and the GSL itself, enhancing the efficiency and usability of the language.

The development of GeometrySL serves as a valuable case study that demonstrates the practical application of immediate, bi-directional visual feedback within an engineering context. The lessons learned from this project can inspire future research efforts and innovations in domain specific languages with live graphical feedback for CPS.

This research mainly focuses on graphically representing textual differences of 3D robot models. In our evaluation of the tool we had diverse feedback. The main challenge we faced was how to visualize changes made to invisible properties such as tolerances, mass inertia.

A potential direction for future work is to address this question and further enhance our research. Specifically, we aim to explore innovative methods for visualizing changes to non-visual properties such as tolerances, mass, and inertia in robotic models. While transparency has been used to some extent, there is an opportunity to investigate alternative approaches that can effectively convey these modifications without significantly altering the robot's overall visual representation. The current side-by-side view, while useful, is limited in its ability to visualize invisible properties, highlighting the need for more advanced visualization techniques.

As we have seen in our research its heavily subjective to what a user perceives as intuitive. Implement options for users to customize the visualization of non-visual properties based on their preferences and specific use cases. This could include adjustable transparency settings, customizable color schemes, or alternative visualization modes tailored to different user needs.

A Appendix

```
data URDF =
    robot(map[str, URDFValue] attributes,
      map[str, list[URDF]] elements)
...
      map[str, list[URDF]] elements) // joint
  | axis(map[str, URDFValue] attributes,
      map[str, list[URDF]] elements) // joint
  | transmission(map[str, URDFValue] attributes,
      map[str, list[URDF]] elements) // robot
  | actuator(map[str, URDFValue] attributes,
      map[str, list[URDF]] elements) // transmission
  | plugin(map[str, URDFValue] attributes,
      map[str, list[URDF]] elements) // robot, link, or joint
  | counterbalance(map[str,URDFValue] attributes,
      map[str, list[URDF]] elements) // joint
  | tolerance(map[str, URDFValue] attributes,
      map[str, list[URDF]] elements) // robot custom property
  ;
```

Listing 1.14. Fragment of UrdfSL Abstract Data Structure

References

1. Addazi, L., Ciccozzi, F., Langer, P., Posse, E.: Towards seamless hybrid graphical–textual modelling for UML and profiles. In: Anjorin, A., Espinoza, H. (eds.) ECMFA 2017. LNCS, vol. 10376, pp. 20–33. Springer, Cham (2017). https://doi.org/10.1007/978-3-319-61482-3_2
2. Albergo, N., Rathi, V., Ore, J.P.: Understanding xacro misunderstandings. In: 2022 International Conference on Robotics and Automation (ICRA), pp. 6247–6252. IEEE (2022)
3. Alique, D., Linares, M.: The importance of rapid and meaningful feedback on computer-aided graphic expression learning. Educ. Chem. Eng. **27**, 54–60 (2019). https://doi.org/10.1016/j.ece.2019.03.001. https://www.sciencedirect.com/science/article/pii/S1749772818300435
4. Alur, R.: Principles of Cyber-Physical Systems. MIT Press (2015)
5. Ben-Ari, M.: Principles of the Spin Model Checker. Springer (2008)
6. Bolwerk, T.: Improving the workflow for hardware engineers at philips with a domain-specific language and graphical feedback (2023). https://www.cs.ru.nl/masters-theses/2023/T_Bolwerk___Improving_the_workflow_for_hardware_engineers_at_Philips_with_a_domain-specific_language_and_graphical_feedback.pdf
7. Bolwerk, T., Alonso, M., Schuts, M.: Using a textual DSL with live graphical feedback to improve the CPS' design workflow of hardware engineers. In: 2024 19th Conference on Computer Science and Intelligence Systems (FedCSIS), pp. 301–312. IEEE (2024)
8. Bray, T., Paoli, J., Sperberg-McQueen, C.M., Maler, E., Yergeau, F.: Extensible markup language (XML) 1.0 (1998)

9. Cazzola, W., Favalli, L.: Scrambled features for breakfast: concepts of agile language development. Commun. ACM **66**(11), 50–60 (2023)
10. Cook, C., Burnett, M., Boom, D.: A bug's eye view of immediate visual feedback in direct-manipulation programming systems. In: Papers Presented at the Seventh Workshop on Empirical Studies of Programmers, ESP 1997, pp. 20–41. Association for Computing Machinery (1997). https://doi.org/10.1145/266399.266403
11. Cooper, J., Kolovos, D.: Engineering hybrid graphical-textual languages with sirius and xtext: requirements and challenges. In: 2019 ACM/IEEE 22nd International Conference on Model Driven Engineering Languages and Systems Companion (MODELS-C), pp. 322–325 (2019). https://doi.org/10.1109/MODELS-C.2019.00050
12. Fowler, M.: Domain-Specific Languages. Pearson Education (2010)
13. Gray, J., Neema, S., Tolvanen, J.P., Gokhale, A.S., Kelly, S., Sprinkle, J.: Domain-specific modeling. In: Handbook of Dynamic System Modeling, vol. 7, p. 7-1 (2007)
14. Green, T.R.G., Petre, M.: Usability analysis of visual programming environments: a 'cognitive dimensions' framework. J. Vis. Lang. Comput. **7**(2), 131–174 (1996). https://doi.org/10.1006/jvlc.1996.0009. https://www.sciencedirect.com/science/article/pii/S1045926X96900099
15. Hoffmann, B., Urquhart, N., Chalmers, K., Guckert, M.: An empirical evaluation of a novel domain-specific language - modelling vehicle routing problems with athos. Empirical Softw. Eng. **27**(7), 180 (2022). https://doi.org/10.1007/s10664-022-10210-w
16. Horowitz, J., Heer, J.: Live, Rich, and Composable: Qualities for Programming Beyond Static Text (2023)
17. Inostroza, P., van Der Storm, T., Erdweg, S.: Tracing program transformations with string origins. In: International Conference on Theory and Practice of Model Transformations, pp. 154–169. Springer (2014)
18. Kahraman, G., Bilgen, S.: A framework for qualitative assessment of domain-specific languages. Softw. Syst. Model. **14**(4), 1505–1526 (2015). https://doi.org/10.1007/s10270-013-0387-8
19. Klint, P., Van der Storm, T., Vinju, J.: RASCAL: a domain specific language for source code analysis and manipulation. In: Proceedings of the 2009 Ninth IEEE International Working Conference on Source Code Analysis and Manipulation, pp. 168–177. IEEE (2009). https://doi.org/10.1109/SCAM.2009.28
20. Kosar, T., et al.: Comparing general-purpose and domain-specific languages: an empirical study, vol. 7, no. 2, pp. 247–264. https://doiserbia.nb.rs/Article.aspx?ID=1820-02141002247K
21. Kunze, L., Roehm, T., Beetz, M.: Towards semantic robot description languages. In: 2011 IEEE International Conference on Robotics and Automation, pp. 5589–5595 (2011). https://doi.org/10.1109/ICRA.2011.5980170. ISSN 1050-4729
22. Lozano, A., Mens, K., Kellens, A.: Usage contracts: offering immediate feedback on violations of structural source-code regularities, vol. 105, pp. 73–91 (2015). https://doi.org/10.1016/j.scico.2015.01.004. https://www.sciencedirect.com/science/article/pii/S016764231500012X
23. Lyle, J.: Stimulated recall: a report on its use in naturalistic research, vol. 29, no. 6, pp. 861–878. https://www.jstor.org/stable/1502138
24. Munzner, T.: Visualization Analysis and Design. CRC Press (2014). google-Books-ID: NfkYCwAAQBAJ
25. NDC Conferences: Real-time prototyping using visual programming languages - rui martins (2018). https://www.youtube.com/watch?v=cAiFJEcqwm4

26. Onwubolu, G.: Mechatronics: principles and applications. Elsevier (2005)
27. Pérez Andrés, F., de Lara, J., Guerra, E.: Domain specific languages with graphical and textual views. In: Schürr, A., Nagl, M., Zündorf, A. (eds.) AGTIVE 2007. LNCS, vol. 5088, pp. 82–97. Springer, Heidelberg (2008). https://doi.org/10.1007/978-3-540-89020-1_7
28. R. Thorne, D.: Throughput: a simple performance index with desirable characteristics, vol. 38, no. 4, pp. 569–573. https://doi.org/10.3758/BF03193886
29. van Rozen, R., Dormans, J.: Adapting game mechanics with micro-machinations: international conference on the foundations of digital games. Society for the Advancement of the Science of Digital Games (2014)
30. van Rozen, R., van der Storm, T.: Origin tracking + text differencing = textual model differencing. In: Kolovos, D., Wimmer, M. (eds.) ICMT 2015. LNCS, vol. 9152, pp. 18–33. Springer, Cham (2015). https://doi.org/10.1007/978-3-319-21155-8_2
31. van Rozen, R.: Cascade: a meta-language for change, cause and effect (2022). https://ir.cwi.nl/pub/32568
32. van Rozen, R., Reijne, Y., Julia, C., Samaritaki, G.: First-person realtime collaborative metaprogramming adventures (2021). https://ir.cwi.nl/pub/31301/
33. van Rozen, R., van der Storm, T.: Toward live domain-specific languages: from text differencing to adapting models at run time, vol. 18, no. 1, pp. 195–212 (2019). https://doi.org/10.1007/s10270-017-0608-7
34. Schuts, M., Aarssen, R., Tielemans, P., Vinju, J.: Large-scale semi-automated migration of legacy C/C++ test code. Softw. Pract. Exp. **52**(7), 1543–1580 (2022)
35. Schuts, M., Alonso, M., Hooman, J.: Industrial experiences with the evolution of a DSL. In: Proceedings of the 18th ACM SIGPLAN International Workshop on Domain-Specific Modeling, pp. 21–30 (2021)
36. Shelly, G.B., Vermaat, M.E.: Microsoft Office 2010: Introductory. Course Technology Press (2012)
37. Shen, L., Chen, X., Liu, R., Wang, H., Ji, G.: Domain-specific language techniques for visual computing: a comprehensive study, vol. 28, no. 4, pp. 3113–3134 (2021). https://doi.org/10.1007/s11831-020-09492-4
38. Shih, R.H.: Parametric Modeling with Creo Parametric 2.0. SDC Publications (2013)
39. Steenvoorden, T., Stutterheim, J., Barendsen, E., Plasmeijer, R.: Visual support for learning monads, pp. 130–139. Global Science and Technology Forum. https://doi.org/10.5176/2251-2195_CSEIT17.64
40. van der Storm, T.: Semantics engineering with concrete syntax. In: Eelco Visser Commemorative Symposium (EVCS 2023). Schloss Dagstuhl-Leibniz-Zentrum für Informatik (2023)
41. van Rozen: Live game programming with micro-machinations and rascal (2014). https://www.youtube.com/watch?v=YzsKaJEX4D4
42. Vandierendonck, A.: A comparison of methods to combine speed and accuracy measures of performance: a rejoinder on the binning procedure, vol. 49, no. 2, pp. 653–673. https://doi.org/10.3758/s13428-016-0721-5
43. Witte, T., Tichy, M.: A hybrid editor for fast robot mission prototyping. In: 2019 34th IEEE/ACM International Conference on Automated Software Engineering Workshop (ASEW), pp. 41–44 (2019). https://doi.org/10.1109/ASEW.2019.00026. ISSN 2151-0830

44. Woltz, D.J., Was, C.A.: Availability of related long-term memory during and after attention focus in working memory, vol. 34, no. 3, pp. 668–684. https://doi.org/10.3758/BF03193587
45. Xue, D., Chen, Y.: System simulation techniques with MATLAB and Simulink. Wiley (2013)

Embedded Systems Security Co-design: Modeling Support for Managers and Developers

Alexander Fischer[1](✉)[iD], Juha-Pekka Tolvanen[2][iD], and Ramin Tavakoli Kolagari[1][iD]

[1] Nuremberg Institute of Technology, Nuremberg, Bavaria, Germany
{a.fischer,ramin.tavakolikolagari}@th-nuernberg.de
[2] MetaCase, Jyväskylä, Finland
jpt@metacase.com
https://www.metacase.com/

Abstract. The proliferation of connected and autonomous vehicle technologies has significantly increased cybersecurity risks. Modern vehicles, as complex and networked computer systems, require comprehensive protection against malicious ejpt@metacase.comxternal attacks, much like conventional computers. Addressing these challenges requires robust tools that align established automotive model-based development approaches with the ISO/SAE 21434 standard for automotive cybersecurity, which became mandatorpublication in 2021.

Building on prior research, this paper introduces key innovations in the conceptual framework and the tool support that integrate seamlessly into existing automotive development methodologies. These advancements are rooted in extensions to the Security Abstraction Model (SAM) informed by the ISO/SAE 21434 standard. Notably, SAM now incorporates advanced methods for score calculation, including an attack potential-based approach for assessing attack feasibility and the computation of risk scores using risk matrices.

Usability improvements are also a contribution, achieved through the introduction of BPMN-style (Business Process Model and Notation) diagrams tailored for the accessible visualization of otherwise complex security models. These diagrams make multifaceted attack trees easier to interpret, enabling managers and other non-technical stakeholders to intuitively understand security vulnerabilities and make informed decisions.

Additionally, the tool supports updated metrics for impact and risk analysis, demonstrated through practical applications involving automotive subsystems such as braking. These examples illustrate improved traceability between SAM and functional design, ensuring that cybersecurity requirements are effectively integrated into the broader development lifecycle.

Keywords: Embedded security · Model-based engineering · Security modeling

© The Author(s), under exclusive license to Springer Nature Switzerland AG 2025
G. Kardas et al. (Eds.): FEDCSIS-S3E 2024/KKIO 2024, LNBIP 542, pp. 206–232, 2025.
https://doi.org/10.1007/978-3-031-84913-8_8

1 Introduction

Security considerations must be holistic to the development of complex systems to ensure long-term reliability and operational safety. Embedded systems, integrated in modern vehicles, are often designed for extended use without frequent updates, leaving them vulnerable to exploitation. For instance, automotive control units, which facilitate inter-device communication, present potential attack surfaces that, if compromised, could result in significant harm. The increasing digitization and networking of modern vehicles demand robust cybersecurity measures to protect systems against potential cyber-attacks. As vehicles evolve to include advanced software and connectivity features, the attack surface expands, making it critical to identify vulnerabilities and develop effective countermeasures early in the design process. The ISO/SAE 21434:2021 standard "Road Vehicles-Cybersecurity Engineering" [11] provides a framework for assessing risks and implementing cybersecurity throughout the automotive lifecycle. Real-world incidents of unauthorized vehicle access, such as attacks on insecure encryption systems, underscore the importance of proactive risk mitigation strategies (refer to Sect. 2).

In order to address these challenges, model-based engineering (MBE, see Sect. 3) has emerged as a state-of-the-art methodology in automotive software development. MBE facilitates the design, analysis, and validation of complex systems by representing their components and relationships through models. However, traditional system models often remain disconnected from security models, limiting the integration of cybersecurity into the overall system architecture. Collaborative approaches that combine system design and cybersecurity models are essential to implement "security-by-design" principles effectively (refer to Sect. 4). The Security Abstraction Model (SAM) addresses this need by providing a unified approach for modeling security threats and countermeasures in automotive systems (refer to Sect. 7).

This paper builds upon our earlier research [8] and introduces two key extensions to SAM and the modeling support (refer to Sect. 5), enhancing its applicability to ISO/SAE 21434. First, we incorporate additional score calculation methods, including an attack potential-based approach for assessing attack feasibility and a risk score computation using risk matrices (refer to Sect. 6). Second, we enhance the tool's usability by creating BPMN-style (Business Process Model and Notation [16]) diagrams specifically tailored for accessible visualization of security models. These diagrams enable managers and other non-IT stakeholders to intuitively understand complex attack trees (refer to Sect. 8). Significant sections were published in the Proceedings of the *19th Conference on Computer Science and Intelligence Systems (FedCSIS)* (refer to [8]). This work additionally contains the Subsects. 7.5 and 8.5 as well as additional scores and metrics described in the respective sections.

The primary contribution of this work is the development of tool support for SAM using the MetaEdit+ modeling tool. This tool not only aligns with ISO/SAE 21434 but also integrates cybersecurity metrics such as impact ratings, attack feasibility scores, and risk assessments. Additionally, it enables collaborative development between system and security engineers, enables ISO 21434-compliant reporting, and offers enhanced visualization for decision-makers. The paper demonstrates the feasibility and practical application of these extensions with concrete examples (refer to Sect. 8).

2 Security Relevance

The increase in cyber-attacks on vehicles reveals a need for action in the automotive sector to protect system components from external attacks. In particular, cases in which attackers were able to gain access to vehicles and start the engine by transmitting the radio key signal have been reported on by public media [13]. Vehicle owners must be made aware that unlocking doors is easier than generally assumed and that even major manufacturers have been using insecure encryption systems for years [9]. In addition, the secrecy of data sheets does not ensure greater security, but makes thorough security verification more difficult [21]. The increasing connectivity of vehicles and the introduction of convenience features such as e.g. infotainment systems provide further attack vectors that lead to new challenges in identifying and addressing vulnerabilities [6].

Moreover, the trend towards vehicle-to-everything (V2X) communication, which includes vehicle-to-vehicle (V2V) and vehicle-to-infrastructure (V2I) interactions, introduces additional risks. These systems rely on the exchange of information between vehicles and infrastructure to improve traffic flow and enhance safety. However, they also create new opportunities for attackers to intercept and manipulate data, potentially leading to collisions or traffic disruptions.

The proliferation of electric vehicles (EVs) also brings unique cybersecurity challenges. EVs often come with connected charging stations, which can be targeted to disrupt charging infrastructure or gain access to the vehicle's internal network. This not only affects the availability of charging but also raises concerns about the potential for large-scale attacks on the power grid.

In response to these threats, it is crucial for the automotive industry to adopt a multi-layered security approach. This includes implementing robust encryption methods, regular security updates, comprehensive testing of all systems, consideration of social engineering attacks, and an integration into the state-of-the-art automotive software systems development approach, i.e., model-based engineering, see the following section.

3 Model-Based Development in the Automotive Domain

A key advantages of model-based development is its ability to enhance communication and collaboration among development teams. By using models, engineers from different disciplines (such as software, hardware, security, and systems engineering) can work together more effectively, sharing a common understanding of the system under development. This collaborative development approach helps to reduce errors and misunderstandings, leading to higher quality software and faster development cycles.

Model-based engineering currently represents the state of the art in the field of automotive software engineering. The primary reasons for model-based approaches are managing complex engineering tasks in better ways and effective communication [10]. In addition to support for collaboration it makes possible to design, analyze and validate complex systems by using models that represent different aspects of the system. It has proven to be extremely effective in supporting the development of automotive software as it enables the systematic design and analysis of functions [5]. The models are typically created with some general-purpose modeling language like UML or SysML [17,18], or with domain-specific languages targeting automotive systems like:

- Architecture Analysis & Design Language (AADL) [7] is a domain-specific language used for modeling the architecture of embedded systems, including automotive systems. It allows for the representation of both software and hardware components and their interactions. AADL is beneficial for performing performance analysis, such as timing and resource utilization critical in automotive applications.
- AUTOSAR (AUTomotive Open System ARchitecture) [1] is a standardized automotive software architecture framework that allows for the design and development of vehicle software with interoperability and scalability. It defines a set of specifications for software architecture, enabling the integration of components from multiple suppliers. AUTOSAR models are used to specify software components, their interfaces, and communication patterns, ensuring consistency and compatibility across different ECUs (Electronic Control Units).
- EAST-ADL (Electronics Architecture and Software Technology—Architecture Description Language) [4] is a domain-specific language tailored for automotive electrical and electronic systems. It provides a framework for modeling the architecture of vehicles, focusing on requirements engineering, functional analysis, dependability, and system design. It covers a more abstract design level compared to AUTOSAR. EAST-ADL supports the development process by linking requirements to design models and analysis tools, facilitating traceability and verification.

It is worth noticing that these well-known modeling languages applied in automotive do not recognize security, cybersecurity or support for ISO/SAE 21434:2021 standard (see languages used in the automotive industry [1,4,7]). We see that model-based development provides a basis for also supporting cybersecurity engineering and it can be done with an integrated manner. We introduce The Security Abstraction Model (SAM) in more detail in Sect. 7, as an extension to the EAST-ADL providing an integration and traceability between models of system development and cybersecurity.

4 Need for Integration of Security Design into Systems Modeling

The increasing use of software components instead of mechanical components in vehicles and the development of autonomous vehicle systems require robust cybersecurity measures. Models allow system engineers and security engineers to collaborate and thus put the principle of "security-by-design" into practice. This collaborative modeling approach ensures that security considerations are embedded from the very beginning of the design process, rather than being retrofitted after the fact.

[3] gives an overview of the following advantages of the integrated approach:

- Models provide a structured way to document and trace system functions and requirements throughout the development lifecycle. By incorporating security requirements alongside functional requirements, engineers can ensure that security is treated as a core aspect of the system. This traceability allows better management of dependencies and the identification of potential security impacts arising from changes in system functionality.
- Security objectives need to be clearly defined to protect critical system assets and ensure the overall safety and privacy of vehicle occupants. Models can help in articulating these objectives in a precise manner, providing a clear roadmap for implementing necessary security measures. This includes specifying access control policies, data protection mechanisms, and secure communication protocols.
- To defend against potential cyber-attacks, specific security measures must be integrated into the system design. Models facilitate the systematic design and evaluation of these measures. For instance, threat modeling techniques can be used to identify potential attack vectors, and countermeasures can be designed and validated within the model. This proactive approach helps in mitigating risks before they materialize in the physical system.
- Continuous vulnerability analysis is crucial for maintaining the security of automotive systems. Models enable the simulation and analysis of various attack scenarios, helping engineers to understand the potential impact of different vulnerabilities. By analyzing these scenarios within the model, engineers can prioritize vulnerabilities based on their severity and likelihood, and implement appropriate mitigation strategies.
- The automotive industry is subject to stringent regulatory requirements regarding safety, e.g., ISO 26262, and security, e.g., ISO 21343. Integrating security within the design models ensures that the development process aligns with these regulations and industry standards. This alignment is essential for achieving certification and ensuring that vehicles meet legal and market requirements.

5 Need for Tool Support

Collaborative development work creating specifications, analyzing, checking and versioning them as well as transforming models to code, reports etc. requires tool support. In this paper we apply MetaEdit+ tool [15] to create and use modeling support for cybersecurity. MetaEdit+ is applied because it already supports existing automotive system development languages such as EAST-ADL and AUTOSAR.

Second reason for using MetaEdit+ is that it can generate code directly from the models as well as allows creating generators for various purposes other then producing code, like checking, reporting, as well as producing input to other tools like simulators and analysis tools. This function not only provides considerable time and cost savings in development effort, but also improves the overall quality of the system developed.

Thirdly, and crucial for our work on security modeling, MetaEdit+ can extend and combine languages via metamodels, as well as create new domain-specific modeling languages. This flexibility allows for the customization of modeling languages to suit specific domain requirements. Once a metamodel is defined, developers can use it as their domain-specific language for modeling [19].

In Sect. 8 we describe how modeling support was created by defining security-related language concepts, rules and notation. We also present the generators that calculate security scores and produce relevant security documents as in ISO 21434. We demonstrate resulting tool support with examples.

6 ISO Standard 21434

ISO/SAE 21434 contains objectives, requirements and guidelines related to cybersecurity engineering and can be used to implement a cybersecurity management system that also involves cybersecurity risk management [11]. The standard specifies the technical requirements for managing the cybersecurity risk of electrical and electronic systems (E/E-Systems) in road vehicles, including their components and interfaces. No specific technologies or solutions for cybersecurity are prescribed. ISO/SAE 21434 mandates risk treatment for all identified risks using classical options: risk avoidance, reduction, sharing, or retention and permits risk acceptance up to a defined threshold, as long as the decision is documented along with the retained risks [12]. According to ISO 21434, road vehicle cybersecurity is achieved when assets are adequately protected against threat scenarios. Assets worthy of protection include the various tangible and intangible components of systems such as software and hardware components, sensitive information and communication links. Threat scenarios are the potential cause for the compromised protection objectives of one or more assets [11]. ISO 21434 defines item as one or more components that implement a function at vehicle level, whereby a component is defined as a logically and technically separable part [11]. The item definition defines the target development system, which is subject to a cybersecurity-oriented development process, as precisely as possible and specifies the physical limits of the system under consideration as well as the areas to be protected. Based on the item definition, a threat analysis and risk assessment (TARA) is carried out from the perspective of affected road users. It serves to systematically identify threats and analyze the attack and defense mechanisms in the examined system and essentially consists of the following elements:

1. Item Definition [11, section 9.3]
2. Asset Identification [11, section 15.3]
3. Identification of Threat Scenarios [11, section 15.4]
4. Impact Rating [11, section 15.5]
5. Attack Path Analysis [11, section 15.6]
6. Attack Feasibility Rating [11, section 15.7]
7. Risk Value Determination [11, section 15.8]
8. Risk Treatment Decision [11, section 15.9]
9. Cyber Security Goals [11, section 9.4]
10. Cyber Security Claims [11, RQ-09-06]
11. Cyber Security Concept [11, section 9.5]

Cybersecurity engineering analysis identifies and explores potential actions that an abstract attacker could perform maliciously and the damage that could result from compromising the cybersecurity of a vehicle's E/E systems. Cybersecurity monitoring, remediation and incident response depend on changing environmental conditions, i.e. there is a constant need to identify vulnerabilities in road vehicle E/E systems and counteract new attack techniques.

The abbreviation CAL stands for Cybersecurity Assurance Level and, similar to the ASIL (Automotive Safety Integrity Level) in the ISO 26262 standard, is used to appropriately adjust the effort and care required for subsequent activities in the area of cybersecurity. The ISO/SAE 21434 standard specifies that an appropriate CAL should be defined for each threat scenario based on the associated impact and attack vectors. This is similar to setting risk values. While the risk value is dynamic and can change during the development process, the CAL is intended to remain stable during development as it is an integral part of a development requirement.

7 Security Abstraction Model with Extensions

Security Abstraction Model (SAM) provides concepts for modeling security aspects of automotive systems. Figure 1 describes the metamodel of SAM illustrating which kind of security aspects are specified when modeling automotive systems with security considerations. In this figure, we present the complete metamodel so that the relationships between the entities become visible, as this is relevant for the reporting described later.

Originally SAM [22] did not recognize the later published ISO 21434 standard but this is now integrated into SAM and its metamodel [2]. This creates a link between the security requirements of the ISO 21434 standard and the models created based on SAM. Similarly, SAM was not originally developed explicitly for modeling social engineering but an extension has been developed that enables the modeling of social engineering attacks and maps the relationship of these

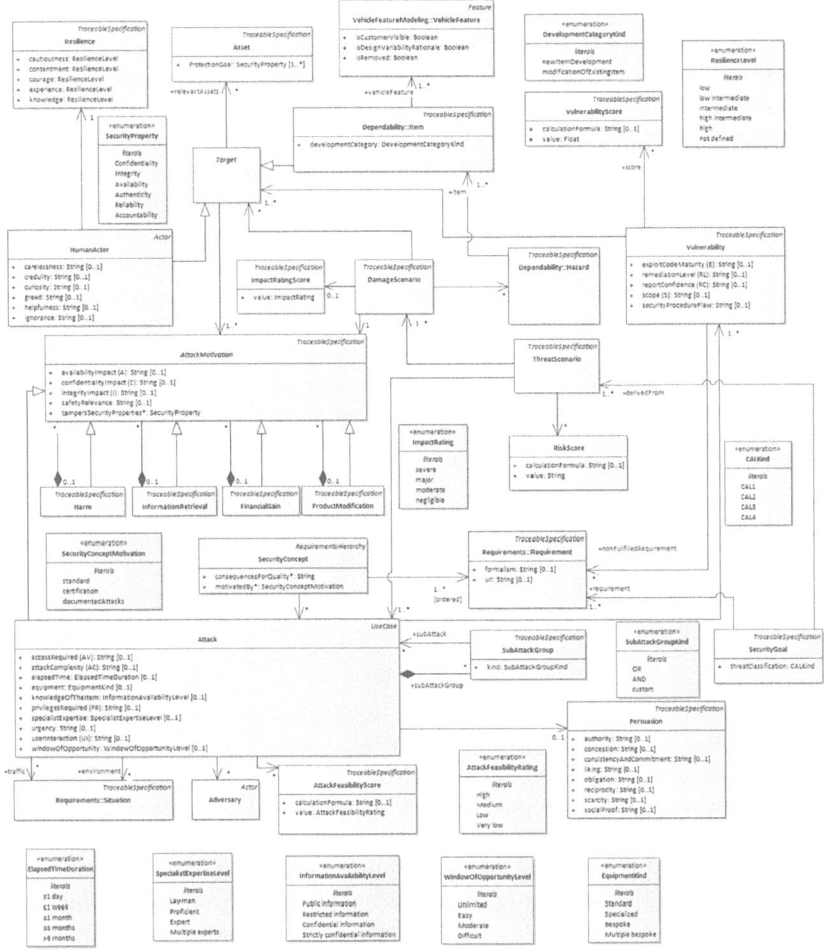

Fig. 1. SAM metamodel. View Online at https://bitbucket.org/east-adl/sam/

attacks to the actors and the rest of the model [3]. These extensions enable a more comprehensive specification of cybersecurity aspects, their reporting as in ISO 21434 and calculating related metrics and scored. We describe these extensions in the next subsections, and their implementation to the modeling tool in Sect. 8.

7.1 Integration with System Design

EAST-ADL [4] is a language for describing the system architectures of software-intensive automotive systems using an information model that represents technical information in a standardized way. The descriptions cover vehicle functions and features as well as functional and hardware architecture. The EAST-ADL model is structured according to abstraction levels, with each sub-model representing the relevant details of the complete embedded system of the respective abstraction level.

Security Abstraction Model and EAST-ADL are linked by the common concept of item. In EAST-ADL, item represents a functional or non-functional requirement of the system that is being described and modeled. SAM extends the concept of item by incorporating security properties. This enables SAM to specify security requirements that are necessary to fulfill the overall system requirements. These security requirements are integrated into the model to enable a comprehensive security analysis and to identify potential vulnerabilities and threats in the system.

Although SAM is developed as part of the EAST-ADL, it is not necessarily bound to EAST-ADL, offering flexibility in its application. SAM can be used independently of the rest of the system model to provide an overview of security-critical system parts before or at the beginning of the system engineering process. This independent utility allows engineers to identify and address potential security vulnerabilities early in the development cycle.

7.2 Scores

The latest version of SAM used at the time of writing includes a number of entities from ISO 21434 to enable a detailed risk assessment. These entities include Asset, Damage Scenario, Threat Scenario, ImpactRatingScore, RiskScore, AttackFeasibilityRating and AttackFeasibilityScore (see Fig. 1). By integrating ISO 21434, not only can vulnerabilities now be assessed, but so can potential attacks and their impact on the system. For this purpose, the AttackFeasibilityScore, ImpactRatingScore and RiskScore are included in SAM. Attack feasibility, a critical component of threat analysis, can be calculated using two distinct methods [11]. The first approach is based on the Common Vulnerability Scoring System (CVSS) formula, which provides a standardized way to estimate the severity. The second approach, based on attack potential, aligns with ISO/SAE 21434 and evaluates feasibility using five core parameters:

- Elapsed Time: The amount of time required to identify a vulnerability and develop and (successfully) apply an exploit.
- Specialist Expertise: The level of technical skill needed to execute the attack.
- Knowledge of the Item or Component: The extent of information the attacker has acquired about the item or component.
- Window of Opportunity: The combination of access type (e.g. logical and physical) and access type (e.g. unlimited and limited) during which the attack can be executed.
- Equipment: The tools and resources necessary to discover the vulnerability and/or to execute the attack.

In addition to the previously mentioned scores, ISO 21434 contains further scores that are available in the SAM metamodel. The ImpactRatingScore evaluates the severity of an attack based on factors such as the extent and duration of system compromise. The RiskScore, in turn, combines the impact and attack feasibility ratings to prioritize threats and guide the implementation of security measures. These scores enable a holistic understanding of the system's security posture, helping engineers identify critical vulnerabilities and prioritize mitigation strategies effectively.

7.3 Social Engineering

SAM provides a basis for the assessment of social engineering attacks by including various scores and entities. A qualitative scoring system has been developed to specifically focused on social engineering. Integrating a scoring system further improves the assessment and understanding of risks associated with social engineering, helping to develop appropriate security measures to minimize the impact of these attacks. Extensions to SAM were implemented at different levels, including new meta-entities, extensions to existing meta-entities, and supplementary documentation, enabling greater consideration of social engineering and standards.

Due to the existing integration of CVSS scores and other assessments in the Security Abstraction Model, it was necessary to investigate whether the extension and harmonization would create redundancy. Redundancy is beneficial if there are reasons for mapping an issue in different ways. The social engineering entities were integrated into the metamodel to ensure a clear capture of security aspects without creating unnecessary duplication or repetition of metrics.

7.4 Reporting

Reporting is essential in the context of ISO 21434, which explicitly requires it. Specifically, a cybersecurity assessment report (RQ-06-31) serves as appraisal of the level of cybersecurity. Although the standard does not provide explicit guidelines on the format or structure of such reports, our implementation of the report generation adheres closely to the principles described in ISO 21434. This ensures that the cybersecurity assessment report effectively communicates the findings and recommendations derived from the assessment process.

In accordance with ISO 21434, the report is primarily focused on assets, reflecting the standard's emphasis on asset-oriented cybersecurity management. Its structure is closely based on the example in Annex H of the standard. However, by integrating the social engineering aspect of SAM, we have also introduced reporting that focus on human actors and recognize the importance of the human element in cybersecurity. In addition, we have included a section dealing with miscellaneous items and how they relate to vulnerabilities and the associated vulnerability scores. While the report sections relating to social engineering and miscellaneous are not explicitly included in the standard, their inclusion broadens the scope of the report and provides stakeholders with a holistic reporting of cybersecurity risk and mitigation.

There are several advantages to automatic report generation:

- It enables the hierarchical organization of multiple models, facilitating the creation of comprehensive reports that cover different aspects. This hierarchical structuring enables a systematic and coherent presentation of information across different levels of abstraction.
- Automated report generation can incorporate item definitions by linking to EAST-ADL architecture models, providing insight into potentially at-risk vehicle features and their interrelationships. This integration increases the depth and specificity of the report.
- By selecting relevant properties, the calculation and reporting of scores is automatically generated, which ensures efficiency and accuracy. In cases where multiple values are applicable, these are aggregated, with the maximum value being reported.

7.5 Visualization as SAM Lane Diagram

The Security Abstraction Model (SAM) allows an alternative visualization method called the **SAM Lane Diagram**, designed for intuitive understanding without requiring deep knowledge of SAM modeling. This visualization approach is inspired by UML [17] and BPMN [16], making it accessible for stakeholders at various decision-making levels. It is particularly useful for quickly exchanging information about an attack across diverse organizational hierarchies.

The SAM Lane Diagram builds upon a swimlane diagram (refer to Fig. 2) and integrates an Attack Tree to represent the processes and relationships involved in an attack. An Attack Tree illustrates one or more attack vectors, starting with a root attack and branching into subattacks. Each subattack represents a necessary condition that must be fulfilled for subsequent attacks to occur. In this diagram, affected components, such as control units or networks, are depicted as swimlanes. Attacks are placed within these swimlanes, associating them with the specific components (referred to as "Items") they target.

To execute an attack, an adversary must exploit the vulnerability of the corresponding Item (depicted in the swimlane) and potentially complete prerequisite subattacks. Logical causal relationships between attacks are represented by arrows: the arrow points towards the subsequent attack, indicating the required sequence. For instance, in the representation shown in Fig. 2, "Attack 1.3" is a subattack of "Attack 1.2", which, in turn, is a subattack of "Attack 1.1". An example of a specific attack can be seen in Fig. 8.

The SAM Lane Diagram also accommodates complex scenarios involving:

- **AND** relationships, where multiple subattacks must occur simultaneously as prerequisites for an attack.
- **OR** relationships, where alternative paths can achieve an attack.
- **CUSTOM** relationships, allowing users to define specific logical connections to meet individual requirements.

This visualization method enables a clear depiction of attack sequences and their associated items. It provides a structured and scalable way to analyze and communicate cybersecurity risks, enhancing collaboration and decision-making in complex system environments.

The SAM Lane Diagram is especially useful for:

- **Cross-functional collaboration**: By presenting security data in a visually intuitive format, the diagram facilitates discussions between technical and non-technical teams, ensuring alignment on risk mitigation strategies.
- **Decision-making support**: Managers can use SAM Lane Diagrams to understand attack scenarios without delving into technical details, enabling faster and more informed decision-making.
- **Scenario modeling**: Complex attack scenarios involving multiple components and dependencies can be modeled comprehensively, aiding in both planning and response efforts.

While SAM Lane Diagrams are currently derived from detailed SAM security models, future work aims to enable the reverse process: generating SAM security models from high-level SAM Lane Diagrams. This functionality would allow stakeholders to collaboratively design intuitive, high-level attack representations and derive actionable security models without requiring extensive manual effort. Additionally, expanding support for advanced visualization features, such as real-time updates based on threat monitoring data, would further enhance the utility of SAM Lane Diagrams in dynamic environments.

The SAM Lane Diagram thus represents a powerful tool for analyzing, communicating, and addressing cybersecurity risks, bridging the gap between detailed technical models and accessible visual representations.

8 Tool Support: Language Definition and Usage

This section presents the tool support for security modeling. We first describe the implementation of support for SAM, including the modeling language, score calculators and the reporting of security threats in accordance with ISO standard 21434. Subsequently, we provide two examples demonstrating the use of the developed modeling tool, alongside score calculation, reporting and tracing to other system design models.

Our implementation of tool support began by extending the existing language definition of EAST-ADL and its associated security language. Although EAST-ADL is supported by various tools, we applied in MetaEdit+ the latest version of EAST-ADL (v2.2)[1]. Since MetaEdit+ enables the co-evolution of metamodels and models [20], the changes made to the modeling support were automatically updated to already existing models.

The language definition covered all parts needed for obtaining tool support: Not only the metamodel and related constraints, but also the notation, guidance for creating and editing models, as well as updating older versions or notifying modelers to make changes when automatic update were not considered feasibly,

---
[1] https://east-adl.info/.

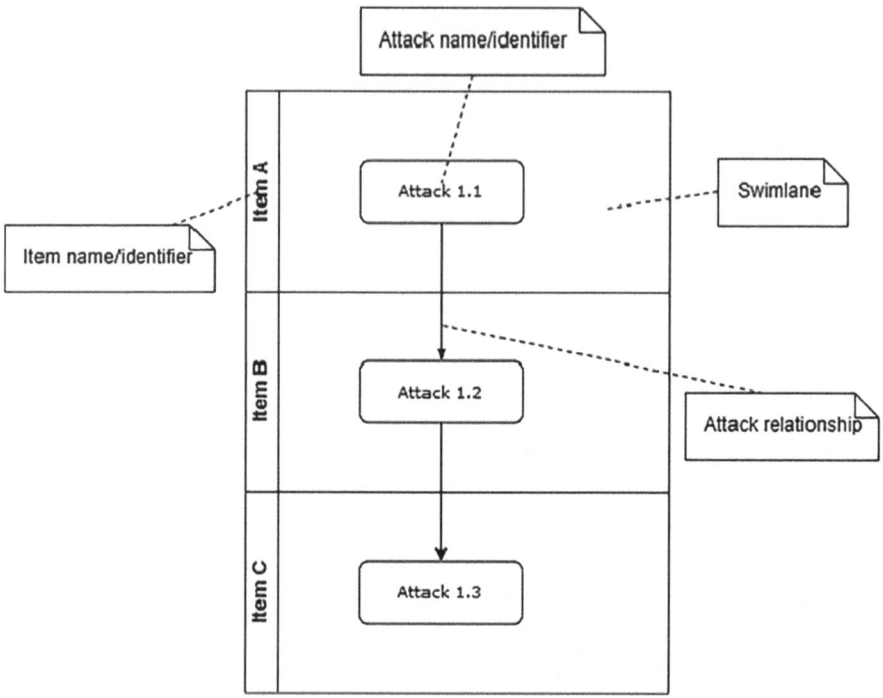

Fig. 2. Conceptual representation of the SAM Lane Diagram

such as when there was a risk of losing relevant data. Finally, generators for various score calculations and threat security reporting were defined, in addition to those available in MetaEdit+ for EAST-ADL, such as Simulink, Hip-Hops and ReqIF, or defined by users targeting external tools like SPIN, UPPAAL, Stateflow and Reliability Workbench[2].

8.1 Metamodel Extensions

For modeling support, the metamodel of SAM was defined by two person with MetaEdit+ Workbench, and then tested by other modelers by using the same language with the modeling editors, browsers, and collaboration tools of MetaEdit+. We created several security models as test cases including the Brake-By-Wire example presented here later[3] Figure 3 shows the elements of the security modeling language in MetaEdit+. The list of Objects shows the key modeling objects, the list of Relationships shows the connections between these elements, and the list of Roles shows how an object participates in the relationships, such as being directed or undirected, having constraints, or detailed properties.

---

[2] https://metacase.com/solution/east-adl.html.
[3] SAM implementation can be accessed at https://bitbucket.org/east-adl/sam/src/master/MetaEdit-Extension/Reporting_Examples.

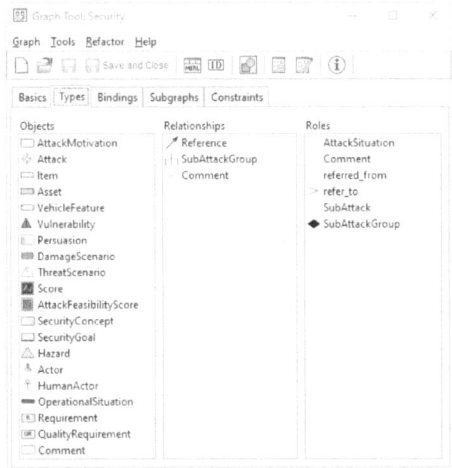

Fig. 3. Extended SAM definition

Figure 4 details the definition of HumanActor, which has 11 properties. The first three are inherited from EAST-ADL and AUTOSAR metamodels. These three properties have rules and constraints, such as 'Short name' being mandatory and starting with an alphabetical character followed by possible characters, numbers, or underscores and constraint with maximum length (defined as a regular expression: [a-zA-Z][a-zA-Z0-9_]{0,127}). These are followed by the characteristics of HumanActor in SAM (see Fig. 1): Curiosity, Helpfulness, Credulity, Greed, Ignorance, and Carelessness - all of which are fixed value enumerations. The definition also includes a description of language element and having them all detailed provides help system available for security model creators and readers within the tool.

While the metamodel in Fig. 1 identifies many language concepts as individual objects, such as resilience or metrics elements, we aimed to minimize the modeling effort not only in terms of creating model elements but also in terms of updating, deleting and checking specifications. As a result, the implementation as a modeling language exhibits some differences from the metamodel illustrated in Fig. 1. This is mainly to minimize the modeling effort and improve usability. The main differences are:

- Since Resilience is a mandatory item for a human actor, it is a property of HumanActor. This way language user is expected to add - and later edit - just one element in a model rather than two and a connection between.
- The same approach is also applied for the 4 metrics elements: while they can be added to and visualized in the model, they are not mandatory. Modeling editor can calculate the metrics even if those metric elements are not explicitly added to the model. Figure 5 illustrates this in the user interface at the bottom of the screen by showing individual metric values for vulnerabilities

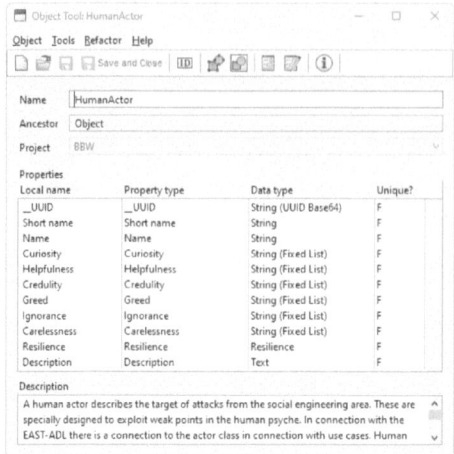

Fig. 4. Definition of HumanActor in metamodel of MetaEdit+

and attacks yet showing CVSS basic and temporal scores for vulnerability as well as ISO 21434 feasibility scores (both CVSS-based and potential-based) for the attack directly in the diagram, which is what the user wanted in this case.
- Attack motivation is an element of the modeling language, and its subtype is selected from the property with mandatory value. Thus, the type of Attack-Motivation (Harm, Financial Gain etc.) can be changed without deleting the old one and creating and re-connecting a new one.
- While the metamodel of SAM defines directed associations among security concepts, the modeling language does not expect models to be created in that order: the created editor shows the correct direction regardless of how the user opts to link model items. In other words, the model is created correctly independently of the order in which the modeler decides to create relationships.
- Default values for enumerations are provided.
- Properties of model elements are listed in the order that would be the order that would be most natural for considering the security properties.

We did not enforce all rules as mandatory, such as requiring each HumanActor to have a defined Resilience. Instead, we allowed for more flexibility in modeling, but we also provided guidance to language users to complete the security model. We defined 17 checks derived from the metamodel to provide warnings, which were shown to the language user during modeling. As an example, at the bottom of Fig. 5 is shown a warning that SecurityConcept is not related to any Requirement. Additionally, we defined recommendations for creating security models that deal with optional links: linking Attacks to Actors, SecurityConcepts with Attacks, and DamageScenarios to Hazards - the last been shown as a recommendation by the tool for the security model in Fig. 5.

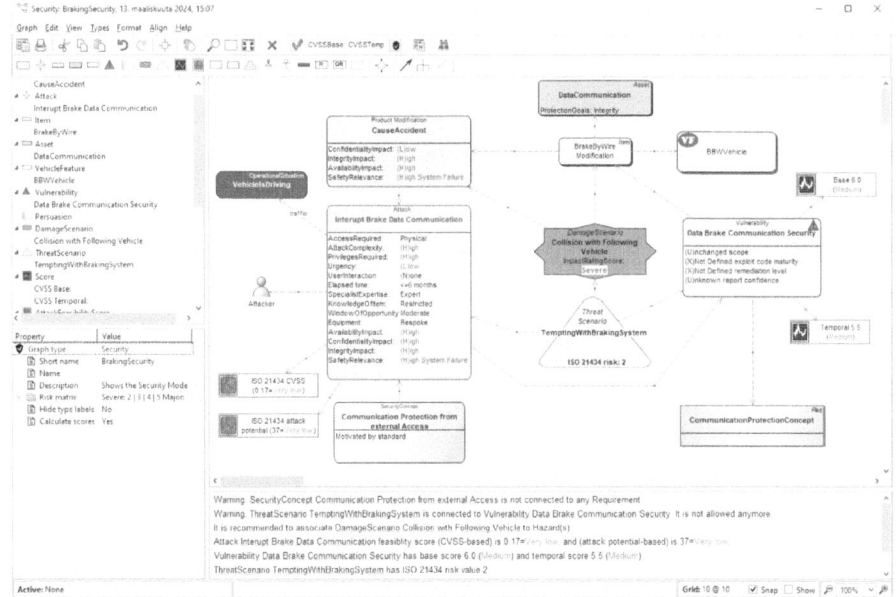

Fig. 5. Security model in modeling editor illustrating checks, recommendations and calculated metrics

8.2 Notation and Guidance

The security model example in Fig. 5 also illustrates the notation: How models are presented for humans to read, edit and use for communication. Our tool implementation therefore covered creating notation for the respective language elements. Figure 6 shows the definition of notational symbol for DamageScenario: It shows the name that user enters and given impact rating score. The notation also shows the type of model element as a part of the notational symbol. Such guide is useful when creating or reading the models in the first place but for experienced modelers it becomes redundant text that consumes extra space and thus can be hidden by the language user from the diagrams if desired.

In addition to providing guidance during modeling, the defined metamodel thoroughly describes individual language elements. These descriptions are accessible directly in MetaEdit+ through the help system, which is available from the editor's toolbar or individually for each language element when used.

8.3 Co-evolution

Given that SAM itself also evolved, we implemented guidance to update the existing security models to be compliant with the latest language version. MetaEdit+ manages with in-built functionality automatically model changes that are caused by adding and renaming items in the metamodel, constraints and notation (for details see [20]). However, some changes to models may require

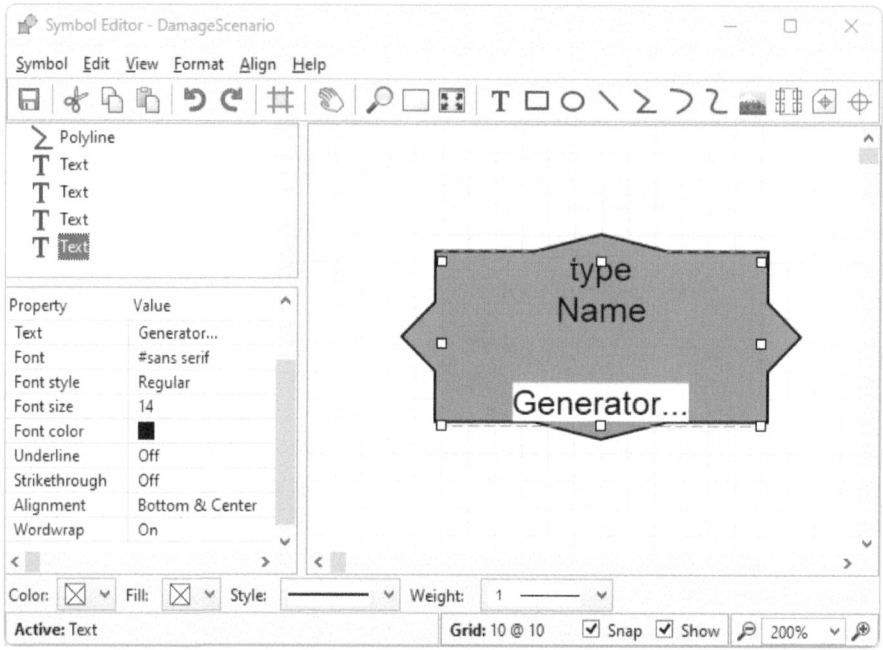

Fig. 6. Defining the notation for DamageScenario

human intervention when automatic updates are not feasible. To prevent the loss of critical model information, we followed a deprecation strategy: existing models can still be used, but all new models follow the latest language version. Additionally, we implemented guidance within the modeling editor to assist users in updating their models. This feature is illustrated at the bottom of the editor in Fig. 5: "Warning: ThreatScenario TemptingWithBrakingSystem is connected to Vulnerability Data Brake Communication Security. It is not allowed anymore." Similar co-evolution support could be applied in the future when support for cybersecurity modeling evolves or new versions of the ISO standard or SAM are developed.

8.4 Metrics

As models provide detailed information on security aspects, they can be used for various assessment purposes. We implemented support for SAM-based security models integrated with CVSS. Once a security model is created with the required data, the modeling tool automatically calculates various scores. For example, in Fig. 5, the vulnerability of Data Brake Communication Security has a Base CVSS score of 6.0 (Medium) and a Temporal CVSS score of 5.5 (Medium). For the specified attack, the ISO 21434 CVSS score is 0.17 (Very Low), while the ISO 21434 attack potential-based score is 37 (Very low).

Since attacks can consist of subattacks, calculating vulnerability metrics must take the entire attack tree into account. In our implementation of CVSS, we considered the most severe case by using the most severe attack within the attack tree as the basis for calculation. The same principle is applied when different types of individual attacks are related to the same vulnerability.

Scores for vulnerability and attack feasibility are calculated during modeling and displayed either directly on the diagram or in a separate report pane below it. Figure 5 illustrates these scores at the bottom of the screen, along with two different Attack Feasibility Scores shown next to the Attack element.

The tool calculates the risk value by combining the impact ratings (set for Damage scenarios) and the feasibility scores assigned to related attacks in the attack trees. Since ISO 21434 suggests that organizations define their own rating scales, the tool supports the use (and reuse) of a Risk Matrix with numerical values (1–5) assigned to the ratios. Based on this, the risk value (2) is calculated and displayed inside the symbol of the Threat Scenario (as shown in Fig. 5) and included in the generated reports (see Sect. 8.6).

In SAM, a Threat Scenario can relate to multiple Damage Scenarios, each of which contributes an Impact Rating Score. Similarly, a Threat Scenario can also relate to multiple Attacks, each of which is associated with an Attack Feasibility Rating. The feasibility score is an aggregated property of the Attack and considers all the subattacks within the attack tree.

To determine the risk value for a Threat Scenario:

- **Impact Rating**: The most severe Impact Rating Score among all associated Damage Scenarios is used.
- **Feasibility Rating**: The most severe feasibility score among all related Attacks is used. If the Threat Scenario corresponds to more than one attack path, the feasibility scores of these attack paths are appropriately aggregated, taking the maximum value as per the standard.

Feasibility ratings in SAM can be either CVSS-based or attack potential-based. For risk value determination, the highest (most severe) feasibility rating is always selected, regardless of the rating method. This approach aligns with the requirements of the ISO/SAE 21434 standard, ensuring that the most critical feasibility rating is reflected in the overall risk value.

The calculated risk value is derived using a risk matrix, combining the most severe Impact Rating and Feasibility Rating. This ensures a consistent and methodical approach to risk value determination. Additionally, we allow the definition of custom risk scores and the assignment of multiple risk values for a single Threat Scenario, covering different categories such as financial impact, safety, or operational disruption. This flexibility enables organizations to tailor the risk assessment process to their specific requirements and priorities.

8.5 Alternative Visualizations

As it can be overwhelming for beginners to see all the details of security models at once, we applied two techniques to show partial data. In MetaEdit+ it is possible to create different and parallel views to the same model and hide wanted element types from the model. For instance, a user may want to see just items, attacks and vulnerabilities hiding all the rest (as in Fig. 7). This can be done by choosing the desired elements from the view menu.

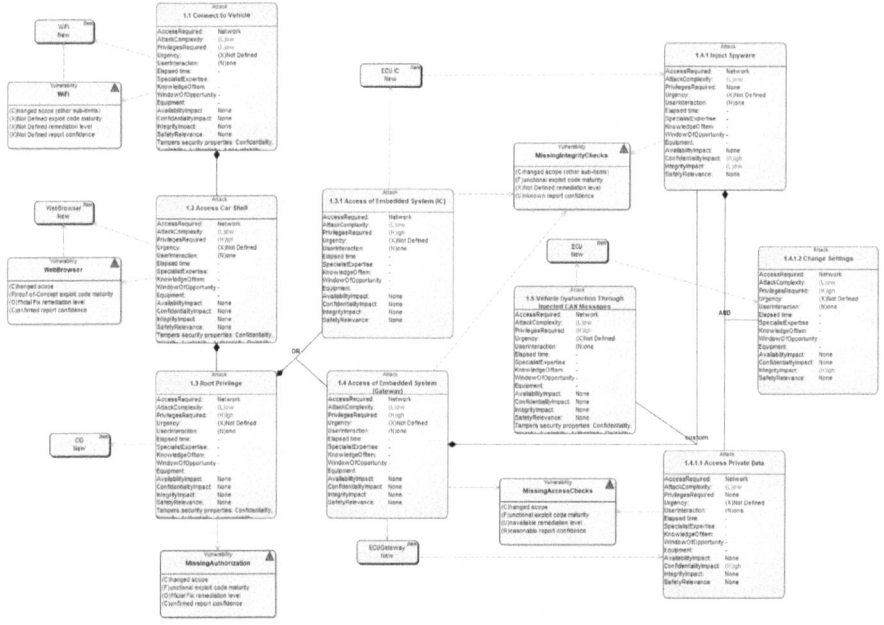

Fig. 7. Attack tree in SAM

Another alternative to managing complexity is to create models showing selected elements using some other, and possible already familiar, language. We implemented a transformation that creates a diagram in BPMN (Business Process Modeling Notation) based on attack trees and their related items and vulnerabilities. Figure 8 shows an attack tree automatically created as a BPMN diagram from security models—from Fig. 7 in this example. This functionality is created with the MetaEdit+ generator system applied to produce metrics and reports. The mappings between the SAM and BPMN element types can be adapted and extended by the MetaEdit+ users.

In SAM, an attack can relate to many items, and MetaEdit+ allows an attack to appear in multiple swimlanes (representing different items). While this flexibility is supported in SAM and MetaEdit+, it deviates from the BPMN metamodel defined by OMG, where tasks are typically confined to a single swimlane. Our approach allows this flexibility, ensuring that tasks spanning multiple swimlanes can still be visualized. To remain methodologically consistent we point out that:

– An attack only refers to a specific item if it represents a concrete attack, i.e., the leaf of an attack tree.

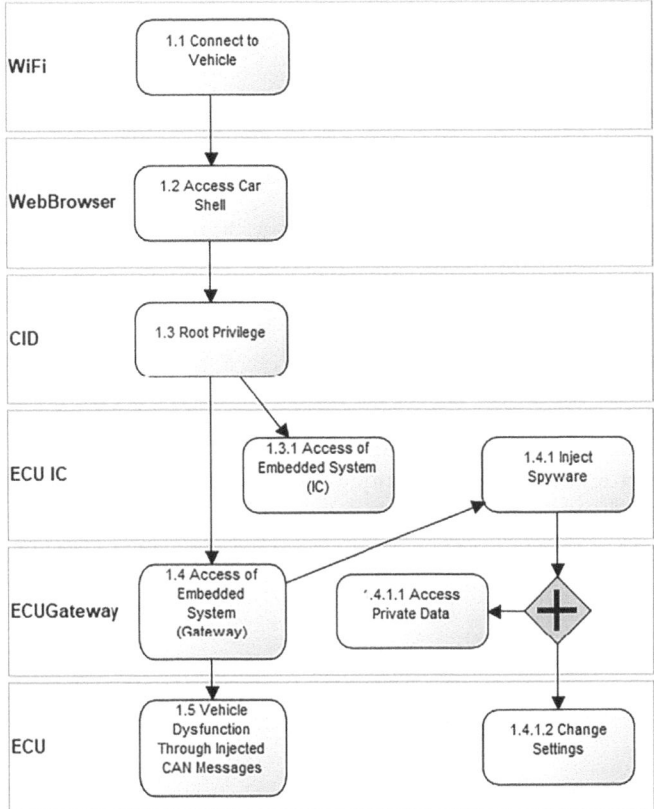

Fig. 8. Attack tree presented in BPMN

- Otherwise, the attack should reference generalized items, such as "vehicle".

This methodological restriction ensures compatibility with the BPMN metamodel but does not restrict the user in generating BPMN diagrams as they can be edited afterwards.

The standard use case involves exporting a complex SAM diagram into a BPMN diagram for a simplified, process-focused view. However, our tooling also supports exporting multiple SAM graphs from a hierarchy into BPMN. This is particularly valuable in hierarchical structures where individual diagrams contribute to an overarching security model.

In scenarios where items are shared among multiple SAM diagrams, the resulting BPMN diagram can become significantly more complex. However, this complexity highlights the value of automation and tooling in producing comprehensive, scalable visualizations. These tools enable the generation of detailed models that might otherwise be infeasible to create manually.

8.6 Documenting and Reporting

Existing documentation generators were available in MetaEdit+ for the purposes of reporting. These generators, however, did not recognise the needs of ISO 21434. Given that the SAM was made to recognize explicitly cybersecurity, we defined a threat reporting generator based on the reporting requirements (as in Sect. 7.4).

Figure 9 shows the result of this generator produced from Fig. 5 and from the related system design specifying the vehicle features (Fig. 10) and the system functions (Fig. 11). Reports are provided also in RTF and Word formats but illustrated here in plain text format to show their details. Figure 10 shows a small part of the model specifying features related to the braking system. These features are realized by some design functions and hardware functions of EAST-ADL. Figure 11 illustrates a part of the logical design functions of the braking system that are also recognized in the generated security report. Both security report and metric calculators were implemented with generator system of MetaEdit+ [15].

Standard ISO/SAE 21434
There are currently 1 Items with 1 Features and 0 Human actors affected by overall 0 Hazards and 1 Attacks. 2 of the Development Ph:

Item definition
The item BrakeByWire:
BrakeByWire is linked to DesignFunctionType BBW_FDA (DesignFunctionArchitecture for Braking from Pedal to ABS) via feature BBV
BrakeByWire is linked to HardwareComponentType HDA (Hardware architecture for braking system.) via feature BBWVehicle and to H:

Asset identification
Asset DataCommunication is related to DamageScenario Collision with Following Vehicle with the following security properties: Integrit

Impact rating
DamageScenario Collision with Following Vehicle has impact rating: Severe

Threat scenario identification
DamageScenario Collision with Following Vehicle is related to ThreatScenario TemptingWithBrakingSystem.

Attack analysis
ThreatScenario TemptingWithBrakingSystem is related to: Attack Interupt Brake Data Communication

Attack feasibility rating
Interupt Brake Data Communication has attack feasibility rating (CVSS-based) 0.17=Very low and (attack potential-based) is 37=Very

Risk value determination
TemptingWithBrakingSystem has aggregated attack feasibility rating (CVSS-based) 0.17=Very low and Impact rating Severe with risk value(s) ISO 21434 calculated risk value: 2

Targets
Target BrakeByWire is related to Data Brake Communication Security

Vulnerability analysis
Vulnerability Data Brake Communication Security has vulnerability base score 6.0 (Medium), temporal score 5.5 (Medium)

Fig. 9. Sample of Security Analysis Report

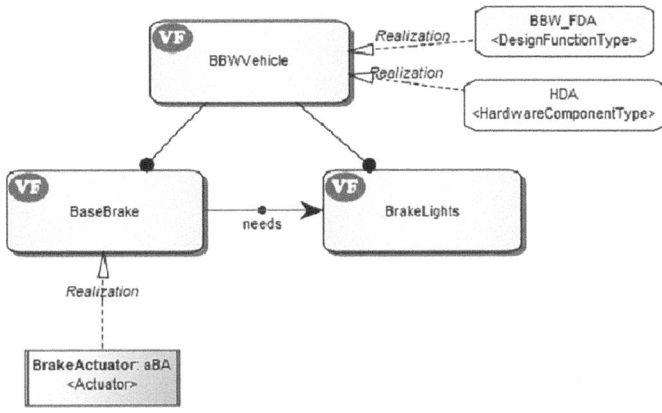

Fig. 10. Vehicle feature model: braking (fraction)

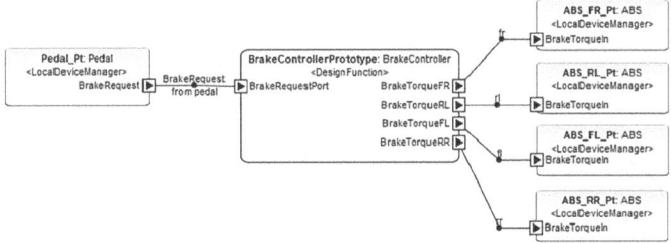

Fig. 11. Design level functions of braking system (fraction)

Traceability from security models to system design is visible in the security analysis report. For example, in Fig. 9 the item definition at the beginning of the report is linked to the design functions and hardware functions of the braking system. Also the summary at the beginning of the generated report shows that security models are related to two different development phases of EAST-ADL, namely to the vehicle level in which features related to items are defined as well as to the design level functions realizing those features.

Figure 12 shows another report targeting analysis of social engineering threats in automotive systems. This report is generated from a security model shown in Fig. 13 representing a social engineering attack that affects the braking system. It shows a baiting attack in which the braking system is compromised through deception maneuvers. The report identifies the human actors involved, their vulnerabilities and their resilience to such attacks. Additionally, it provides insights into the persuasion methods used in the social engineering attack, improving understanding of the potential dangers posed by human manipulation tactics. This holistic approach to reporting provides valuable insight into the intricacies of cybersecurity risks associated with social engineering and helps develop robust countermeasures to protect automotive systems from such vulnerabilities.

Social engineering
There are currently 1 Human actors with 5 exploitable human weaknesses. 1 Principles of Persuasion are used in 1 attacks.

Human actors
Car Owner has the following properties:
Curiosity: (L)ow
Helpfulness: (H)igh
Credulity: (H)igh
Greed: (N)one
Ignorance: (L)ow
Carelessness: (H)igh
with resilience:
Cautiousness: (H)igh
Contentment: (L)ow
Courage: (LI) Low lintermediate
Expereince: (H)igh
Knowledge: (H)igh

Persuasions
Related to Attack Interrupt Brake Data Communication through baiting
Persuasion Persuasion has the following properties:
Reciprocity: (H)igh
Obligation: (H)igh
Concession: (H)igh
Scarcity: (H)igh
Authority: (H)igh
Consistency and Commitment: (I)ntermediate
Liking: (L)ow
Social Proof: (L)ow

Miscellaneous
There are currently 1 Items and 1 Vulnerabilities. The highest vulnerability score is 7.1.

Fig. 12. Sample of social engineering report

The reports illustrated in Figs. 9 and 12 show that they provide links from reported items back to the security models and other system development models. This clear traceability shows that security aspects do not need to be addressed in isolation, but can be linked to the rest of the system development. These reports can be produced directly to external files like used for word processors or web browsers.

In addition to reporting on individual security model – as illustrated in the previous examples – security threat reporting is also available for all EAST-ADL models: It can be generated for any selected hierarchy of EAST-ADL models combining multiple security models into a single security threat report. This capability enhances collaboration by allowing traces from system designs to be followed to all vulnerabilities and attacks across the entire developed system. Linking security models with system models in the same repository, accessible to all engineers simultaneously, significantly improves collaboration, feedback

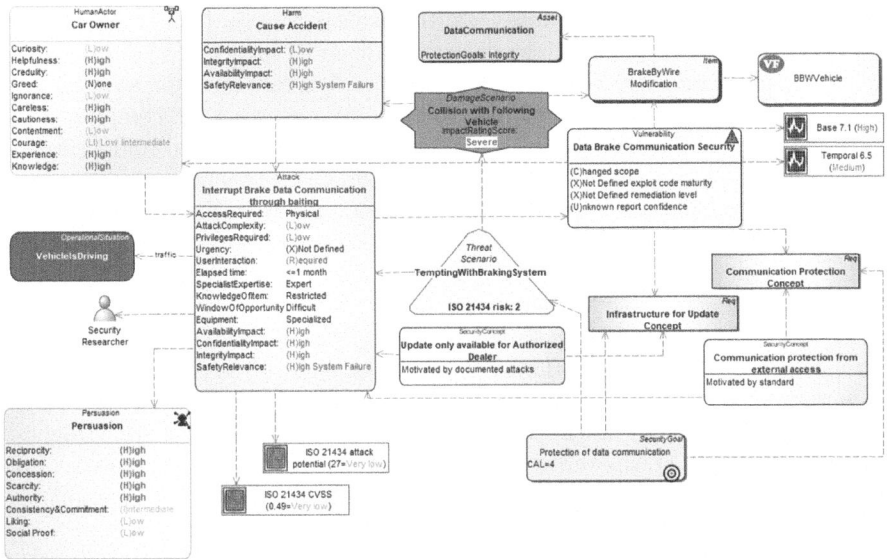

Fig. 13. Security model in modeling editor illustrating a social engineering attack

efficiency, and the quality of specifications compared to people working separately and using different formats and tools.

9 Conclusion

This paper presents a tool support for model-based cybersecurity engineering in the automotive domain. It shows how tool support can meet the requirements of ISO/SAE 21434 standard in model building, calculating metrics and security threat reporting. Our tool, built on the EAST-ADL language with security extensions, provides a solution to support these model-based approaches. By integrating system and security modeling, along with capabilities for calculating security metrics and generating ISO-compliant reports, the tool enables engineers to navigate the complexities of automotive cybersecurity with confidence. Furthermore, the tool's ability to guide engineers in defining and integrating security models with system models underscores its user-centered design and practical utility.

The contributions of this work are multifaceted. First, the integration of advanced scoring mechanisms into SAM, such as the CVSS-based attack feasibility analysis and the attack potential-based method, enables precise evaluation of threats. The latter approach considers additional parameters, including elapsed time, required expertise, knowledge of the target system, available window of opportunity, and equipment needs. This dual scoring system provides flexibility, allowing users to choose or combine methods based on the specific cybersecurity scenario.

Second, this research introduces additional visualization techniques like the SAM Lane Diagram. By adopting conventions from BPMN, the SAM Lane Diagram facilitates intuitive understanding of attack trees, even for stakeholders without deep technical expertise. This capability ensures that complex security scenarios can be effectively communicated across technical and decision-making levels, fostering better collaboration. The inclusion of swimlanes to represent affected items and vulnerabilities, alongside logical relationships between attacks, enhances the clarity and usability of these diagrams. For instance, the ability to model complex AND, OR, and CUSTOM logical relationships makes this tool highly adaptable for real-world scenarios.

The significance of this work extends beyond its immediate application in automotive cybersecurity. As the latest enhancements to the metamodel enable a complete representation of the ISO 21434 standard, it lays the groundwork for broader adoption across industries where cybersecurity standards are of highest importance. Moreover, the versatility of the extensions, particularly those related to social engineering attacks, positions it as a valuable resource for compliance with various cybersecurity standards beyond ISO 21434.

While the modeling support is readily available our plan is to apply it to model various security cases to evaluate it and identify possible areas for extensions. Another direction for future research is to extend tool support, and possibly the metamodel of SAM, to support the latest versions of metric calculators like version 4.0 of CVSS.

One of the possibilities for further research is extending SAM's capabilities to enable bidirectional model generation. Currently, SAM Lane diagrams can be generated from security models, providing a high-level visualization of complex attack scenarios. Future work will focus on the reverse process-generating detailed security models from SAM Lane diagrams. This functionality would support workflows, enabling engineers and decision-makers to collaboratively draft high-level representations and derive actionable security models.

Future research could investigate the automatic creation of models based on attack data. This approach has the potential to rationalize the modeling process and enable not only security engineers but also automotive engineers to contribute to the creation of security models. By automating the generation of parts of the models that currently require manual modeling, such as specific attack scenarios and vulnerabilities, significant time savings can be achieved.

Other extensions to the metamodel could relate to the implementation of specific mechanisms, such as cryptography. Although the metamodel already allows the modeling of requirements and security concepts, these additions could allow a more detailed and accurate modeling of the internal relationships of these mechanisms.

The Cybersecurity Assurance Levels (CALs) from the ISO 21434 standard can be specified in the tool for a security goal. However, these security goals and other entities from the concept phase, such as requirements, are not currently included in the reporting, as the current reports focus primarily on risk assessment. For CALs, it is important to note that no consensus has yet been reached on how to determine and treat such a parameter, so this aspect has been relegated to the Annex only [14]. This could be a potential future extension, allowing for the creation of reports that encompass requirements, security goals, and concepts, even though this is not explicitly required by the standard.

References

1. AUTOSAR: Enabling continuous innovation (2024). https://www.autosar.org/
2. Bergler, M., Tavakoli Kolagari, R.: Automotive software security engineering based on the ISO 21434. In: Proceedings of the 2023 5th World Symposium on Software Engineering, WSSE 2023, pp. 17–26. Association for Computing Machinery, New York (2023). https://doi.org/10.1145/3631991.3631994
3. Bergler, M., Tolvanen, J.P., Zoppelt, M., Tavakoli Kolagari, R.: Social engineering exploits in automotive software security: modeling human-targeted attacks with SAM. In: 31st European Safety and Reliability Conference | 19–23 September 2021, Angers, France, pp. 2502–2509 (2021). https://doi.org/10.3850/978-981-18-2016-8_720-cd
4. Blom, H., et al.: East-ADL - an architecture description language for automotive software-intensive systems (2013). https://www.maenad.eu/public/conceptpresentations/EAST-ADL_WhitePaper_M2.1.12.pdf
5. Broy, M., Feilkas, M., Herrmannsdoerfer, M., Merenda, S., Ratiu, D.: Seamless model-based development: from isolated tools to integrated model engineering environments. Proc. IEEE **98**(4), 526–545 (2010). https://doi.org/10.1109/JPROC.2009.2037771
6. Costantino, G., La Marra, A., Martinelli, F., Matteucci, I.: CANDY: a social engineering attack to leak information from infotainment system. In: 2018 IEEE 87th Vehicular Technology Conference (VTC Spring), pp. 1–5 (2018). https://doi.org/10.1109/VTCSpring.2018.8417879
7. Feiler, P., Gluch, D., Hudak, J.: The architecture analysis & design language (AADL): an introduction (2006). https://doi.org/10.1184/r1/6584909.v1
8. Fischer, A., Tolvanen, J.P., Tavakoli Kolagari, R.: Automotive cybersecurity engineering with modeling support. In: 2024 19th Conference on Computer Science and Intelligence Systems (FedCSIS), pp. 319–329 (2024). https://doi.org/10.15439/2024F5017
9. Garcia, F.D., Oswald, D., Kasper, T., Pavlidès, P.: Lock it and still lose it - on the (in)security of automotive remote keyless entry systems. In: Proceedings of the 25th USENIX Conference on Security Symposium, SEC 2016, pp. 929–944. USENIX Association, USA (2016)
10. Gustavsson, H., Enoiu, E.P., Carlson, J.: Model-based system engineering adoption in the vehicular systems domain. In: 2022 17th Conference on Computer Science and Intelligence Systems (FedCSIS), pp. 907–911 (2022). https://doi.org/10.15439/2022F47
11. International Organization for Standardization: ISO/SAE 21434:2021, Road vehicles - Cybersecurity engineering (2021). https://www.iso.org/standard/70918.html
12. Jakobs, C., Werner, M., Schmidt, K., Hansch, G.: Heuristic risk treatment for ISO/SAE 21434 development projects. In: 2022 17th Conference on Computer Science and Intelligence Systems (FedCSIS), pp. 653–662 (2022). https://doi.org/10.15439/2022F136

13. Li, J., Dong, Y., Fang, S., Zhang, H., Xu, D.: User context detection for relay attack resistance in passive keyless entry and start system. Sensors **20**(16), 4446 (2020). https://doi.org/10.3390/s20164446
14. Macher, G., Schmittner, C., Veledar, O., Brenner, E.: ISO/SAE DIS 21434 automotive cybersecurity standard - in a nutshell. In: Casimiro, A., Ortmeier, F., Schoitsch, E., Bitsch, F., Ferreira, P. (eds.) SAFECOMP 2020. LNCS, vol. 12235, pp. 123–135. Springer, Cham (2020). https://doi.org/10.1007/978-3-030-55583-2_9
15. MetaCase: Metaedit+ 5.5 user's guides. https://metacase.com/support/55/manuals/. Accessed May 2024
16. OMG: Business process model and notation (BPMN) version 2.0.2 (2013). https://www.omg.org/spec/BPMN/2.0.2
17. OMG: Unified modeling language specification version 2.5.1 (2017). https://www.omg.org/spec/UML/2.5.1/
18. OMG: Systems modeling language specification version 1.6 (2019). https://www.omg.org/spec/SysML/1.6/
19. Tolvanen, J.P., Kelly, S.: Effort used to create domain-specific modeling languages. In: Proceedings of the 21th ACM/IEEE International Conference on Model Driven Engineering Languages and Systems, MODELS 2018, pp. 235-244. Association for Computing Machinery, New York (2018).https://doi.org/10.1145/3239372.3239410
20. Tolvanen, J.P., Kelly, S.: Evaluating tool support for co-evolution of modeling languages, tools and models. In: 2023 ACM/IEEE International Conference on Model Driven Engineering Languages and Systems Companion (MODELS-C), pp. 914–923. IEEE (2023)
21. Wouters, L., Marin, E., Ashur, T., Gierlichs, B., Preneel, B.: Fast, furious and insecure: Passive keyless entry and start systems in modern supercars. IACR Trans. Cryptogr. Hardw. Embedd. Syst. **2019**(3), 66–85 (2019). https://doi.org/10.13154/tches.v2019.i3.66-85
22. Zoppelt, M., Tavakoli Kolagari, R.: SAM: a security abstraction model for automotive software systems. In: Hamid, B., Gallina, B., Shabtai, A., Elovici, Y., Garcia-Alfaro, J. (eds.) Security and Safety Interplay of Intelligent Software Systems, pp. 59–74. Springer International Publishing, Cham (2019)

Author Index

A
Alonso, Marco 167

B
Bolwerk, Twan 167
Bucaioni, Alessio 64

F
Fischer, Alexander 206
Flammini, Francesco 64

H
Henriques, Pedro Rangel 135
Holzheuser, Anna 113
Humm, Bernhard G. 113

K
Kardas, Geylani 87
Kolagari, Ramin Tavakoli 206

N
Neto, Alvaro Costa 135
Neumann, Michael 3

O
Ochodek, Mirosław 30

P
Partovian, Sania 64
Pereira, Maria João Varanda 135
Pham, Kevin Phong 3

S
Saritas, Hidayet Burak 87
Schuts, Mathijs 167

T
Thornadtsson, Johan 64
Tolvanen, Juha-Pekka 206

W
Wysocki, Włodzimierz 30

Z
Zender, Alexander 113

The manufacturer's authorised representative in the EU is Springer Nature Customer Service Centre GmbH, Europaplatz 3, 69115 Heidelberg, Germany. If you have any concerns regarding our products, please contact ProductSafety@springernature.com

Printed and bound by CPI Group (UK) Ltd, Croydon, CR0 4YY
26/03/2026
02078962-0004